Psychological Bases of Sport Injuries

David Pargman
Editor

Fitness Information Technology, Inc.
Morgantown, WV 26504

Library of Congress Catalog Card Number: 92-73668

ISBN 0-9627926-3-2

Cover Design: Brian Caudill
Copy Editor: Sandra R. Woods
Printed by: BookCrafters

Printed in the United States of America
10 9 8 7 6 5 4 3 2 1

Fitness Information Technology, Inc.
P. O. Box 4425, University Avenue
Morgantown, WV 26504 USA
(800) 477- 4FIT (4348)
(304) 599-3482

To the memory of my father, Sidney J. Pargman

CONTENTS

Contributing Authors

William Carroll, J.D., A.T.C. is currently chair of Sports Medicine at the United States Sports Academy in Daphne, Alabama. He received a M.S. from Indiana University and J.D. from the Birmingham School of Law. He is a NATA certified athletic trainer and formerly head trainer of the Indiana Pacers of the World Hockey Association, head trainer at the University of Illinois in Chicago and trainer at Northeastern University in Boston.

Kelly Crace is a staff psychologist at the Counseling Center of the College of William & Mary. He received his M.A. in sport psychology and his Ph.D. in counseling psychology from the University of North Carolina at Chapel Hill. He has published and presented nationally in the areas of performance enhancement, team development, social influence processes, career development, and stress management. He has consulted in these areas for academic, sport and business groups from the entry to the elite levels. In regards to sport injury, he has conducted research on the psychological aspects of career ending injuries, provided individual counseling to injured athletes and facilitated support groups for athletes dealing with the stress of injury.

Edward Etzel is a licensed psychologist with the West Virginia University Counseling and Psychological Services Center where he serves as psychologist for the Department of Intercollegiate Athletics. He is also an assistant professor within the School of Physical Education where he teaches applied sport psychology and research methods. Ed is a 1984 Olympic Gold Medalist in Shooting. He was also coach of the five-time NCAA Champion WVU Rifle Team.

A.P. "Budd" Ferrante is the psychologist for athletics at The Ohio State University. He is a Diplomate in counseling psychology of the American Board of Professional Psychology and is listed on the U.S. Olympic Committee's Registry for the Psychology of Sport. Budd served as sport psychologist for the U.S. Olympic Team in Seoul, Korea

Perry Fine is an associate professor of Anesthesiology at the University of Utah School of Medicine. He is an attending physician in the University Pain Management Center. He serves as a sports medicine consultant to the University Athletic Department with special interest in pain management and head injury assessment.

Frances Flint has been a faculty member at York University in the Department of Physical Education, Recreation, and Athletics since 1977. She obtained both her master's degree and Ph. D. from the University of Oregon. Her doctoral work involved an integration of sport psychology and sports medicine and focuses on the injured athlete. After her coaching career, she earned certification as an Athletic Trainer (NATA) and continues her work with injured athletes at York University. She has recently developed a Sports Therapy certificate program at York University for the training of future therapists in sport.

Lance B. Green is currently an assistant professor in the Exercise and Sport Sciences Department of Tulane University. His particular interests include the application of imagery to exercise and sport settings as well as the psycho-social context within which individuals pursue physical activity. He received his doctorate from the University of Northern Colorado in Greeley and has held a position at the University of Hawaii-Hilo where he taught and coached baseball.

J. Robert Grove received his master's degree from Southern Methodist University and the Ph. D. from Florida State University. He has published 25 articles in refereed journals to date, serves on the Editorial Board of the *Journal of Sport Psychology* and is an Associate Editor of the *Australian Journal of Science and Medicine in Sport.* Dr. Grove's main interests relate to personality and attribution theories in regard to sport and exercise behavior. He is currently a Senior Lecturer in Exercise and Sport Psychology in the Department of Human Movement Studies at the University of Western Australia.

Charlie Hardy is an associate professor in the Department of Physical Education, Exercise and Sport Science at the University of North Carolina at Chapel Hill, where he coordinates the Exercise and

Sport Psychology Laboratory and teaches classes in sport psychology and research methodology. He received his Ph.D. in sport psychology from Louisiana State University and completed a post doctoral fellowship at the University of North Carolina at Chapel Hill. His research interests are in social influence processes and emotions within exercise and sport. He is a Certified Consultant, AAASP, President of the AAASP, and has been a visiting sport psychologist at the United States Olympic Training Center.

John Heil is a psychologist with Lewis-Gale Clinic in Roanoke, Virginia specializing in sport psychology, pain and behavioral medicine. He is Coordinator of Psychological Services for the Lewis-Gale Hospital Pain Center. He serves on the United States Fencing Association Sports Medicine Committee and the ASTM Committee on Sports Equipment and Facilities. Dr. Heil is also Director of Sports Medicine for the Commonwealth Games of Virginia.

Jane C. Henderson teaches physical education at John Abbott College in Ste. Anne de Bellevue, Québec, Canada. She received the M.S. from Southern Illinois University and a Ph.D. in Sport Psychology from Florida State University. Among her research interests is physiological manifestations of psychological stress. She has served as assistant trainer to the Canadian Judo Team and currently competes as a distance and marathon runner.

Keith P. Henschen is a professor at the University of Utah in the Department of Exercise and Sports Science, where he teaches courses in the psycho-social aspects of sports. He is a member of the American Psychological Association (APA); The American Alliance of Health, Physical Education, Recreation and Dance (AAHPERD); and is on the United States Olympic Committee Sport Psychology Registry. Dr. Henschen has worked with two Olympic governing bodies, numerous professional and collegiate teams, and consulted for a variety of world-class athletes.

Lydia Ievleva is a former Master's student of Terry Orlick with whom she collaborated in writing a chapter, and is currently a doctoral candidate with David Pargman in the Department of Educational Psychology at Florida State University, specializing in Sport Psychology. She has consulted with over 100 athletes from 15 different sports at the amateur, collegiate, and professional level, varying from developmental to world class levels.

Lou M. Makarowski has been in full-time private practice as a licensed psychologist since 1976. He is founder of Achievement Place, Pensacola, Florida, which specializes in performance enhancement, psychotherapy and consultation. Dr. Makarowski received the Ph.D. degree from the University of Iowa while specializing in pediatric, school and clinical psychology. He currently serves as a member of the Behavioral Science staff of the Navy Family Practice Residency Program in Pensacola and is a trauma psychologist at Baptist Hospital, Pensacola.

Bruce C. Ogilvie is professor emeritus in the Department of Psychology at San Jose State University. Dr. Ogilvie is a world-renowned pioneer in applied sport psychology. He has researched, consulted, and published in the area of performance and the high-performance person since 1955. He has contributed over 140 publications on issues ranging from children in sport, identification of psychological factors that contribute to performance success, and the development of performance-enhancing strategies. Dr. Ogilvie has served as a team psychological consultant for numerous U.S. Olympic teams, as well as for professional football, baseball, hockey, and soccer teams. He has also been a private consultant for elite athletes from various sports.

Terry Orlick is an internationally recognized mental training consultant and researcher in applied sport psychology as well as other performance related fields. He is a professor in the School of Human Kinetics at the University of Ottawa, and has been working in the field of applied sport psychology for over 20 years. Orlick is a consultant to numerous Olympic teams, as well as many others pursuing personal excellence in a variety of domains including medicine, professional and amateur sport, music, law, aerospace mission control, the military, sales, children and parenting. He is the current president of the International Society for Mental Training, and the author of numerous articles and 15 books including most recently the second edition of *Pursuit of Excellence,* and *Nice on My Feelings.*

David H. Perrin is associate professor and director of graduate athletic training education and research at the University of Virginia. He is editor of the *Journal of Sport Rehabilitation* and serves on the editorial board of three additional sports medicine periodicals. He has authored one textbook and has written chapters in several others. His research focuses on the assessment of human muscular performance and the treatment and rehabilitation of athletic injuries. He is a practicing athletic trainer at the University of Virginia where he cares for the men's lacrosse team.

John Rickell is currently teaching Ethics and Philosophy of Human Behavior at the University of West Florida where he is affiliated with the Departments of Communication Arts, Philosophy and Religious Studies. He has studied human behavior throughout his professional career and is currently involved in developing and implementing an Applied Ethics Institute at the university. Professor Rickell worked for many years as a consultant to the Morale, Welfare and Recreation (MWR) programs for the U.S. Air Force in the areas of human behavior and ethics. He has lectured to numerous organizations on counseling and ethics.

Robert J. Rotella is an associate professor and director of sport psychology in the Department of Health and Physical Education at the University of Virginia. His research writings have focussed on stress, anxiety, self-confidence, performance enhancement, and the psychology of injury rehabilitation. In addition, Dr. Rotella has co-authored six books and numerous chapters in sport psychology and sport medicine texts. Throughout his career Dr. Rotella has emphasized the application of sport psychology to enhance the lives and performances of highly committed athletes.

Michael L. Sachs is an associate professor in the Department of Physical Education, Temple University, specializing in exercise and sport psychology. He received his Ph. D. in sport psychology from Florida State University, and previously taught at the University of Québec at Trois-Rivières. He served as a Research Project Coordinator in the Applied Research and Evaluation Unit in the Department of Pediatrics, University of Maryland School of Medicine. He is a licensed psychologist in Maryland, as well as a Certified Consultant, AAASP. Dr. Sachs has served as the President of the Association for the Advancement of Applied Sport Psychology.

Gerry Schwille is the Head Athletic Trainer in the Department of Intercollegiate Athletics at Temple University. He was the Director of the Valley Hospital Sports Institute, Ridgewood, NJ, and Head Athletic Manager for the New Jersey Generals of the United States Football League. He received his master's degree in Physical Education/Sports Medicine from Oklahoma State University, and is currently a doctoral candidate in the Sports Administration Department of Temple University. He is a member of the American College of Sports Medicine, a Certified Athletic Trainer of the National Athletic Trainers' Association, and a Licensed Athletic Trainer in Pennsylvania and New Jersey.

Gregory A. Shelley received his master's degree in sport psychology from the University of Iowa. While at Iowa, he worked with Deidre Connelly on a variety of research projects pertaining to sport injuries. Greg is currently working on his doctorate degree in sport psychology at the University of Utah under the direction of Keith Henschen. In addition to his work in the area of athletic injuries, special research interests include: termination from sport, person perception, and group dynamics in sport. Greg enjoys weight training, hunting, fishing, and wildlife photography.

Michael R. Sitler is an assistant professor in the Department of Physical Education, Temple University, specializing in athletic training/sports medicine. He received his Ed. D. in sports medicine from New York University. Prior to his arrival at Temple University, he was an Assistant Professor at the United States Military Academy, West Point, NY for six years. He is a certified member of the National Athletic Trainers' Association (NATA) and is currently the Program Director of the NATA approved undergraduate Athletic Training Education program at Temple University. One of his primary research interests is injury intervention in athletics, and his work in prophylactic ankle and knee bracing is recognized both nationally and internationally. Dr. Sitler is currently serving as the Chair of the Pennsylvania Athletic Trainers' Society Research Committee and is a member of the Eastern Athletic Trainers' Association Research Committee.

Aynsley M. Smith is a nurse counselor in sport psychology at the Sports Medicine Center of the Mayo Clinic in Rochester, MN. She earned the M.A. and R.N. degrees, and is currently completing her Ph. D. degree in Kinesiology at the University of Minnesota-Twin Cities. Ms. Smith has published in journals such as the *Mayo Clinic Proceedings* and *Sports Medicine*; her research is primarily focused on the post-injury emotional responses of athletes, and on the epidemiology of injury in ice hockey. Her applied work centers on counseling interventions with injured athletes.

Bruce W. Tuckman is a professor at Florida State University where he teaches courses in educational psychology, sport psychology and research methods. He has published numerous textbooks, a novel about the rehabilitation of an injured marathon runner and many research articles. He is working on a book about self-motivation, is a former marathon runner and competes as a racewalker.

Diane M. Wiese-Bjornstal is an assistant professor in the Division of Kinesiology at the University of Minnesota-Twin Cities, where she teaches undergraduate and graduate courses in sport psychology. She received her Ph. D. in physical education, with emphases in the social psychology of sport and biomechanics, from the University of Oregon. Dr. Wiese-Bjornstal has published in a variety of journals such as *The Sport Psychologist, Journal of Sport and Exercise Psychology, Research Quarterly for Exercise and Sport,* and *Sports Medicine.* Her primary research interests in the sport injury area center on the role of athletic trainers and coaches in the injury recovery process and, in collaboration with Ms. Smith, the development of a theoretical model of post-injury psychological response and recovery.

Preface

This book comprises 15 chapters that center upon causal and rehabilitative factors associated with athletic injury. Although injury is multidimensional, only a psychological orientation toward injury is adopted here.

Needless to say, the incidence of sport injury is very high and its consequences frequently formidable. A case need not be made here for the importance of minimizing the physical and mental debilitation that traumatized athletes endure. To this end, innumerable articles, books, and research reports have been produced by biomechanicians, athletic trainers, orthopaedic physicians, and sport equipment manufacturers. However, within the past 15 years or so, a rather impressive body of work has taken a different perspective. Rather than viewing injury from structural, anatomical, or physical environmental directions, this approach emphasizes elements of the psychological domain wherein special attention is given to affective, perceptual/cognitive, and personological factors. Many of these early efforts were directed toward the prediction and prevention of athletic injury, with considerably less attention given to rehabilitative considerations. However, within the past few years, the latter area in particular has been emphasized, and a number of effective, creative therapeutic methods structured on established, or at least fairly widely accepted, psychological theory have been advocated.

The contributing authors in this volume are persons of considerable professional experience. With reference to the chapters they have written, their expertise may be categorized into three general areas. They are either psychologists or mental health professionals with keen interests in sport-related behavior; sport psychology experts per se (many of whom have to their credit personal histories of athletic participation either as athletes or coaches); and lastly, some of the authors are athletic trainers. The daily concerns of those in the latter category are with injured skeletal muscle, fractured bones, damaged corrective tissue, and faulty joints. But trainers are also obliged to understand motivation for rehabilitative behavior and principles underlying compliance and adherence.

Although contributing authors proceed in different directions in their respective chapters, some overlap in their individual reviews of related literature may be evident. Rather than purge this occasional duplication of effort, an editorial decision was made to permit authors to integrate conclusions and interpretations from the existing literature in a fashion that was personally meaningful.

The chapters are presented in four sections. Chapter assignments are, of course, based upon relevance to the major thrust of a section. In some cases, although of obvious importance to the book's mission, a clear-cut section assignment for a chapter was difficult to determine. That is, some of the chapters could logically have been located in other sections. Such choice not withstanding, all chapters have been solicited from highly knowledgeable persons with considerable experience in their topical areas.

Section 1 consists of material that is conceptual or descriptive of experiences, assertions, and premises upon which later chapters or sections are predicated. It is, by and large, introductory and provides insight into the general psychological nature of athletic injury.

In **Section 2** various relationships between athletic injury and psychological variables are discussed. These relationships imply the existence of measures that are, or can be, incorporated into preventive as well as rehabilitative methods.

Section 3 comprises chapters that describe counseling approaches recommended for use with injured athletes. **Section 4** does the same, but for permanently disabled athletes.

Preceding each section is an editorial commentary that describes its contents and attempts to place its chapters in perspective.

Although the book may be responsive to many professional needs and interests, its primary target is those persons who work frequently with injured athletes. The book's paramount goal, therefore, is to provide caveats and clues to counsellors, athletic trainers, and those preparing for such careers, who stand to benefit from the insights and wisdom of those with considerable experience in this area.

Finally, I wish to acknowledge the efforts of persons who have contributed meaningfully to the preparation of this volume: Lydia Ievleva, one of my doctoral students who tackled a variety of relevant tasks with enthusiasm and efficiency; Steve Heyman and Craig Fisher who reviewed an early draft of the book; and Andy Ostrow, President, Fitness Information Technology, Publishers, who conceived the idea for this project and provided a good deal of advice along the way.

David Pargman
Tallahassee, Florida

SECTION 1
Injury and Sport—
the Problem: Conceptual
and Practical Approaches

SECTION 1

Injury and Sport—the Problem: Conceptual and Practical Approaches

The purpose of this section is to present important injury-related factors that are basic to chapters in the following three sections of the book. This section begins with an introductory chapter written by the book's editor, **David Pargman**, which, in effect, is a brief review of psychological factors that researchers have investigated in an effort to improve our understanding of sport injury. Most of these issues are also discussed in considerably greater detail in subsequent chapters.

The second chapter by **Jane Henderson** and **William Carroll** also addresses the relationship between sport injury and psychology but emphasizes the injury side of the equation. Helpful case studies are provided.

John Heil and **Perry Fine**'s chapter elucidates a perceptual experience that is all too often part of the injury experience, namely pain. Their perspective is biopsychological.

The last chapter in this section by **Louis Makarowski** and **John G. Rickell** deals with ethical issues facing professionals who counsel and work in other ways with injured athletes. It raises a number of provocative issues that are often not considered by such individuals.

Chapter 1

Sport Injuries: An Overview of Psychological Perspectives

David Pargman
Florida State University

This chapter briefly overviews selected psychological factors associated with athletic injury that are discussed in greater detail in the subsequent chapters. Among the variables addressed are personality traits, self-concept, and response to psychosocial stress stimuli in an athlete's life. In addition, a number of basic terms and concepts are defined and clarified.

Is there anything redeeming about athletic injury? If there is, it is assuredly of a secondary or indirect benefit, at least where athletes are concerned. Certainly, good things may accrue from physical debilitation. Victims may be compelled to reorder their lives and life-styles or to develop creative and fulfilling logistical strategies to meet the demands of heretofore uncommon physical challenges. New and meaningful relationships may also be established with others whom the injured may never have encountered were it not for their sport-related trauma. All of this notwithstanding, physical injury is essentially a negative experience that athletes typically and fervently try to avoid. But the rigorous, physical, competitive nature of organized sport often belies these avoidance attempts. Sport is clearly a breeding ground for physical injury.

What follows in this chapter is an overview of selected psychological factors that are hypothesized to be related to the experience of sport injury.

Subsequent chapters will discuss these factors in greater depth. Included will be certain perceptual/ cognitive, affective, and personological considerations that have received attention in the general psychological and sport psychological (in particular) literature. Thus, the contents of this chapter emphasize causes and consequences of sport injury other than those that are structural, organic, and physiological. The tendency for all too many sport enthusiasts as well as for medical or paramedical personnel is to dwell upon an injury's physical dimensions. Although they recognize the realities of compulsory withdrawal from sport and its financial and competitive consequences (especially to collegiate and professional athletes and their teams), medical experts, more often than not, attend to the physical consequences of injury. Behavioral, cognitive, and emotional psychological dimensions of sport injury, from both causal and rehabilitative points of view, are often overlooked or minimized. This chapter, then, deals specifically and pointedly with the psychological dimensions of athletic injury.

The intensity with which sport proceeds, the attractive incentives offered to its successful participants, and the dangerous terrain and burdensome climatic conditions under which it often occurs account for a high incidence of sport injury.

Although various operational definitions of the term "injury" becloud descriptive statistics, published estimates for secondary and collegiate levels in the United States alone are close to 3/4 of a million injuries per year (Bergandi, 1985). Other estimates are for more than 850,000 per year at the high school level alone (Noble, Porter, & Bachman, 1982; Wrenn & Ambrose, 1980). When sport injury is examined out of the secondary and collegiate context (recreational activities and professional sport), the incidence may be as high as 3-5 million annually (Kraus & Conroy, 1984). Ironically, these numbers are expected to rise despite advancements in athletic equipment and rule changes (Tator & Edmonds, 1986). This may be due to an ever-increasing number of participants, greater societal interest in sport, and greater availability of leisure time. Despite the well-intentioned efforts of the amateur and professional sport establishments, athletic injury continues to undermine the aspirations and achievements of some participants. For them it is a bane.

Whereas the term "accident" suggests something unforeseen, as in a totally random occurrence (equipment failure, slippery playing surface, etc.), "injury" may involve aggressive behavior with an intent to do harm (to oneself or to another). Indeed, results of some older studies point to personality and social adjustment variables as underlying causal factors (Brown, 1976; Conger, Gaskill, Glad, Hassell, Rainey, & Sawrey, 1959; Levine, McHugh, Lee, & Rahe, 1977; Shaffer, Schmidt, Zlotowitz, & Fisher, 1977; Shaffer, Towns, Schmidt, Fisher, & Zlotowitz, 1974; Tillman & Hobbs, 1949). Accordingly, sport injury may be, at least in part a function of psychological predisposition, which in turn, may clarify the incidence, type, or intensity of athletic injury. Indeed, a number of published papers include findings in support of the relationship between psychological factors and sport injury (Bergandi, 1985; Burckes, 1981; Gould, Weiss, & Weinberg, 1981; Kerr & Minden, 1988; Pargman, 1976; Pargman & Lunt, 1989; Valliant, 1981; Weiss & Troxell, 1986; Yukelson, 1986).

In addition, attempts to clarify "injury proneness" in sport have been attempted with psychodynamic explanations (Sanderson, 1977). Burckes (1981) suggested that some athletes may facilitate their own injury by volitionally entering high-risk situations. In such instances injury satisfies a need for sympathy that resides at low levels of consciousness. Guilt, related to poor previous performance, or a need to escape anxiety associated with competition may be additional motives that operate at low levels of awareness. Deutsch (1985) presented case studies that supposedly reveal underlying symbolic representations of sport injury that he suggests correlate with basic needs in other aspects of life. Beisser (1967) also described injury-related problems that appear to have psychiatric bases.

Psychological Factors Believed To Be Related To Sport Injuries

A number of behavioral factors believed to be related to sport injury have been studied. Among these are: personality, compliance, self-concept, and social factors.

Personality

Among the unusually large number of personality studies reported in the sport psychology literature are some that use trait inventories and other personality variables to assess injury frequency and intensity (Brown, 1971; Jackson, Jarrett, Bailey, Kausek, Swanson, & Powell, 1978; Kraus & Gullen, 1969; Pargman, 1976; Valliant, 1981). Results from some of these studies point to significant relationships between variables such as time missed from games or practice due to injury, and scores on trait personality scales. However, such alleged links are, at best, tenuous and far from definitive. Unfortunately, this literature, although thought-provoking, has not yet generated conclusions that coaches, athletes, and trainers may find useful.

Anderson and Williams (1988) have suggested that some personality traits "... may dispose one to be less susceptible to the effects of stressors" (p. 301). Thus, they suggest an association between psychology (particularly the stress variable) and sport injury. Their hypotheses have been supported in football but not in many other sports. Their model, similar to one proposed by Smith (1986), emphasizes an integration of cognitive, physiological, attentional, behavioral, intrapersonal, social, and stress history variables that may yet permit some prediction of sport injury. However, additional research is necessary.

Compliance

Yet another dimension of the relationship between sport injury and human psychology is athlete compliance with rehabilitation programs. In view of remarks made in the beginning of this chapter about the large numbers of athletes injured annually, it may be assumed that many are also engaged in, or should be engaged, in physical rehabilitative efforts. However, little investigation has been done with regard to athlete adherence to such programs (Fisher, Domm, & Wuest, 1988; Wiese & Weiss, 1987). This is an area in dire need of empirical investigation as what has been reported to date is essentially anecdotal (e.g., Wiese & Weiss, 1987).

Self-Concept

Yaffe's (1978) suggestion that the psychological impact of an injury is better understood by explaining the self-concept, deserves consideration, and a number of studies have explored this relationship. For instance, Young and Cohen (1981) reported a significant difference in total self-concept score and four subscale scores, between injured and noninjured female high school basketball players. Interestingly, the injured athletes demonstrated a more positive view of themselves (identity), their state of health, their physical appearance, and physical skills and a more positive sense of personal worth than did the noninjured players. Their overall self-concept was also higher. These findings were interpreted by the authors as suggestive of greater physical risks being taken by the injured athletes during competition and practice because of the positive views held about themselves. Supposedly, this inclination resulted in greater vulnerability to injury. In contrast, the noninjured players expressed greater receptivity to mild derogatory statements included in the Tennessee Self-Concept Scale (TSCS). This may indicate lower self-confidence or esteem with regard to sport skill performance. Perhaps the noninjured players felt comparatively more inadequate than their injured counterparts and were therefore more receptive to criticism. Consequently, they may have behaved in a safer or more conservative way on court.

This attractive speculation is, however, inconsistent with results from a previous study conducted by the same researchers. Young and Cohen (1979) used female college tournament basketball players as subjects. No differences were observed between injured and noninjured athletes with regard to total self-concept or other subscale scores.

Results reported by Lamb (1986) suggest an inverse relationship between self-concept and injury in college female varsity field hockey players as measured by the TSCS. Lamb concluded that a low self-concept level was related to a high frequency of injury.

Relationships between self-concept and sport injury should be investigated further. Additional findings from multivariate research designs with larger subject samples in a wider variety of sport areas may ultimately yield findings that are of practical application to athletic trainers, physical therapists, and coaches. Unlike personality traits, self-concept is a psychological variable that may fluctuate within short time-frames and is, therefore, amenable to strategic manipulations. It may have important implications for injury prevention and rehabilitation.

Social Factors

The direct or indirect interaction with others in the environment may exert both negative and positive influences upon individuals. For instance, an argument with a teammate or coach prior to or during competition may arouse an athlete to the extent that he or she plays havoc with attentional or cognitive functions, thereby impeding performance and causing movement to be mechanically incorrect. The intensity and frequency of social stressors may thus have an impact upon vulnerability to sport injury.

Bramwell, Minoru, Wagner, and Holmes (1975) administered The Social and Athletic Readjustment Rating Scale (SARRS), consisting of 57 events likely to occur in an athlete's life, to 82 collegiate football players. Some of the events, such as making a serious mistake in a game or having "trouble with the coach," are sport related . Others are unrelated to sport. The responses are indicative of the psychosocial disturbances in an athlete's life. Bramwell et al. observed that subjects with low Life Events Scores had the lowest injury rates (35%); those with medium scores showed an injury rate of 44%; and those whose Life-Event Scores were high had an overwhelming injury rate of 72%. Coddington and Troxell (1980) modified the SARRS to make it appropriate to high school football players. Using 114 subjects, they concluded that subjects with emotional conditions associated with high scores on family instability and parental divorce or death incurred more "significant" injuries than did those whose scores were not elevated. These conclusions were also supported by subsequent work done by Cryan and Alles (1983), who used college football players.

However, evidence contrary to the above findings is also available. Passer and Seese's (1983) work casts a shadow of doubt on the relationship between psychological factors and sport injury. In working with two different collegiate football teams, they observed a meaningful relationship between these variables in but one of the groups. Williams, Tonyman, and Wadsworth (1986) also failed to observe support for this association in male and female college volleyball players. Perhaps the interaction of attentional, cognitive-perceptual, and personality demands of certain sports, in combination with psychological attributes of individual athletes, should be carefully incorporated in future research designs in order to dispel uncertainty about the relationship between psychosocial factors and sport injury.

It seems appropriate to conclude by saying that additional well-conceived research will undoubtedly decrease conflicts and shortcomings in the existing literature related to the psychological bases of athletic injury. However, currently available findings strongly suggest that injury prevention and the development of rehabilitation programs for injured athletes should be approached from psychological directions as well as anatomical, mechanical, and biological directions. Those who work professionally with athletes of all skill levels should strive to acquire insight into the emotional, perceptual, personological, and social psychological factors suggested in this chapter as potentially related to sport injury.

REFERENCES

Anderson, M.B., & Williams, J.M. (1988). A model of stress and athletic injury: Prediction and prevention. *Journal of Sport and Exercise Psychology, 10*, 299-306.

Beisser, A.R. (1967). *The madness in sport.* New York: Appleton-Century-Crofts.

Bergandi, T.A. (1985). Psychological variables relating to the incidence of athletic injury. *International Journal of Sport Psychology, 16,* 141-149.

Bramwell, S.T., Minoru, M., Wagner, N.N., & Holmes, T.H. (1975). Psychosocial factors in athletic injuries. *Journal of Human Stress, 1*(2), 6-20.

Brown, R. (1971). Personality characteristics related to injury in football. *Research Quarterly, 42,* 133-138.

Brown, T.D. (1976). Personality traits and their relationship to traffic violations. *Perceptual and Motor Skills, 42,* 467-70.

Burckes, M.E. (1981). The injury-prone athlete. *Scholastic Coach, 6*(3), 47-48.

Coddington, R., & Troxell, J.R. (1980, December). The effect of emotional factors on football injury rates–a pilot study. *Journal of Human Stress.* pp. 3-5.

Conger, J.J., Gaskill, H.S., Glad, D., Hassell, L., Rainey, R.V., & Sawrey, W.L. (1959). Psychological and psychophysiological factors in motor vehicle accidents. *Journal of the American Medical Association, 169,* 1581-1587.

Cryan, P.D., & Alles, W.F. (1983). The relationship between stress and college football injuries. *Journal of Sports Medicine and Physical Fitness, 23,* 52-58.

Deutsch, R.E. (1985). The psychological implications of sports related injuries. *International Journal of Sport Psychology, 16,* 232-237.

Fisher, A.C., Domm, M.A., & Wuest, D.A. (1988). Adherence to sports-injury rehabilitation programs. *The Physician and Sports Medicine, 16,* 47-52.

Gould, D., Weiss, M., & Weinberg, R. (1981). Psychological characteristics of Big Ten Wrestlers. *Journal of Sport Psychology, 3,* 69-81.

Jackson, D.W., Jarrett, H., Bailey, D., Kausek, J., Swanson, J.J., & Powell, J.W. (1978). Injury prediction in the young athlete, a preliminary report. *American Journal of Sports Medicine, 6*(1), 6-14.

Kerr, G., & Minden, H. (1988). Psychological factors related to the occurrence of athletic injuries. *Journal of Sport and Exercise Psychology, 10,* 167-173.

Kraus, J.F., & Conroy, C. (1984). Mortality and morbidity from injury in sports and recreation. *Annual Review of Public Health, 5,* 163-192.

Kraus, J.F., & Gullen, W.H. (1969). An epidemiological investigation of predictor variables associated with intra-mural touch football injuries. *American Journal of Public Health, 59*(12), 2144-2156.

Lamb, M. (1986). Self-concept and injury frequency among female college field hockey players. *Athletic Training, 21*, 220-224.

Levine, J.G., McHugh, W.B., Lee, J.O., & Rahe, R.H. (1977). Recent life changes and accidents aboard an attack carrier. *Military Medicine, 27*, 469--471.

Noble, H.B., Porter, M., Bachman, D.C. (1982). Athletic trainers: Their place in the health care system. *Illinois Medical Journal. 162*, 41-44.

Pargman, D. (1976). Visual disembedding and injury in college football players. *Perceptual and Motor Skills, 42*, 762.

Pargman, D., & Lunt, S. (1989). The relationship of self-concept and locus of control to the severity of injury in comparatively lower ability level collegiate football players, *Sports Training, Medicine and Rehabilitation, 1*, 203-208.

Passer, M.W., & Seese, M.D. (1983, December). Life stress and athletic injury: Examination of positive versus negative events and three moderator variables. *Journal of Human Stress*, pp. 11-16.

Sanderson, F.H. (1977). The psychology of the injury prone-athlete. *British Journal of Sports Medicine, 11*(1), 56-57.

Shaffer, J.W., Schmidt, C.W., Zlotowitz, H.I., & Fisher, R.S. (1977). Social adjustment profiles of female drivers involved in fatal and nonfatal accidents. *American Journal of Psychiatry, 134*, 801-804.

Shaffer, J.W., Towns, W., Schmidt, C.W., Fisher, R.S., & Zlotowitz, H.I. (1974). Social adjustment profiles of fatally injured drivers: A replication and extension. *Archives of General Psychiatry, 30*, 508-511.

Smith, R.E. (1986). Toward a cognitive-affective model of athletic burnout. *Sport Psychology, 8*, 36-50.

Tator, C.H., & Edmonds, V.E. (1986). Sports and recreation are a rising cause of spinal cord injury. *The Physician and Sports Medicine, 14*, 157-167.

Tillman, W., & Hobbs, G. (1949). The accident-prone automobile driver: A study of psychiatric background. *American Journal of Psychiatry, 106*, 321-331.

Valliant, P.M. (1981). Personality and injury in competitive runners. *Perceptual and Motor Skills, 53*, 251-253.

Weiss, M.R., & Troxell, R.K. (1986). Psychology of the injured athlete. *Athletic Training, 21*, 104-109.

Wiese, D.M., & Weiss, M.R. (1987). Psychological rehabilitation and physical injury: Implications for the sports medicine team. *The Sport Psychologist, 1,* 318-330.

Williams, J.M., Tonyman, P., & Wadsworth, W.A. (1986, Spring). Relationship of life stress to injury in intercollegiate volleyball. *Journal of Human Stress,* pp. 38-43.

Wrenn, J.P., & Ambrose, D. (1980). An investigation of health care practices for high school athletes in Maryland. *Athlete Training, 15,* 85-92.

Yaffe, M., (1978). Psychological aspects of sports injuries. *Research Papers in Physical Education, 67*(3).

Young, M.L., & Cohen, D.A. (1979). Self-concept and injuries among female college tournament basketball players. *American Corrective Therapy Journal, 33*(5), 139-142.

Young, M.L., & Cohen, D.A. (1981). Self-concept and injuries among female high school basketball players. *Journal of Sports Medicine, 21,* 5-11.

Yukelson, D. (1986). Psychology of sport and the injured athlete. In D.B. Bernhart (Ed.), *Clinics in Physical Therapy* (pp.175-195). NY: Churchill Livingstone.

Chapter 2

The Athletic Trainer's Role In Preventing Sport Injury And Rehabilitating Injured Athletes: A Psychological Perspective

Jane Henderson
John Abbott College
William Carroll
United States Sports Academy

In this chapter we describe various responses to sport injury in athletes with whom we have worked, as well as selected psychological factors that may contribute to sport-related injury. Our perspective is that of the athletic trainer. It is our contention that insufficient attention has been allocated to this view. We additionally discuss intervention tactics that we have used with athletes and the measure of success achieved.

Athletic trainers realize the importance of understanding psychological factors involved in injury. Eight out of every 10 athletes will be injured at some time in their career, frequently while at college, and will miss at least three weeks of practice and competition (Dulberg, 1988). The intimacy of the relationship between athlete and trainer may frequently provide trainers with an opportunity to enjoy a rapport with injured athletes that may enhance opportunities for insights into an athlete's psychological make-up. Therefore, athletic trainers may notice that some athletes insist on playing while in pain, and there are some who may fake an injury on Tuesday, miss practice all week, and play Saturday. For some the evaluative dimension of sport performance may be paramount, and these athletes seem to be dependent upon a competitive experience to determine their identity. Because of these factors and the multidimensionality of injury itself, it is very difficult to ascertain the precise nature of the interplay between physiological and psychological makeup.

The academic preparation of athletic trainers typically emphasizes treating injuries and understanding physical rehabilitation. However, it is also important for trainers to understand the psychological dimensions of rehabilitation and injury.

Identity Problem

Often an individual's identity is contingent upon his or her role as an athlete. The danger in such a narrow identity focus is that an athletic career is short-lived with injuries often viewed as major crises. This kind of threat to one's self-worth is often so highly stressful that other attributes of the individual may be totally overshadowed by the athletic identity.

An example of this phenomenon is the case of a senior linebacker on a Division II football team. The linebacker suffered a potential grade III ankle sprain in the next-to-the-last game of the season. Instead of waiting for assistance, he immediately limped off the field and refused to talk to the athletic trainer, but stood on the sideline yelling obscenities at the officials until an unsportsmanlike conduct penalty was called. The player agreed to use crutches but did not show up for therapy, or keep a scheduled appointment with a physician. He was absent from practices the next week and from the final game of the season. The week after the final game, the player dropped out of school needing less than thirty credit hours to graduate.

Indications of this athlete's impending withdrawal from sport were evident. More attention should have been directed towards his entire concept of self and not focused exclusively on his athletic prowess. Although this identity problem was the product of many years of personal development, recognition of other attributes of the individual could well have alleviated some of that negative conditioning. This athlete's identity revolved entirely around performance.

It is necessary for athletes to recognize the multidimensional character of their lives. They are more than just athletes. Athletes must have separate identities as students, teammembers, friends, and contributors to society. Athletes must realize the importance of self-worth, despite what occurs within athletic performance. Also, coaches, parents, and athletic administrators would do well to appreciate this point.

The training room is an unusual environment. For many athletes the opportunities for comradeship, the relaxed atmosphere, and the casual attire or nudity are conducive to the expression of emotions and personal thoughts in contrast to the practice or competitive milieu. Therefore, the trainer must be able to identify potential problems and take steps to ensure that the athlete receives the necessary professional guidance.

One of the functions of a trainer, although not often overtly recognized, is to act as a first-line counselor. The trainer needs to be available to assess more than just physical injuries. Certain psychological problems will demonstrate recognizable signs and symptoms. However, it is very important for trainers to be able to identify their professional limitations. When trainers reach the limit of help that they are capable of providing, they may still serve athletes in two important ways: (a) by providing assurance that seeking professional psychological help is not a sign of weakness but rather a step toward taking charge of one's life and (b) by recommending a competent counselor or psychologist who is capable of leading the athlete to a resolution of the problem.

Unfortunately, the athletic trainer may often be isolated from the coaching staff and the rest of the medical team. It is important that lines of communication be kept open between the trainer and the coaching staff, doctors, psychologists, and administrators. Because the first hints of physical-psychological problems are often demonstrated in the training room it is extremely important for the trainer to communicate regularly with all team personnel.

Due to their unique and central position in the sports community, alert trainers may be able to avert some potential injuries that are related to psychological functioning. The athletic trainer has access to physicians' reports and has the experience of having dealt with many athletes suffering from numerous types of injuries. The trainer is then in an excellent position to be realistic about each athlete's physical strengths and weaknesses. At the same time the trainer must be sensitive to the athletes' subtle expressions of self-doubt and fear. Athletes may drop many veiled hints about their desire to step back from competition. The astute trainer, the one who actively listens and integrates the meaning of verbal clues with physical symptoms, may be able to discern unspoken messages and begin to provide help or relief to the athlete who is either faking an injury or who truly believes that he or she has one although no physical symptoms are evident. Such an athlete may be saying in fact, "Help, I don't think I want to continue playing." This strategy is exemplified by the following example, the case of George.

George came from a very well-known football family. His grandfather was an All-American at a major institution as were his father and uncle, both of whom went on to play professionally. Although he possessed superior size, by the time he became a senior in high school, it was apparent that his skill levels were no better than average. Although he earned a starting position in his senior year, he was graded poorly in preseason scrimmage films. During the first game, he was consistently outplayed by the player opposing him on the line of scrimmage. Subsequently he was pulled from the game and replaced by a substitute. After the game, he presented himself in the training room complaining of intense low back pain. He was examined by the team physician and given an appointment for the following Monday. All diagnostic tests were negative, but the subjective complaints continued. The physician prescribed a regimen of medication and moist heat, and withheld George from practice for the week. The following week, the subjective complaints were elevated; therefore, diagnostic tests were repeated. Again results were negative. This continued for three weeks accompanied by increased posturing prior to palpation. Diagnostic tests were repeated (five weeks after initial complaints) and were again negative. The decision was made at that time to withhold the athlete for the remainder of the season for "medical" reasons. The athlete continued therapy three times per week until the end of the season but never returned for therapy thereafter.

George's injury may have been a conscious defense used to legitimize his diminished position. The overt symptoms and complaints were treated, but the underlying psychological trauma was totally overlooked. Athletic trainers cannot afford to provide "assembly line" sports medicine. Trainers must not only recognize the psychological aspects of an injury but must also foresee their possibility and counteract the potential negativity. In George's case the cognitive approach of defining recovery parameters and involving the athlete in the planning of the rehabilitation protocol could have been a healthy diversion. The achievement of short-term goals in the rehabilitation process would have allowed a sense of accomplishment and could well have led to a more desirable result. In contrast to this outcome is the case of Alice.

Alice arrived on campus as a freshman with a bubbling personality, very outgoing and full of life. Alice had been All-State in track, volleyball, and softball during her high school career. Her talent exceeded that of her teammates and opponents; however, college athletics proved to be a different matter. She had trouble making the volleyball team and spent most of the fall season on the bench. As the season progressed and Alice's playing time did not increase, changes in Alice's demeanor and actions signalled adaptation problems. She became quiet and withdrawn. Answers to direct questions became one word or were not forthcoming at all. She appeared very despondent.

Alice decided that she needed to be stronger physically to compete at the college level. Without seeking proper guidance, she embarked on an ill-conceived strength program. She was doing weight sets to exhaustion two times a day. After two months of this self-designed program, she presented herself in the training room. She was emotionally distraught and could not understand why she had not gained strength and actually appeared to be losing it. She had "hit bottom" and was finally reaching out for help.

The weight program was the easy part to correct. Her own program had left the muscle tissue in a constant "tear-down" mode. After giving her some basic information on proper strength training techniques and explaining that more training was not necessarily better training, a new program was developed for Alice. As she continued using the new program, Alice was able to discern positive gains during interim testing. This experience was basically her first athletic success at the collegiate level, and it gave her a great deal of confidence in the trainer. Her attitude began to improve, and her earlier outgoing nature began to return. By spring, she was a successful member of the track team and also one of the leading hitters on the softball team.

Self-Esteem

Self-esteem problems may manifest themselves in various ways, as in the case of Joe. Joe was not a particularly physically attractive person, but he did possess a combination of natural physical ability and skill educability that made him an exceptional athlete. His major focus was on playing professional football. Throughout his prep career, he had played on very successful teams. He was therefore highly recruited and chose a major institution with a winning tradition.

Unfortunately, because of factors not within Joe's control, such as team violation of NCAA rules, team probation, and scholarship limitations, Joe's team did not fare well during the years of his participation. By the start of his senior year, the team had won only seven games in the previous three years and was picked to finish last in the conference for the coming season. Because of the team's mediocrity, Joe felt he had received much less attention from the professional scouts than his individual performance statistics merited. He therefore believed that the team's success during his senior year would be a major factor in determining whether he would be selected in the professional football draft.

By the midpoint of the season, the team was winless, and general team motivation appeared very low. Joe, however, was still performing at a high level. In the sixth game, Joe suffered an acromioclavicular sprain to his right shoulder. Due to the severity of the injury (Grade II) and the shortness of the remainder of the season, Joe's injury proved to be season ending. At first, he reacted very angrily, blaming everything and everyone for his injury. Although he threw himself with furor into the rehabilitation program in order to show full recovery by draft time and attained all intermediate rehabilitation goals in record time, there were still danger signals. He had to be watched closely to prevent him from exceeding prescribed resistance (weight training) standards. However, he insisted on doing the rehabilitation program during times when other team members were not in the training room, weight room, or pool. His affect appeared much flatter than during previous encounters. His attire became less meticulous, and his general hygiene appeared to be at a lower level than before.

After numerous discussions with the athletic trainer during which Joe exhibited danger signs, such as the lack of interest in schoolwork and campus events, and a general decline in his formerly positive attitude, the need for referral became evident. Joe was convinced to keep an appointment with the psychologist at the student health center. He was subsequently referred to a sport psychologist and remained under his tutelage throughout the school year. Problems were then identified involving self-esteem and perceived status. Although not chosen highly in the draft, Joe did sign a professional contract and went on to play professional football for seven years.

The personality traits that most likely contribute to an athlete's success may also be factors related to the injury process and rehabilitation (Eby & Van Gyn, 1987). The compulsive, highly motivated, single-mindedness that is required for many athletes to succeed may also enable them to view injury as another part of the game. To reach their present level of success many athletes have had to overcome substantial physical and psychological barriers and be able to view the injury process as another hurdle to be taken in stride.

A prime example of this was Troy. Troy was an overachiever. His athletic talents were marginal, but his motivation and work ethic were beyond question. By his junior year, after two years of primarily special team and scout team experience, he became the starting cornerback for a northeastern Division I college football team. In the fourth game of the year, Troy suffered what was later diagnosed as a Grade II sprain of the lateral collateral ligament. At first, Troy was extremely apprehensive, trying to mask the pain upon palpation and insisting the diagnosis was incorrect. The team physician and trainer spent a great deal of time with Troy explaining the nature of his injury and the course of his rehabilitation. Troy was in rehabilitation twice a day, with the second session always scheduled at the same time as the team was preparing for practice. During practice, Troy was allowed and encouraged to go on the field where he kept abreast of game plans and defensive strategies. Three weeks after his injury, Troy could produce a full pain-free range of motion of the injured knee and was able to begin functional activities. He was reexamined weekly by the team physician and was given permission to return to activity, wearing a protective brace, 24 days after the injury.

Troy continued his rehabilitation on a daily basis for the rest of the season and on a three times per week schedule in the off-season. When Troy was physically examined during the next preseason period, his knee was pronounced totally sound. Troy enjoyed a very successful senior year, was named to several postseason all-conference teams and played in the Hula Bowl. To his credit, Troy continued rehabilitation twice per week throughout his senior year.

Troy's recovery time was rapid, considering the nature of the injury. The only logical explanation for the unusual speed of his recovery was his degree of maturity and willingness to accept a plan to overcome the present barrier, the injury. He had overcome barriers regarding his size and speed, while maintaining high self-efficacy and successfully dealing with injury. Troy's rehabilitation was successful because (a) he followed the plan constructed for him by the medical team, (b) he sustained a high degree of confidence in his ability to recover from injury, and (c) he never lost sight of his long-term goal to complete rehabilitation and return to play. In view of Troy's very high motivation for rehabilitation therapy, certain considerations were involved. For instance, any type of isolation from the team environment would have been detrimental to his recovery. Therefore, a cognitive approach by the medical team was employed. This consisted of involving the athlete in the planning of his rehabilitation program by defining parameters and interim goals to be achieved at various times in the rehabilitative process. The mystery was taken out of the injury; and this helped Troy realize that injury was not insurmountable, that the same tenacity he showed on the athletic field would contribute to successful rehabilitation.

Athletes, of course, differ in regard to many psychological factors. These relate to their personal reactions to the injury as well as the recovery process. The athlete's psychological strengths and weaknesses may well determine the course of recovery. For example, two college football players, John and Dave, suffered ankle injuries in the same game. Both athletes were similar in size and played the same type of position (i.e., defensive line). Dave's injury was initially believed to be a fracture because of point tenderness. He was therefore transported to the hospital immediately for X-rays. John's ankle was iced, a compression wrap was applied, and he was issued crutches. The eventual official diagnoses by the team physician was that both athletes had suffered second degree inversion ankle sprains.

The course of rehabilitation for these two athletes, however, was totally different. John was able to tolerate some isometric contraction within 24 hours of the injury. Dave could tolerate no motion of the ankle joint for eight days following the injury. John was able to begin modified cardiovascular exercise on a stationary bike and in the pool within four days after the injury. He was able to apply full body weight five days after injury. On the other hand, Dave reported pain upon any attempts to mobilize the injured joint and subsequently was treated with electrical stimulation to prevent atrophy and to promote muscle reeducation.

John was able to perform functional tests within 10 days of the injury and returned to full activity within 14 days after injury occurrence. Dave remained non-weight bearing on crutches for seven days after the injury. His edema was slower to resolve due to his inability to tolerate even mild range of motion. Dave was unable to perform functional tests without pain 26 days after the injury and was not permitted to return to full activity until

38 days.

Reasons for these differential recovery experiences most likely relate to the athletes' psychological characteristics. John obviously was better prepared psychologically not only to cope with but also to recover from his injury. On the other hand, Dave was fearful; he tended to worry and focus on the pain, thus avoiding rehabilitation for fear of experiencing discomfort. Rather than viewing rehabilitation as a necessary steppingstone to recovery, he saw it only as a negative, stressful experience. John, however, was able to accept his setback as a temporary condition. He put his faith in the trainer and team physician and viewed the rehabilitation procedure as one more necessary step involved in the achievement of his ultimate goal, playing football. He accepted pain and was able to deal with it because he trusted those in charge of his rehabilitation and appreciated the need to be completely involved in the process.

The competitive sport experience provides for varying sensations, the least desirable of which is pain. The perception of pain is variable among athletes with regard to intensity (Meyers, Bourgeois, Stewart, & Leunes, 1991). Athletes also vary with regard to pain tolerance and threshold. Such variation is likely to be a function of personality, self-concept, and the degree of internalization of the athlete. Although every injury involves physical damage to a bodily structure, it is just as important to understand that every athlete is going to suffer psychologically as a result of an injury. To properly assist an athlete in injury rehabilitation the athletic trainer must understand certain psychological factors involved in the rehabilitation process.

An injured athlete often feels defenseless, stripped of identity and self-esteem. During the rehabilitation program the athletic trainer should be looking for verbal and nonverbal signals of psychological problems that may not only hamper the recovery but also have a profound effect on the athlete's day-to-day functioning. Some sport psychologists believe that athletes demonstrate injury response similar to grief reactions to death and dying (Nideffer 1989; Rotella & Heyman, 1986). Although this model is in need of more research and testing, to date it is very helpful in explaining athlete responses to injury. Athletes may first typically respond with disbelief and denial, followed by anger, bargaining, depression, and finally, acceptance. Therefore, denial, fear, anger, depression, and even shame are experienced by some athletes as a result of an injury. Of course many variables may affect this response. These include team position, age, skill level, past injury experience, and reactions of others.

Athletes differ in their capacity to address pain. Pain threshold may well be a product of a combination of psychological traits. Results from a study of athletes by Meyers, Bourgeois, Stewart, and Leunes (1991) indicate that pain threshold may be a function of coping (dealing positively with a situation) and cognitive appraisal (intellectually dealing with a situation in a problem-solving manner). Therefore, the use of imagery could be a very effective intervention; for example, "I imagine that the pain is outside of the body." This active visualization combines the intellectual aspect with coping responses and allows the athlete to feel some power over the healing process.

When an athlete experiences injury, the actions of significant others, friends, spouses, etc. often influence motivation for recovery. The injury itself may permit reinforcement that appears positive, but in the long run becomes negative. The secondary gain attributable to reactions by others may well be a stronger reinforcer for maintaining pain than being pain-free. This obviously would have a detrimental effect on recovery time.

Injury Prevention—Attentional Focus And Stress

An injury can occur solely due to lack of appropriate attentional focusing on the part of the athlete. Research has shown a positive, although questionable, connection between stress perception and injury occurrence. A link between these variables may be the athlete's attentional style. As defined by Nideffer (1989), attentional behavior in sport requires that an athlete integrate and respond mentally, emotionally, and/or physically to a variety of internal and external cues. Inappropriate responses due to stress may influence attentional processes and the athlete's ability to interpret appropriate and necessary cues for proper execution of a sport skill, thus leaving the athlete vulnerable to injury.

Athletic trainers need to be aware of inappropriate attentional characteristics in athletes. Signs of stress-related attentional problems might be (a) inability to perform tasks that are usual and routine, such as dropping easy passes, missing the basket completely in basketball, making fundamental mechanical errors; (b) changes in patterns of behavior such as uncharacteristic tardiness, decline in personal hygiene, daydreaming; (c) somatic complaints; (d) irritability and mood swings; (e) apparent diminished motivation. These signs often indicate a deleterious impact of stress upon the athlete's attentional focus. None of these signs alone is evidence of a problem. However, unheeded attentional difficulties may become casual factors in injury occurrence.

Jay is a good example of this. A highly recruited prep football athlete, Jay chose to attend a major southeastern university. In preseason practice, his running speed and playing skills were outstanding. In his first intercollegiate game, he set a school record for rushing yardage.

As school started, Jay began to have problems adjusting to college life. He had difficulty sleeping, and his relationships with other players and fellow students became strained. He became indecisive about his academic goals. His performance at practice and in games suffered as a result of these distractions. In the third game of the season, he attempted to make a cut toward the center of the field and suffered a knee injury subsequently diagnosed as a rupture of the medial collateral ligament and the anterior cruciate ligament. Although the rehabilitation process after surgery went well, this athlete was never able to fulfill his potential. As a result of this injury Jay lost at least a full step in comparison to his pre-injury speed. Because of the nature of his position, this loss of speed eventually eliminated him from achieving his projected potential of athletic success at the collegiate level. Retrospectively, the signs of Jay's attentional difficulties due to his adjustment problems to college life were obvious. At that time, however, the sport medicine orientation took only a physiological perspective. The important part psychology may play in injury prevention was only beginning to be explored. Furthermore, the adaptation process to college life is a universal experience, one that university athletic trainers see on a daily basis. The generalization is made that every athlete will eventually "handle" this problem. However, if the athlete's attentional focus is sufficiently diverted during this coping process, injury potential is greatly enhanced. Unfortunately coping with this experience is a very individual experience.

It is important not to generalize reactions of athletes to situations, but to regard every situation as creating a potential injury problem.

Training Room Dependency

All athletic trainers have come across individuals who, because of the attention afforded by the training room environment, attempt to prolong the injury process beyond its logical course. Usually this involves a perception on the athlete's part that he or she is not receiving adequate attention on the playing field (playing time, or reinforcement). One of the most difficult challenges for the trainer is to wean such individuals from the security provided by the training room atmosphere. Cooperation of the coaching and medical staff is essential to this process.

Trainers may assist athletes in conquering training room dependency by (a) tapering the treatments; (b) encouraging the athlete to develop self-treatment practices, that is, icing after practice on the field, stretching in the locker room prior to and after practice, and using a prescribed home maintenance program; (c) minimizing psychological stress felt by the athlete; (d) enhancing the athlete's self-efficacy for recovery by positively reinforcing successful rehabilitative attempts while encouraging independence.

Practical Applications For Trainers
Involved In The Injury Process

1. Expect and encourage some emotional reaction to injury as a normal response. According to Dr. Richard Parker of the San Diego Sports Medicine Center, the normal flow of chemicals in the brain alters with the sudden cessation of exercise (Mora, 1990). This imbalance affects everything one feels and does. Depression, then, could be a natural by-product of injury and a hindrance to healing and recovery.

2. Recognize that there is no "average" injury because there is no "average" person. Everyone is an individual and reacts differently to similar stimuli. Each person is a product of heredity, environment, and learning. Although there are some common traits among athletes, they are not, as many have believed, "superhuman." Athletes are required to react to a wide range of stressors and are not necessarily immune from sport-related stressful stimuli. Sociopsychological factors that characterize the noncompetitive sport environment are often magnified in sport as sport participation demands inordinate amounts of physical and emotional effort.

   When the trainer deals with an injured athlete, no one treatment regimen should be used. Of course, one must adhere to certain established protocols. However, evaluation of each athlete by the trainer is necessary in order to determine the best course of treatment. In addition, it should not be assumed that even identical or similar injuries will respond to therapy within the same time frame. Psychological factors, which vary widely among athletes, will influence recovery time.

   It is evident, therefore, that realistic personal goals should be established for each individual. The ultimate goal is to return to full activity, but establishing achievable intermediate goals allows the injured athlete to experience a sense of accomplishment at every step along the rehabilitation path. The use of intermediate goals allows for success attainment at various stages during the injury prevention or rehabilitation process. These goals should be reasonable and attainable for the individual athlete, who should be involved in the goal-setting process.

3. It is also important that the trainer understand that he or she is treating the whole person, not only the physical aspect of the athlete's injury. The trainer should be able to detect signals of atypical behavior by the athlete during rehabilitation and make referrals for specialized assistance–that is, nutritional, financial, psychological counselling, etc.

4. The training room's physical attributes may also contribute to the desired psychological milieu. When visiting the training room the athlete should perceive a positive attitude on the part of staff members. The training room must be an environment wherein the athlete is comfortable in expressing him- or herself with a perceived guaranty of confidentiality. It is incumbent upon the training room staff to establish a trusting relationship. Trainers should emphasize a positive problem-solving attitude in the training room and strive to minimize negativism in themselves as well as in clients. No one enjoys the time and effort invested in rehabilitation, but if these factors are presented in a positive fashion the athletes are much more likely to follow the rehabilitative plan and look to the trainers as a problem-solving resource. Regardless of what is going on in their lives, the athletes should believe that they will find not condemnation in the training room, but rather an attentive listener and competent resource manager.

5. At the time of injury, the trainer is often the first medical or paramedical individual in contact with the injured athlete. The trainer's demeanor must be calm, positive, and professional. This sets the tenor of the entire recovery process. Although not a "cheerleader," the trainer encourages the athlete and projects an image of "enabler" who intends to keep the athlete focused on the major goal: recovery.

    Injury rehabilitation should be handled in a positive and careful manner. Instructions to athletes should be offered thoughtfully and the trainer's personal feelings should be expressed with forethought and care. The training room's physical setting should be strategically arranged. For instance, brightly painted walls, or clean floors are all telling signs of a properly functioning and caring environment.

6. The manner in which the trainer describes the rehabilitation plan and presents it orally to the athlete is often as important as the plan itself.

Just as manufacturers package items attractively to promote sales, trainers must give forethought to the ways in which they present their programs. For instance the trainer's facial expression, vocal inflection, and projected confidence in his or her abilities are all mediators of the injured athlete's psychological framework. Unfortunately, some trainers place too much emphasis on "can't" and "don't" rather than on "do" and "can." This reframing of the negative to the positive, while apparently a simple matter, can meaningfully influence the construction and integration of the rehabilitation plan. It is much healthier for athletes to view their rehabilitation in terms of progress rather than in delimitations.

7. Research has shown that negative emotions are related to diminished physiological functioning, that is, reduced blood flow, muscle constriction, and bracing; and are all contraindications for health and healing (Peterson, Seligman & Vaillant, 1988; Schmale & Iker, 1971; Seligman, 1991). The trainer, by modelling a positive approach, can enhance a healthy outlook.

8. Rehabilitation programs should be varied to maintain the interest of the athlete. Interspersing cardiovascular exercise with weight and stretching programs allows relief from boredom and may prevent burn-out. Many injured athletes benefit from time-limited rehabilitation programs because as competitors, they are accustomed to the need to achieve within rigid time schedules. Instead of attending practice at a certain time the athlete will report to the training room for scheduled workouts. This serves two functions: It maintains the structure of routine to which the athlete is accustomed and promotes socialization with the athlete's teammates. These factors may offset some degree of psychological trauma and allow for the channelling of energies into productive activity.

Some Recommended Psychological Interventions
For Trainers Involved In Injury Rehabilitation

1. **Modelling** - Athletes can be exposed to injured athletes who have successfully recovered from similar injuries. Videotapes may be employed to this end.

2. **Positive attitudes** - The brain does not differentiate between imagined events or events that have actually occurred (Suinn, 1980). Through imagery, athletes may develop neural pathways to the muscles that are used in a particular activity. If the messages are many and negative,

muscle bracing will decrease blood flow, and decreased range of motion will occur, thus limiting healing. However, if through imagery the messages are positive and skill oriented, athletes may actually strengthen the neural pathways for certain movements in their sport (Suinn, 1980). Therefore, it is important to help athletes maintain a positive mental attitude about healing. Athletes should be taught to tune in to their bodies and mentally to direct energy to areas of injury. Imagery, or creative visualization, has the power to work wonders for the healing body. Many psychologists use visualization techniques, focusing on positive future events that prepare the body to heal. Such visualizations as concentrating on imaging a healthy blood flow are effective techniques.

3. Another way to help an athlete develop and sustain a positive attitude is through self-affirmation. This involves using self-talk to affirm the positive abilities of the athlete. The athlete immerses the conscious mind in positive thoughts that are necessary in order to maintain a positive concept of self- throughout adversity. This technique involves the athlete developing a list of positive self statements which he or she may then listen to on tape. Some examples are "I am in control of my healing," "I am healing at an appropriate rate;" "I am confident in my self and will return to sport when I am ready." Statements made by the athlete should be in the present tense and should not merely comprise a "wish list." When the statements are presented in this manner, they help the athletes focus on their present state of confidence. The athletic trainer can help in the preparation of this list by giving praise and credit when it is due and by encouraging athletes to engage in affirmative statements during rehabilitation time. For optimal effectiveness, it is best for the list to be highly personalized. We are not recommending that athletic trainers become involved in providing psychological interventions for athletes, but we feel it is important that trainers be aware of the power of the positive approach. It is advisable that athletic trainers work in conjunction with, or refer athletes to, sport psychologists when interventions are necessary.

CONCLUSIONS

Psychology plays an important role in sport injury rehabilitation. The modern trainer must do more than assist in physiological healing and injury prevention. He or she must be an active and sensitive listener, a counselor, and a referral agent when evidence suggests that the injured athlete requires additional professional attention.

In addition, to provide the best care for their athletes, trainers must be involved in the motivation of athletes, the reshaping of athlete's attitudes, and the maintenance of a positive attitude in the training room environment.

The evolution of athletic training into an allied health profession has necessarily increased the need for more multidimensional individuals to serve as trainers. Athletic training has become more difficult, stressful, and demanding. It is thus imperative for the trainer to understand the psychological aspects of injury, prevention, and rehabilitation, and to develop psychological principles that will result in the best care for the athlete.

REFERENCES

Dulberg, H.N. (1988, September & October). Injury: How athletes deal with hurt. *Sport Care and Fitness,* p. 53.

Eby, C., & Van Gyn, G. (1987). "Type "A" behaviour pattern in varsity athletes. *Journal of Sport Behaviour, 10,* 73-81.

Meyers, M., Bourgeois A., Stewart S., & Leunes A. (1991, October). *Development and assessment of the sports inventory for pain.* Proceedings of the Association for the Advancement of Applied Sport Psychology. Savannah, GA.

Mora, J. (1990, August). Coping with injury, mind over muscles. *Triathlete,* pp. 28, 30, 31, 79.

Nideffer, R.M. (1989). The psychological aspects of sports injuries: Issues in prevention and treatment. *International Journal of Sport Psychology, 20*(4), 241-255.

Peterson, C., Seligman M., & Vaillant G. (1988). Pessimistic explanatory style as a risk factor for physical illness: A thirty-five year longitudinal study. *Journal of Personality and Social Psychology, 55,* 23-27.

Rotella, R.J., & Heyman, S.R. (1986). Stress, injury, and the psychological rehabilitation of athletes. In J.M. Williams (Ed.), *Applied sport psychology: Personal growth to peak performance* (pp. 343-364). Palo Alto, CA: Mayfield.

Schmale, A., & Iker, H. (1971). Hopelessness as a predictor of cervical cancer. *Social Science and Medicine, 5,* 95-100.

Seligman, M. (1991). *Learned optimism.* New York: Alfred A. Knopf.

Suinn, R.M. (1980). Psychology and sports performance: Principles and applications. In R.M. Suinn (Ed.), *Psychology in sports: Methods and applications* (pp. 26-36). Minneapolis: Burgess.

Chapter 3

The Biopsychology of Injury-Related Pain

John Heil
Lewis-Gale Clinic
Perry G. Fine
University of Utah

Pain is a complex and ever-present challenge to the athlete. How effectively pain is managed influences sport performance, injury risk, and injury rehabilitation—and hence, success as an athlete. There are important roles to be played by all members of the sports medicine team in pain and injury management. Effective rehabilitation requires a thorough understanding of the dual, interacting psychological and biological influences that occur with pain and injury. Treatment is facilitated by careful comprehensive assessment, sensitivity to the "meaning" of pain to the athlete, and a psychologically minded treatment approach.

During World War II, military surgeon Lieutenant Colonel Henry Beecher (1946) observed that soldiers wounded in combat needed fewer narcotics for relief of pain than did civilians who suffered similar injuries. In subsequent research (Beecher, 1956) he revised this observation and concluded that there was not a dependable relationship between severity of a wound and the pain experienced. The degree of suffering is a reflection of the *meaning* of pain to the patient. In his work, Beecher comments on the similar ability of athletes to tolerate the severe pain of acute injury.

While widely recognized, this phenomenon is still relatively little understood. Its roots lie in the "culture" of sport where athletes are literally and figuratively reminded "no pain, no gain, no fame" and encouraged to "play with pain" (and sometimes inadvertently with injury). The time-honored nature of these expectations is reflected in the saga of an ancient warrior whose conquest of performance over pain is emulated in modern sport. The Greek soldier Pheidippides allegedly ran from the site of the battle to the home city of Athens to announce a critical victory over an invasion force, then collapsed and died. His efforts today are honored in the marathan, which covers the 26 miles and 385 yards of his run.

The conquest of pain is a many-sided challenge to the athlete. There is routine performance pain, the nuisance of minor aches and soreness, the intense pain of sudden severe injury, the grind of rehabilitation, and the uncertainty of chronic injury. In sum, there are high expectations that athletes will tolerate pain effectively. Health professionals have an important role to play in helping the athlete cope with routine performance pain and the pain associated with injury, and most importantly in helping the athlete understand the difference between the two. This, in turn, relies on a thorough understanding of the nature of the biological and psychological substrates of pain.

The biopsychological nature of pain is clearly reflected in the definition offered by the International Association for the Study of Pain (Merskey, 1986) in which pain is described as a "sensory and emotional" experience. In spite of such unequivocal statements, there is a strong tendency in the medical and sport communities to try to define pain either as physical or mental, that is, as real or in one's head. This overly simplified and misleading conceptualization of a complex process is clearly a disservice to athletes.

Herein, "pain" refers to a perception that is an end product of a stimulus that is received and mediated by a complex biological system. The process of perception further elicits attempts to find the meaning of the pain and to guide one's behavior accordingly.

This chapter is written to provide the athletic trainer (or other sports medicine specialist) with an appreciation of pain as a biopsychological phenomenon and of the impact it may have on injury rehabilitation. Initial sections that identify the biological and psychological substrates of pain are followed by overviews of pain assessment and management. These latter sections focus on psychological factors, to complement the athletic trainer's existing knowledge concerning the objective assessment of injury.

Biological Factors

The sensation, transmission and perception of pain are the function of a distinct division of the nervous system, the **nociceptive system.** Nociception is a multistage process built on complex anatomic networks and chemical mediators that constitute the fundamental substrates of the pain experience.

Pain is triggered by the activation of two identifiable sets of receptors, high threshold mechanoreceptors and polymodal nociceptors. High threshold mechanoreceptors respond to strong mechanical stimuli transmitting pain signals with relative speed. In contrast, polymodal nociceptors respond to thermal, chemical and mechanical stimuli, and are relatively slow in transmission. This latter group of receptors continues to fire for a time after the cessation of the pain-provoking stimulus. In addition, these have a lower threshold of response when subsequently exposed to similar stimuli. This process, known as sensitization, may cause heightened sensitivity to pain-producing stimuli and also to pain in response to ordinarily nonpainful stimuli.

Sensitization is most likely to occur when there is repeated exposure to severe pain over days and weeks. Persistent pain syndromes such as myofascial pain and sympathetically maintained pain appear to have roots in this process. Myofascial pain syndrome is a musculoskeletal dysfunction with points of tenderness that when activated trigger referred pain (Fine & Petty, 1986). Sympathetically maintained pain most commonly occurs in the arm or leg. This syndrome is characterized by hypersensitivity of the skin and spontaneous burning pain that appears to be reflexively driven by sympathetic nervous system activity (Roberts, 1986). In essence, these syndromes evolve as the nociceptive system comes to behave in a new way to old or otherwise ongoing pain stimuli. These syndromes often go unrecognized and as such are the cause of suffering and diminished performance. For more information, see Fine (in press).

Pain stimuli are transmitted via peripheral nerves to the spinal cord, which functions as a neurosensory switching station. Here pain and other sensory stimuli from the periphery, as well as information received centrally (via descending tracts) from the brain, converge upon common neurosensory pathways. The investigation of these interactions led Melzack and Wall (1965) to propose the **Gate Control Theory** of pain. It holds that processing centers in the spinal cord may either decrease or increase the intensity of pain as a neuroelectric phenomenon, and so result in the perception of relatively lesser or greater pain than that initially signalled. Subsequent research suggests that a similar process of modulation potentially occurs at other locations in the nociceptive system. The Gate Control Theory has been used to explain the efficacy of pain control of various therapeutic modalities ranging from cryotherapy to ultrasound to acupuncture.

Modulated pain signals then ascend to the brain along any of several pathways. These transmit information with varying speed and directness to higher cortical centers, conveying a sensory as well as an emotional-reactive component of pain. The final perception of pain is based upon a summation of inputs from multiple brain centers including those that serve emotion and memory. As a consequence, even at its initial awareness, pain gains some of its meaning from prior experience and present state of mind. Once registered as perception, pain inputs also set off a cascade of electrochemical events via feedback loops within the nociceptive and autonomic nervous systems that influence subsequent pain transmission and psychological status. This feedback system is directly triggered by the onset of pain-inducing stimuli.

Although firmly rooted in physiology this system has a potentially wide range of psychological sequelae. Phenomenon ranging from enhanced mood following exercise to "runner's high," as well as remarkable feats of pain tolerance during sport, and the placebo response to treatment, have been explained via the action of this feedback system. Why such effects may be profound under some circumstances and absent under others remains a mystery.

The important role of naturally occurring opioids, known as endorphins, in pain inhibition is well accepted. However as the pathways and mediators of the pain system are more fully elucidating, the complexity of the interactions of these substrates only becomes more evident (Pasternak, 1988). For the sake of real understanding any temptation toward oversimplification needs to be resisted. For instance, endorphins represent only one class of the many neurotransmitters that are involved in pain modulation. Serotonin, which also influences emotion and sleep, is a prominent pain-processing intermediary. Like serotonin, the endorphins also subserve a variety of other neuroendocrine functions.

The characteristics of the nociceptive system--sensitization, spinal gating, and pain as a summative perception (of multiple physiological factors)–underscore the complexity of the biology of pain. To arrive at a better understanding of the actual experience of pain, the interplay and integration of psychological influences upon these characteristics must be explored.

Psychological Factors

At the instant of perception pain emerges as a more distinctly psychological phenomenon with intrapsychic and social components. Perception sets off a psychologically driven chain of reactive events (in contrast to the biologically driven events of nociception proper), the goal of which is to give meaning to pain. This complex process, subserved by multiple brain centers, yields an interpretation that is influenced by prior experience and current context, and that has cognitive and affective components. Pain is essentially a private intrapsychic experience and can remain so–although it seldom does. When pain becomes social communication (in the form of pain report or nonverbal display) it takes on an added dimension. An additional element of meaning arises as significant others (teammates, coaches, friends, health providers) react to the athlete's expression of pain. The importance of the social component in pain has led some to characterize pain as a biopsychosocial phenomenon (Fordyce, 1988).

Pain is most simply understood in terms of location, intensity and sensory type. Pain comes to have meaning as this basic information is evaluated in light of functional limits on physical ability; memory of similarly painful events; and assessment of the impact of injury on current and future activity. The single most important element of meaning is the assumed status of pain as benign, or alternately, as a sign of injury. A simultaneously evolving emotional understanding incorporates cognitive evaluative information and leads to response on a continuum ranging from relief ("No problem! This is routine pain") to distress ("Oh no! I'm really hurt"). In the latter case some degree of negative emotion in the form of fear, anxiety or sense of loss is likely to follow.

Out of this cognitive-emotional understanding of pain comes action. Intrapsychically, this triggers psychological coping. Actions in the form of reports of pain and demonstrated limits in functional activity also carry pain into the social sphere. The way an athlete displays pain is a important determinant of the way others respond. However, this is ultimately influenced by a host of factors ranging from cultural differences to the specific expectations of a given sport environment. In the immediate time frame this influences how promptly what type of care will be given. More protracted response to the athlete's pain may be helpful or harmful. Such attention may be useful in the form of ongoing social support which functions as a buffer against the psychological sequelae of injury. Conversely, overattention by significant others may elicit guilt, fear of reinjury, or potentially lead to maladaptive secondary gain.

As pain gains meaning, it also gains complexity as social and psychological factors build upon the nociceptive imprint that is the basis of pain. In the end, pain may be experienced in its most useful form as a transient phenomenon heralding a self-limited relatively inconsequential event. Alternately, it may take a pathological form leading to a highly disruptive life-altering disease process of indeterminable proportions.

Pain Assessment

Pain is a complex multidimensional phenomenon. Assessment should reflect the circumstances surrounding injury and the athlete's response to it. The more complex and subjectively distressing they are, the more important a comprehensive approach to assessment becomes.

The basis of pain assessment is the athlete's subjective report of pain intensity (e.g., rated on a "'0' to '10' scale") and quality (e.g., burning, stabbing, electric, aching, etc.). The self-report "'0' to '10' scale" is quite versatile and allows pain to be assessed across a variety of situations. Measures of "average daily pain," pain at its "worst," and pain at its "least" can be obtained. It is also useful to identify those specific factors or situations that lead to an increase or decrease in pain. This line of inquiry provides insight into the challenges the athlete faces in sport, rehabilitation, and activities of daily living. It also offers a perspective on the athlete's coping methods and how effectively they are working.

It is of paramount importance to understand the specific meaning the athlete attaches to pain and how this influences behavior. Consider the situation where an athlete fears that pain experienced during muscular rehabilitation is a sign of reinjury (when in fact it is benign, non-tissue-damaging pain). As a consequence, the athlete may unwittingly erect a serious barrier to rehabilitation. A vicious cycle can ensue, undermining the rehabilitation process. Self-confidence in the ability to recover effectively and trust in the ability of treatment providers to safely direct rehabilitation may be undermined. Resultant, compliance problems may then be interpreted by treatment providers as a lack of motivation. It can be seen how this common, fairly simple, misunderstanding of pain may trigger a variety of other difficulties.

An altogether different problem may arise when the athlete fails to heed pain messages that do in fact signal reinjury. In this situation, rehabilitation can be marred by treatment setbacks.

The more severe or enduring the pain, the progressively greater becomes the role played by factors such as attention, expectation, autonomic arousal and muscle tension. With chronicity also comes greater suffering (Fordyce, 1988). Over time, complaints of pain are increasingly likely to reflect an overall "distress quotient," a measure of suffering that combines pain *and* distress about the pain.

Where inconsistency is noted in athlete's behavior and reports of pain, there is a natural tendency to question the athlete's sincerity and even to challenge complaints of pain. ("Doesn't he want to get better?" "Maybe she is not a serious competitor.") There is relatively little to be gained, and potentially much to be lost, in adopting such a strategy, especially in regard to treatment rapport and trust. As pain persists, it becomes increasingly situation specific. It can be triggered by circumstances that elicit fear, anxiety, or lack of confidence, independent of tissue injury. In this situation, it is recommended that the athlete's complaints of pain still be accepted as a sign of a true problem and that a vigorous effort be made to understand the full scope of the pain as a biopsychological problem. For more on this treatment difficulty see Rotella and Heil (1991).

Often the source of such pain problems arises from implicitly held distorted "cognitive schema." These are essentially misinterpretations of injury that are rooted in a poor understanding of pain and the recovery process. A true problem occurs where the perspectives of the athlete and treatment providers diverge. For example, the athlete may interpret continuing pain as a sign of unresolved injury while treatment providers assume that objective signs of recovery mean there is no basis for pain. The potential problems this may cause are evident. Assessment of the injured athlete begins with a focus on understanding pain as a normative consequence of injury. As problems develop, it is useful to supplement this perspective with a secondary focus on adjustment problems caused by intractable pain or nonhealing injury.

Pain Management

There are a wide variety of practices commonly used by athletic trainers and therapists during rehabilitation that serve the purpose of pain management (e.g., ice, ultrasound, TENS, diathermy, electrical stimulation, acupressure, massage). However, with pain and injury, psychological sequelae are inevitable. These require the athlete to mobilize coping resources. The athlete's efforts are usually sufficient, and recovery proceeds on course and without complication. Yet, at times, psychological adjustment problems will arise. The athletic trainer or therapist who adopts a psychologically minded approach to rehabilitation will facilitate recovery and pain management in both routine and complicated injury situations.

There are four pillars of psychological rehabilitation that enhance speed of recovery and maximize the athlete's sense of well-being. These are education, goal setting, social support, and mental training. The first three of these are quite natural extensions of the role of the athletic trainer or other sports medicine specialist. Mental training techniques fall more within the province of psychology. They offer a potentially valuable intervention in regard to pain control, as well as stress management and mental readiness for return to play. Collaborative intervention between the psychologist and athletic trainer will optimize their effectiveness.

A variety of self-directed pain management techniques have been devised for use in general medical settings (Turk, Meichenbaum, & Genest, 1983). These are most effective when the athlete is at rest. Their utility in an action-oriented athletic setting is generally limited. Research on the mental strategies used by distance runners during training and competition (e.g., Morgan, 1978; Schomer, 1987) offers insight into approaches to pain management that are suitable for athletic performance. However, their utility in injury management situations is limited.

The work of these two traditions is integrated and extended to an action-oriented injury management scheme in the "pain-sport attentional matrix" (Heil, in press). This conceptual scheme identifies four broad classes of pain coping methods. These are defined by whether the athlete "focuses on" or "focuses away from" both pain and sport simultaneously—or whether there is a separation of attention between sport and pain (e.g., "focus on" sport and "focus away from" pain). The key role played by the athletic trainer is in differentiating benign pain from signs of reinjury, and in determining a relatively safe level of physical activity—and guiding the way through positive reinforcement of effective behavior.

At the time of injury it is important to create a sense of calm and security in the midst of the potential pain and fear of injury. Once rehabilitation commences, the athletic trainer or therapist should take on the role of educator, describing the nature of injury as well as the why and how of

Table 1. Guidelines For The
Psychological Management Of Pain

Situation: At the occurrence of injury (especially if severe or psychologically traumatic)
•Establish rapport and create positive realistic expectations
•Shift focus from pain to thoughts of a positive outcome or to the next necessary step in injury management

Situation: During otherwise uncomplicated rehabilitation
•Educate the athlete regarding the mechanisms of injury and treatment
•Identify pain as a routine aspect of rehabilitation

Situation: With treatment plateaus or setbacks
•Clarify treatment goals and encourage conscientious adherence
•Reassure athlete of the benign status of pain

Situation: At failed return to play
•Acknowledge discouragement and provide support
•Differentiate routine pain from dangerous pain (which signals reinjury).

Situation: Chronically failed rehabilitation
•Treat pain complaints as real even if inconsistent
•Review the rehabilitation program with respect to all factors identified above, searching for mitigating or sabotaging factors.

rehabilitation. With treatment setbacks, it is important to focus on encouraging the athlete and helping him or her understand how to proceed with successful rehabilitation. Where there is failed return to play, the trainer or therapist should acknowledge the athlete's disappointment (and distress), clarify the cause of the problem, and readjust treatment regimens and recovery time lines accordingly. In case of chronically failed rehabilitation, trainers and therapists must work vigorously to maintain athlete trust and confidence, be alert to psychological complications, and reevaluate diagnosis and treatment plans. Psychological consultation should be provided--if it has not been thus far. Table 1 offers a brief summary of recommendations for pain management across differing rehabilitation situations. For a more detailed treatment of approaches to chronically failed rehabilitation see Sternbach (1987).

SUMMARY

Pain is a complex biopsychological phenomenon. The goal of this chapter is to enhance the athletic trainer's or therapist's knowledge of pain and to broaden skills in pain assessment and management. An understanding of pain is based on knowledge of the anatomic and chemical elements of the pain-processing nociceptive system, and of the interplay of biological and psychological factors. Pain signals are subject to modulation by the nervous system. Pain intensity may be reduced by mechanisms described in the Gate Control Theory. In contrast, sensitization to pain may occur and result in persistent pain syndromes. The perception of pain sets off a psychologically driven chain of events by which behavior is modified according to the meaning assigned to pain. With chronicity, distress about pain increases as does the influence of factors such as attention, expectation, autonomic arousal, and muscle tension. The psychological sequelae of pain and injury will be most readily recognized and effectively managed with a team-based, psychologically minded approach to rehabilitation.

REFERENCES

Beecher, H.K. (1946). Pain in men wounded in battle. *Annals of Surgery, 123*(1), 96-105.

Beecher, H.K. (1956). Relationship of significance of wound to pain experienced. *Journal of the American Medical Association, 161*(17), 1609-1613.

Fine, P.G. (in press). The biology of pain. In J. Heil (Ed.), *The sport psychology of injury*. Champaign, IL: Human Kinetics.

Fine, P.G., & Petty, W.C. (1986). Myofascial trigger point pain: Diagnosis and treatment. *Current Reviews in Clinical Anesthesia, 7,* 34-39.

Fordyce, W.E. (1988). Pain and suffering: A reappraisal. *American Psychologist, 43*(4), 276-283.

Heil, J. (in press). *The psychology of sport injury*. Champaign, IL: Human Kinetics.

International Association for the Study of Pain (IASP) Subcommittee on Taxonomy (1986). Classification of chronic pain: Descriptions of chronic pain syndromes and definitions of pain terms. Merskey, H. (1986), *Pain* (Suppl.3), S1-S226.

Melzack, R., & Wall, P.D. (1965). Pain mechanisms: A new theory. *Science, 150,* 971-979.

Morgan, W.P. (1978, April). The mind of the marathoner. *Psychology*

Today, pp. 38-40, 43, 45-46, 49.

Pasternak, G.W. (1988). Multiple morphine and enkephalin receptors and the relief of pain. *Journal of the American Medical Association, 259,* 1362-1367.

Roberts, W.J. (1986). A hypothesis on the physiological basis for causalgia and related pains. *Pain, 24,* 297-311.

Rotella, R.J., & Heil, J. (1991). Psychological aspects of sports medicine. In B. Reider (Ed.), *Sports medicine: The school-age athlete* (pp. 105-117). Philadelphia: W.B. Saunders.

Schomer, H.H. (1987). Mental strategy training programme for marathon runners. *International Journal of Sport Psychology, 18,* 133-151.

Sternbach, R.A. (1987). *Mastering pain: A 12-step program for coping with chronic pain.* New York: Putnam.

Turk, D.C., Meichenbaum, D., & Genest, M. (1983). *Pain and behavior medicine: A cognitive behavioral perspective.* New York: Guilford Press.

Chapter 4

Ethical and Legal Issues For Sport Professionals Counseling Injured Athletes

Lou M. Makarowski
Achievement Place, Pensacola, Florida
John G. Rickell
University of West Florida

This chapter examines some of the ethical and legal issues relevant to sport professionals who counsel injured athletes.   Particular emphasis is given to issues and scenarios that are pertinent to trainers and other sport medicine specialists who have not received extensive training in counseling theory and techniques. Value-decision making guidelines are described.   Codes and their derivation that are routinely used by professional counselors to guide them when confronted with ethically challenging situations are described as well.

Magic Johnson tested positive for HIV and retired from the Los Angeles Lakers. The sports world was shocked by this disclosure, but how about you? Have you been privy to disclosures that have left you wondering, "What should I do with this information?"

What you do with information you acquire from those in your charge has important implications for individual and team levels of performance as well as for your ethical stress level and liability exposure. This chapter examines some of the ethical and legal issues relevant to those who function as sport counselors but who may not have had extensive training as counselors. Athletic trainers typically fall within this category. Therefore this chapter, although of potential benefit to many kinds of professionals who work with athletes, is basically directed toward trainers.

Trainers are in the forefront of health care in sports. As a health care provider, your service to the athlete is guided by professional, moral, ethical, and legal directives. Your counseling services should also be guided by professional, moral, ethical, and legal principles.

As a professional, you will follow a code of ethical conduct. But as an employee of an organization, your job description may conflict with ethical requirements of your profession (Ungerleider & Golding, 1992; Voy, 1991). Ethical principles are only part of the picture. As a sport health professional, you can be held legally accountable for the way you carry out your counseling responsibilities.

The American Medical Association now recognizes athletic trainers as allied health providers. Twenty-six states license athletic trainers. The scope of the legislation varies from state to state, but the trend toward licensure is very likely to continue. With increasing professional status comes increased vulnerability to lawsuits. Activities of all types that involve tort will increase as trainers are held accountable legally for increasingly higher levels of knowledge.

The fact that licensed athletic trainers may now open free- standing clinics is another indication that athletic trainers are now expected to know a great deal about many aspects of athletic injury. Malpractice insurance costs for trainers have recently increased significantly. This increase is based upon insurers' projections of increased monetary awards paid to plaintiffs who sue trainers for damages. As public knowledge of sports' inner sanctums grows, so will the creativity of lawyers who seek to protect athletes from exploitation and to protect the public from incompetent or unethical sport professionals (Voy, 1991).

In team sports, the trainer may wear several hats. He or she may also be an assistant coach, psychological counselor, and representative of the employing organization. Wearing different hats can increase opportunities for ethical conflicts. Ethical conflicts are a major source of stress and anxiety. Ethical responsibilities are different for a psychologist than they are for a coach, university professor, health club employee, or professional boxing promoter.

Ethical stress occurs when a trainer's personal philosophy of right and wrong differs from that of the client, employer, profession, or employing organization. Ethical stress can produce anxiety or worry. Ethical anxiety may lie dormant until trainers find themselves confronted with some ethical dilemma or legal proceeding. Trainers confront ethical stressors regularly. Sport professionals can minimize ethical stress by developing a strong personal ethical philosophy and a system that guides their personal decision-making.

Derivation of Ethical Codes

The ethical imperative defines who and what you are. Consider the psychology of ethics, including emotional, cognitive, and behavioral components of an individual's will. Conflicts among these may cause stress to anyone with ethical values. Ethical conflict, the source of ethical anxiety, may provide the impetus for changing ethical and legal codes which originate with the principle of justice. Ethical conflict is a result of one's perception of injustice.

First, You *are*. You encompass one body, mind, character, and spirit. You are defined by the interaction of nature, learning, experience, and opportunity. Your behavior is important in defining *you*. Behavior is determined by nature, learning, and volition.

Volition is the exercise of will, and it guides the choices you make. *Will* may be defined as the total conscious process involved in effecting a decision. Decisions may involve action or the absence of action. Your will is influenced by conscious and subconscious energy, images, emotions, and thoughts. Concepts are composed of images and values. Values are priority assignments that greatly influence choices.

The choices we make are the external signs from which the nature of our character is defined and inferred by us and by others. Conscience is a reflection (approval or disapproval) or rational faculty that discerns the moral characteristic of actions (Butler, 1873). Consideration of right and wrong is the subject matter of morality. Morality represents ideal forms of right and proper conduct. Kant concluded that reason is not intended to produce happiness, but to produce good will. Good will is one that acts for the sake of duty (Solomon, 1982).

Ethics, the science, tells individuals what should be, in principle. Organizations also specify what should or ought to be in the ideal sense. Ethics is the science of moral values and duties or the study of ideal human character, actions, and ends.

Freedom of will is a fundamental, theological principle, with respect to the notion of blame. If one is forced to make decisions, one cannot be held responsible or blamed for the result. Freedom to choose is a fundamental principle of morality as well. Freedom to choose is a right implied by the Constitution of the United States. Freedom to choose by no means implies choice is absent of consequences.

Rather, the freedom is one of choice. When people exercise free will and choose a course of action, they are then accountable for the rightness or wrongness of the choice. The concept of freedom is central to the discussion of ethics and legality as well. Obviously, the concept of free will is of paramount importance to consideration of the principle of justice.

Justice is one of the primary principles of civilization and democracy. The perception of justice is also a primary influence on motivation in sport and life. Sport professionals may engage in questionable practices in an attempt to provide a just or, if you will, an equal playing surface for their athlete, team, or organization.

Society's guidelines, rules, regulations, codes, and laws are usually intended to maintain that which is just, right, and fair. The reflective nature of ethical decision-making helps bring objectivity to one's personal definition of justice.

Value-Based Decision-Making Tools

Value-based decision making includes ethics in a behavioral value system made up of values, attitudes, and beliefs. A behavioral value is something one likes like to do. A behavioral attitude consists of physical, intellectual, emotional, social, and spiritual habits. A behavioral belief is simply a value plus an attitude that grows with time. All this leads to one's behavioral potential. The potential to behave, with opportunity, leads to actual behavior.

Behavior is the basis of a moral action that leads one to act morally and ethically. People need to act in accordance with their behavioral value systems. If people do not act in accordance with their value systems, they are said to have acted unethically or immorally. We all have some value system and behave according to it. Our system may be a hedonistic one, where the Pleasure Principle rules. One extreme of this principle is "If it feels good or gives us advantage, regardless of the consequences, do it." Values emphasizing altruism and service exemplify the other extreme. Most of us fall somewhere between the two extremes. The most efficient value system leads to behavior that produces a healthy life-style. A healthy life-style is defined as physical, emotional, intellectual, social, and spiritual health. It is a life-style of high performance with less stress and less risk of injury.

In order to make decisions based on your value system you have to know yourself. To counsel ethically, a clear understanding of your personal value system is crucial. Knowledge of your personal value system will help you to understand yourself and others. You will also be in a better position to communicate value-laden information in a way that you recognize and that the athletes you counsel will accept.

Your personal value system can create ethical stressors if it is in conflict with the decisions you make. Your value system also creates emotional blind spots that incline you to give the benefit of the doubt. Blind spots may also cause you to be overly scrupulous. Trainers who are emotionally close to their athletes will counsel more effectively and ethically if they learn to recognize their own personal value systems as well as the personal value systems of the athletes they counsel.

Value Decision-Making Guidelines

Ask yourself these questions when making decisions that are of value importance.

1. Is my decision/action compatible with my goals, values, and expectations?
2. Does it feel right?
3. Where does the act ultimately lead?
4. What is the track record of others when making a similar decision? Or, what is my track record when making a similar decision?
5. By doing this, what am I saying about myself? Value decision-making is a dynamic process.

Ethical/Legal Issues

Personal morality is certainly an important aspect of an individual's ethical philosophy, but counselors/trainers who set themselves the task of being "Morals Police" may unnecessarily limit their contribution to the client/athlete and to the employing organization. When psychologists counsel, they must make every effort to work within the value system of the client. The psychologist who is unable to listen empathetically and nonjudgmentally has an ethical duty, as well as a professional obligation, to help the client identify a more impartial confidant. The professional psychologist must not breach the client's right to confidential, competent treatment in the referral process, or in the transition to a more appropriate counselor. A trainer who counsels should do likewise.

The penalty for a psychologist who violates the client's right to confidentiality can be extreme. The results of breaching such rights may include being found guilty of malpractice by the legal system with penalties that can include substantial monetary damages. Loss of license may occur in case of conviction for violation of professional statutory proscriptions. For lesser ethical breaches, which do not involve civil or criminal misconduct, the penalties for psychologists may range from censure to expulsion from professional organizations.

Ethical decision-making greatly reduces the likelihood of any form of criminal, civil, or malpractice violation. Ethical codes for counselors routinely define ethical practice as that which occurs within the limits of the law. Conduct that violates legal mandates will almost always be clearly unethical. Your value decision-making tools should help you make choices that are clearly within legal codes.

A trainer who counsels athletes in areas that provoke ethical concerns should consider referring such individuals to a professional counselor without such conflict. Risk is always present in the sport environment. Participants at all skill levels are often attracted to risk because of the challenge it presents. Mastery of risk provides a thrill that makes sport exciting (Tricker & Cook, 1990). In a highly competitive environment, it is easy for athletes and support staff to get caught up in a "win at any cost" mentality. When ends justify means, risks of cheating may be either emotionally denied or considered part of the excitement, a necessary evil or even a demonstration of willingness to pay the price of success.

Sport professionals working with elite athletes will regularly be confronted with evidence of illegal or unethical practices designed to enhance performance (Ungerleider & Golding, 1992; Voy, 1991). An athlete quoted by Ungerleider & Golding reported anonymously:

> My belief is that if I had to take an estimate, about sixty-five percent of the top five, let's say top ten in the world in every event, are doing something illegal. That basically is the growth hormones in the ballistic events and blood doping for the distance events. I think all of the major distance runners that have run really incredible times are blood doping. I think middle distance runners are using a combination of blood doping and steroids (p. 119).

Director of the Olympic drug testing laboratory in Seoul, Dr. Park Jong Sei stated that "as many as 20 athletes at the games turned up positive, but were not disqualified" (Ungerleider & Golding, 1992, p. 119). The ethics of these sport physicians and administrators are questionable if these allegations are valid. Some coaches have been known to refuse to train athletes who wanted to compete "clean" (Voy, 1991). Sport professionals who counsel athletes have obviously chosen to ignore these facts for a long time. With respect to performance enhancement, these professionals may look away because they sincerely believe the athlete who does not cheat will not be able to compete successfully.

Athletic leadership represents an extremely important, yet underestimated factor that influences unethical behavior. Coaches, trainers, and even athletic directors may fit into the following categories:

1. Leaders who INSTRUCT drug usage.
2. Leaders who ALLOW drug usage.
3. Leaders who COVER drug usage.
4. Leaders who are the PROVIDERS of the CAINES. (McGuire, 1990, p.10)

Sport professionals, physicians, or administrators who condone or rationalize substance abuse obviously value winning above societal codes designed to promote mental and physical health.

Unethical behavior is unfortunately commonplace in sport. Manipulating academic eligibility requirements is unethical. Unethical behavior may also include child abuse, some weight loss practices, or sexual barter (Rotella & Connelly, 1984). In the case of moral issues, boundary violations, illegal activity or abusive relationships, the motivation for condoning such practices may also be justified by the belief that everyone is doing it.

Recognizing abuse can be difficult in the competitive environment since personal criteria of abuse are often culture laden and highly subjective. Since the legal criteria are usually clear in sport, abusive behavior may be disguised, tolerated, and at times, celebrated. The need for aggression in sport can lead to acceptance of abusive coaching or parenting activities designed to increase such behavior at game time. Therefore, abusive behavior may be publically abhorred, but privately condoned when it leads to success.

Abusive behaviors may be justified in a sports family as they are in other abusive families. Fear of being rejected typically leads family members to see no evil, hear no evil, speak no evil. There may be an unspoken conspiracy of silence resulting from a fear of job loss or a glorification of the coach, athlete, or abusive sport professional. Many believe the risks from the questionable sport procedures are far less dangerous to the athlete than are other likely alternatives. Sometimes, these people are correct.

Fear of violating a sports family's value system is a powerful motivator, especially when the intensity of the desire some athletes have to succeed is considered. "*Sports Illustrated* reported the results of a survey which asked athletes whether they would take a drug that guaranteed them a gold medal but would kill them within a week after winning. Fifty percent of subjects responded affirmatively!" (Ungerleider & Golding, 1992, p.123)

When sport professionals behave unethically and take risks at the expense of athletes, they gamble dangerously. Without a well developed value-based decision-making system to guide them, they may experience censure by professional or employing organizations even if the ethical violation is not criminal. Criminal penalties or civil suits may follow ethical breaches that violate statutory law as well. The Len Bias tragedy is a case in point.

Ethical Standards

The National Athletic Trainers' Association (NATA) completed a role delineation validation study for the entry-level athletic trainers' certification examination in 1990. "One of the major functions of a certification program is the protection of the public from the practice of the incompetent professional" (p. 4).

NATA considered six major domains as essential components for competent functioning at the entry level:

1. Prevention.
2. Recognition and Evaluation.
3. Management/Treatment.
4. Rehabilitation.
5. Organization and Administration.
6. Education and Counseling. (p. 5)

That education and counseling skills are viewed as critically important competencies for entry-level certified athletic trainers is not at all surprising. The advising of athletes and coaches, as well as that of others interested in athletic endeavor, is clearly within the purview of the work of a trainer.

The trainer's professional experience may be adequate for counseling a cooperative individual who is seeking noncontroversial information.

Situations such as those do not normally pose ethical or legal issues for the sport professional. The more emotionally charged issues however, involving fear, insecurity, depression, anger, drugs, dependency, deceit, boundary violations, sexuality, and secrets tend to be much more taxing ethically and emotionally for the trainer and the athlete.

Typical, daily life situations call for thought, opinion formation, decision making, and action (Simon, Howe, & Kirschenbaum, 1974). Trainers and other sport professionals must frequently make decisions intended to be in the best interest of athletes (Rotella & Connelly, 1984). Therefore, it is imperative that these judgments be guided by ethics based in a workable system for clarifying values that trainers and athletes cannot find in codes. All empowered persons, despite the brevity of their empowerment, need access to guiding ethics (Thompson, 1983). Ethical codes establish restrictions, which when imposed by responsible professions are more desirable than those imposed by external forces (Van Hoose & Kottler, 1985).

Some sport professionals are well aware of the limitations their academic training provides when counseling athletes. Others are willing to counsel on virtually any topic. It might, therefore, be useful to review some of the ethical guidelines that have been imposed upon psychologists by The American Psychological Association (APA). The ethical guidelines discussed in this chapter are drawn from the American Psychological Association's (APA's) Ethical Principles of Psychologists and Code of Conduct (hereinafter referred to as the Ethics Code).

Six general principles state the aspirational norms that guide psychologists toward the highest ideals of psychology:

1. Competence.
2. Integrity.
3. Professional and Scientific Responsibility.
4. Respect for People's Rights and Dignity.
5. Concern for Others' Welfare.
6. Social Responsibility.

This code represents a set of ethical standards for work-related conduct that requires "a personal commitment to a lifelong effort to act ethically, to encourage ethical behavior by students, supervisees, employees, and colleagues as appropriate, and to consult with others as needed concerning ethical problems" (Ethics Code. Preamble, 1992).

Psychologists are expected to supplement, but not violate, the ethical code values and rules based on guidance drawn from personal values, culture, and experience. This ethic has implications for other sport professionals as well.

Counselor's Role

Trainers who counsel injured athletes, should understand the nature of the services to be performed. In turn, any limits of professional competencies and duality of roles should be clarified for the athlete's benefit. The athlete should know whether the counselor is acting as faculty member, coach, or owner. The role taken by the trainer may limit his or her ability to protect the athlete's confidentiality. It may also conflict with his or her interests.

Boundary and role-delineation are also important aspects of the trainer's job. He or she may spend a great deal of time with a team or with an individual athlete during conditioning, practice, travel, and competition. The trainer and athletes eat, sleep, sweat, mourn, and celebrate together and thus, it is easy for boundaries, particularly in matters of a personal nature, to become blurred. The trainer should should be sensitive to the need to keep the athlete informed, at all times, of the nature of the relationship and of changes in the relationship that may occur as a result of changes in the trainer's responsibility. Changes in the nature of information that surfaces as result of the increasing willingness of the athlete to confide in the trainer requires trainers to be in tune with their value blind spots as well as with their guiding ethical codes.

Another issue of ethical significance when counseling athletes pertains to the dangers of developing an overly dependent relationship as opposed to encouraging independent behavior. Van Hoose and Kottler (1985) warned that failure to set and hold to time guidelines, when counseling, may reinforce dependent behavior on the part of clients and encourage them to renege on their responsibility for self-direction. Fostering excessive dependency in response to the trainer's intervention would not only be destructive to the client but could also be ethically questionable.

Contractual obligations pose ethical problems for the sport consultant who provides ongoing personal counseling. Sport psychologists or trainers with a counseling degree should be aware of their contractual obligation to the client. A client may quit the counseling at any time for any reason; however, a psychologist or sports professional who terminates a counseling relationship without sufficient notice may be liable for malpractice if the client sustains damages of a type recognized by law. In other words, when functioning in the role of a counselor, trainers may be held legally accountable if they depart from the standard of care that a jury might consider appropriate for that particular relationship. Obviously, individuals who misrepresent themselves as psychologists are subject to sanction by the state for such misconduct. All professionals, in and outside of sport, counsel in a variety of ways. Coaches frequently consider helping to mold young people's values as the most important and rewarding part of their job. Certainly, they do not consider themselves as providers of psychotherapy (Zeigler, 1987).

Consider the case of the athlete who may deliberately injure himself or herself as a face-saving way to avoid competitive stress (Kane, 1984). NATA would emphasize the importance of recognizing the problem and referring such an athlete to an appropriate professional therapist. When the sports professional uses referral and informal counseling techniques, athletes may leave competition or compete at a reduced level and still maintain their dignity. This type of intervention is not only ethically appropriate but also consistent with NATA recommendations for both competent functioning in the counseling as well as injury prevention domains. You should be sure to complete the transfer process with follow-up, if you believe there is danger to an athlete or another person.

Mentors and counselors should provide services that are within their range of competencies. Trainers, coaches, and other sport professionals who counsel athletes are assumedly helpful, but ethical counseling enhances the quality of this assistance.

A psychologist licensed to provide diagnostic and therapeutic services typically has completed a four-year undergraduate degree in psychology or a related field. An additional three to four years of advanced study in behavioral science, abnormal behavior, and tools of intervention lead to the required doctoral degree. A requirement of two years of supervised practice of these skills under the supervision of a licensed psychologist is the minimum required to take the licensing exam in most states. Once licensed, the psychologist may begin independent practice.

Sport professionals who find themselves questioning their competency to deal with serious psychological situations should be applauded. Being scrupulous may be the best liability insurance. Trainers who feel uneasy should review their value decision-making procedures and consider referring athletes to other professionals whose training and education enables them to deal with highly problematical athlete problems. To direct the athlete to such persons is consistent with NATA and APA guidelines. Knowledge of referral procedures and community resources is specifically referenced as minimum competencies for Certified Athletic Trainers by NATA. In fact, TASK 3 under NATA's Education and Counseling Domain specifically addresses this issue.

NATA further delineates knowledge required to accomplish TASK 3 as follows:

1. Knowledge of situations requiring consultation with professionals regarding the athletes' social and/or personal problems.
2. Knowledge of available professionals for consultation regarding the athletes' social and personal problems.
3. Knowledge of required referral procedures for consultation with professionals for the athletes' social and/or personal problems.

NATA's panel of experts (1990) identified specific skills necessary in order to implement the TASK 3 knowledges as:

1. Skill in recognizing an athlete's need for professional consultation for social and/or personal problems.
2. Skill in communicating to the athlete the purpose or need for professional consultation for social and/or personal problems.
3. Skill in establishing referral procedures regarding social and/or personal problems.
4. Skill in interacting with allied health care professionals.
5. Skill in assisting in intervention as directed by the appropriate allied health care professionals. (p. 62)

Trainers who engage in counseling athletes with social and/or personal problems would be considered incompetent by the standards of NATA were such trainers to exceed the boundaries of their competence to counsel.

This directive from NATA can be a strong tool when referring athletes to professionals more appropriately suited to deal with such problems. The ethic would appear identical, then, both for the psychologists to counsel and deliver psychological services within their level of competence and also the trainer as directed by NATA. There is no other mention in the entire domain of counseling and education competencies for trainers that deals with ongoing personal counseling relationships.

Trainers should understand aspects of psychological readiness for the return to competitive activity and should have skill in evaluating the athletes' present physical and psychological status as it pertains to training and competition. Trainers should also be able to recognize unhealthy personal situations (e.g., substance abuse, eating disorders, assault, abuse, etc.). Lastly, the trainer should be able to recognize the athletes' need for information regarding personal and/or community health topics. Trainers should be skilled in instructional methods as well as information dissemination procedures regarding personal and/or community health topics (NATA, 1990). Clearly, the intent of the counseling mission of the Certified Athletic Trainer is directed toward education, recognition, and referral of athletes for appropriate services in the area of personal, social or mental health problems.

Conflicting Interests

Sport consultants who function as coaches may risk the appearance of conflict of interest. This appearance can be problematic, imposing unnecessary hardship on the athlete and the counselor. The APA Ethics Code Standard 1.21 offers sound guidance:

When a psychologist agrees to provide services to a person or entity at the request of a third party, the psychologist clarifies to the extent feasible, at the outset of the service, the nature of the relationship with each party. This clarification includes the role of the psychologist (such as therapist, organizational consultant, diagnostician, or expert witness) and the probable uses of the services provided or the information obtained, and the fact that there may be limits to confidentiality.

If there is a foreseeable risk of the psychologist's being called upon to perform conflicting roles because of the involvement of a third party, the psychologist clarifies the nature and direction of his or her responsibilities, keeps all parties appropriately informed as matters develop, and resolves the situation in accordance with this Ethics Code. (Ethics Code. Standard 1.21, 1992)

When these ethical guidelines are followed, it is clear for whom the trainer is actually working. Trainers have an obligation to their employers, but they also have a responsibility to the athletes whom they counsel. In performance enhancement settings, it is possible to maintain a very positive relationship with both management and athlete.

Athletes should be assured that what they reveal and discuss remains confidential unless the information impinges upon their safety or health, or that of others. This assurance of confidentiality may be withheld in the case of military or certain organizational or forensic psychologists. The military psychologist must inform his clients of his or her duty to follow the chain of command. Therefore, information may not be kept in confidentiality.

Most employers understand it would be difficult to gain an athlete's trust without the assurance of confidentiality. When positive circumstances prevail, few problems related to confidentiality tend to arise. However, in the face of problems, such as those related to injuries and pressure to win, coaches, owners, or parents, for that matter, may lose sight of ethical requirements. In the heat of competition, a coach might ask an athlete, "What's the matter with Brown? How come he's not putting out in practice?" At this point, the trainer can remind the coach that Brown is working on it. If pressed for more detail, the value decision-making system should be considered before any information is disclosed. The violation of Brown's privilege of confidentiality may easily be the cause of his elimination from the team or from competition.

Every new personal counseling relationship should begin with a review of the limits to which information discussed can ethically be kept confidential. Self-deception on behalf of the trainer as well as the athlete should be avoided at all costs. A psychotherapist's records may be subpoenaed and admitted into evidence in some jurisdictions even where the psychologist/patient privilege is recognized. Most, if not all, jurisdictions recognize, at a minimum, the priest/penitent and psychologist/client relation as confidentially protected.

Too Much, Too Soon

Communication is good. Confession may be good for the soul, and catharsis can alleviate energy-sapping stress. But too much self-disclosure, too soon, can be harmful (Derlega & Chaikin, 1975). Many times, clients will begin talking about stressful situations. Before long, they may blurt out a series of thoughts and feelings that have been on their mind for some time. Beware of clients who seem to say too much, too soon. Particularly, if it is a new client. Listen attentively, but be mindful of the fact that sometimes a client who tells too much too soon may feel violated later.

Self-reliant, emotionally stable, independent people who tend to be cynical may become overwhelmed, stressed, and depressed. Such individuals may often be helped by having the opportunity to talk with someone they trust. Therefore, athletes may frequently appreciate the trainer's or therapist's willingness to just listen.

Occasionally, an athlete who is obviously agitated, anxious and under pressure will come to a trainer. He or she should be assured of the trainer's availability, willingness to help or assist in finding someone who can help.

The athlete does not need to say everything in one meeting. A trainer sometimes needs to put the brakes on self-disclosure. Be sure the athletes are making an informed decision when they attempt to tell all. You have a duty to inform them if their confidential revelations are not legally exempt from discovery by the legal system in the jurisdiction in which you work.

Athletes raised with an aggressive, competitive, racist, or "macho" mentality may feel compromised if they are encouraged to reveal too much of themselves in a moment of weakness. Later, they may feel uncomfortable and therefore resent the counselor, who they may feel robbed them of their dignity or took advantage of them in their moment of weakness. With sensitivity to this kind of result, catharsis can be kept helpful. A confident manner will project a reassuring sense of optimism that a solution will be found. By being there to help, the counselor can easily make any necessary referrals.

It is a counselor's responsibility to have a clearly established protocol when counseling. Consistency in approach, balance between personal morality, ethical principles, and legal responsibilities, ethically and legally correct decisions are likely to be achieved.

Potential Traps

What do you do in a situation where the athlete says, "I have to tell you something, but you must promise not to tell"? It is recommended that the athlete be told, "It is my role to listen. I will be happy to listen to what you have to say, if you trust me to use what you tell me in your best interests." Statements such as those allow the athlete to make the decision on the level of risk and relieve trainers of the burden of getting involved in a bargain they may not be able to keep.

By saying, "I'd like you to tell me anything you trust me to use in your best interest," the trainer offers to be of professional assistance without having his or her hands tied. This approach will be adequate with youngsters, but adults may press for higher levels of secrecy. In this case the limits of privileged confidentiality should be explained and discussed.

Usually athlete/clients will not disengage from the interaction. If they are, however, unwilling to abide by the implied understanding, they should be offered assurance that if they change their mind, the trainer will be happy to listen. At this point, the athlete should be offered the option of speaking to someone. The athlete could be told that there are many persons trained and willing to help—personal physicians, clergymen, mental health professionals, and even anonymous crisis call-in services. In this way, the athlete is not left without the option of help; you are providing the athlete an opportunity to make an informed choice among a variety of options.

Triangles

Triangles can be particularly challenging to many helping professionals. In such a situation a client will share some information about a second party, thereby putting the trainer in a position wherein he or she tries to help someone solve a problem involving someone else without permission to involve that third party. Here again, the best course of action is to be a reflective listener. Avoid the temptation to rescue the athlete from the problem. Do nothing, assuming, that is, that the athlete is not psychotic, suicidal, or homicidal.

Triangle situations require that the listener be accountable for solving a problem without the power or authority to do so. This is a losing proposition. Remember, it is not the counselor's job to solve problems. The counselor is a facilitator who assists athletes to find their own solution. An exception to the facilitator role occurs when the counselor is asked for help by someone who is clearly in danger and who lacks access to a power base adequate to cope with the danger. Children and teenagers who are abused are cases in point. Adult victims of crime also fit this category.

Victims of abuse require immediate action by a counselor of any type. The counselor is to report the abuse to an investigative agent. The counselor should not investigate his- or herself. The goal, when attempting to be helpful, is to stop the abuse. The ethical and legal obligation is to report and thereby attempt to halt it.

Misuse Of Influence

Trainers who coach and counsel on personal matters should also be aware of Ethics Code Standard 1.15.

Misuse of Psychologists' Influence:

Because psychologists' scientific and professional judgements and actions may affect the lives of others, they are alert to and guard against personal, financial, social, organizational, or political factors that might lead to misuse of their influence. (Ethics Code. Standard 1.15, 1992)

This standard might apply to any competitive environment. In highly competitive situations, the perception of value to the cause is of paramount significance. The football depth chart composition is a direct function of such perceptions. Emotional factors influence such perceptions. To use one's influence, gained through personal counseling, to discourage an athlete from questioning his or her access to playing time could be ethically questionable. The same could be said of those who would influence a player to return to competition prematurely following injury.

Cultural Values And Ethical Counseling

Racial bias can prove ethically challenging for those who are counseling athletes. Widespread cultural stereotyping by media, coaches, fans, and athletes has led to a general acceptance of racial stacking in many sports ("Shake," 1991) Trainers who counsel athletes need to be prepared to confront ethical values that involve discrimination. Minorities are advancing to management positions, albeit slowly. Allegations of discrimination will re-emerge; whites attempting to gain a larger market share, will re-enter sports currently dominated by minorities and will complain of prejudice.

Opportunities for value conflicts will increase. Racial disharmonies may attract media attention and thus enhance opportunities for financial gain on behalf of team ownership.

Attitudes about race, or for that matter any personal, values that would conflict with the counselor's ability to provide unbiased consultation are considered reasons to refer the client to someone else. If referral is not practical, the client should be made aware of values that the trainer holds that may be influential in subconsciously slanting his or her counsel.

Gender identity issues have ethical implications for personal counseling. Homophobia is a factor that may lead to ethical conflicts when sexual preference differs for counselor and client. Homophobic beliefs create anxieties that subconsciously or consciously guide statements, as well as nonverbal communication. Favoring individuals of one's sexual preference, is increasingly discussed as a problem among psychologists who counsel and offer services to female sport teams.

Sexual harassment, discrimination, and lack of respect for the values and human differences among those you counsel are clearly unethical and to be avoided. Exploitative relationships are unethical. Sexual relations between counselor and client are considered exploitative, unethical, and are the leading reason for malpractice awards against professional counselors.

Documentation Of Your Work

Ethical and legal considerations require that you keep records and document services performed. This is particularly important in the private sector, although institutional and organizational policies may be similar. If policy doesn't require it, prudence does.

When dealing with sensitive personal information, it is critical to have entries in your confidential file of personal meetings. The notes do not need to be exhaustive, but should include a minimum of a date, who was present, problem addressed, recommendations made, estimates of progress, and your plans for the future. By keeping notes, you will be able to document positions that you have taken should you be ordered to appear in court. You need not keep records for each conversation about every ankle that you tape, but in cases where you develop an ongoing confidential relationship, it is important to keep records. This is particularly true in cases where you see athletes in crises dealing with significant areas of abuse or emotional disturbance, such as depression or suicidal ideation.

It is also quite important to document things that were said and done during rehabilitation of sport injuries. Such documentation may help protect you from litigation. When you are sued, deposed, or brought into court as an expert witness, you will present a much more professional impression if you can cite documents to support your statements. By keeping appropriate records you will be sending a message to the athletes as well. They will know that you have documentation. If they should get angry at you at some point in the future, they might be more willing to be reasonable knowing that you have taken notes. Malpractice situations are not pleasant for anyone. When professionals are sued for malpractice, it is much easier to defend their conduct if they have records. Malpractice and lawsuits may seem to be a long way from the training table, but serious injuries and death of athletes do result in lawsuits. Lawsuits are sometimes brought in revenge for real or imagined slights or offenses. Suing coaches, high schools, universities, and even youth sport associations, has become more widespread (Ball, Robinson, & Narol, 1991).

Consider the case of Len Bias, an outstanding collegiate basketball player. According to press releases, his death was attributable to cocaine use. The Bias family sued Len's university, alleging that the university was in some way responsible for his death. In such a case, a sport psychologist or athletic trainer who counselled Bias might conceivably have been called into court to defend against allegations of professional negligence. Available documentation for what you say and the reasons for saying it, can reduce the counselor's difficulty in responding responsibly.

It is important to realize that the amicable relationship that the trainer maintains with his or her athlete clients will not survive the adversity typically generated by a lawsuit for damages. The lawyers whom the trainer must confront in the courtroom are adversaries. The family of the dead or injured athlete will not be friendly. In a courtroom, you may face witnesses whom you may not even know and may never see again. They will not like you. The attorneys will try to discredit you in order to win a judgment for their client. Having notes to bolster your testimony is professionally correct and, while not a guarantee, will go a long way toward easing your day in court. Ethics Code Standard 1.23 may be useful at this point:

Documentation of Professional and Scientific Work

a) Psychologists appropriately document their professional and scientific work in order to facilitate provision of services later by them or other professionals, to ensure accountability, and to meet other requirements of institutions or the law.

b) When psychologists have reason to believe that records of their services will be used in legal proceedings involving recipients of or participants in their work, they have a responsibility to create and maintain documentation in the kind of detail and quality that would be consistent with reasonable scrutiny in an adjudicative forum. (Ethics Code. Standard 1.23, 1992)

When counseling or referring, be sure to note the problem or issue and your estimate of the client's mental state at time of consultation: Was the athlete lucid and clear or desperate and despondent? Note your recommendation or action, especially if referral was made. The notes do not have to be extensive. They need to include only enough information so that another professional might evaluate the scope of the problem and the appropriateness of your recommendations. This may be enough to convince an adversarial party's attorney and expert that there is no likelihood of deviation from the standard of care.

It is important to recognize that the burden of a plaintiff's proof is not always easy. A tort is a civil wrong. The requirements of proof for a plaintiff in tort are four in number.

The first is duty. This means that there must have been a duty of the defendant to the plaintiff, that duty arising from the particular relationship that they had, for instance, a doctor/patient relationship. Secondly, there must have been a breach of that duty by either an overt act or a failure to act by the person who owes the duty. Thirdly, there must be damages proven that are recognized by law. Lastly, there must be proof that the act or non-act must have resulted proximately in the damages accrued (J.D. Williams, personal communication, April, 1992).

The Privilege
Ethical guidelines of The American Psychological Association and virtually all human relations ethics codes affirm the dignity of the client. Virtually all codes ban discrimination, sexual harassment or other types of harassment, and encourage respect for the rights and diverse values and opinions of the people served. Beyond ethics, it is helpful to realize that we are privileged that our clients choose to share information with us. The act of sharing, particularly sharing sensitive personal information, involves considerable risk on the part of the athlete. It is hoped that by increasing your awareness of values, your work with athletes will be more rewarding to them as well as to yourself.

Authors' Note
The authors acknowledge with gratitude: Medical/legal review of this chapter for accuracy by Jay D. Williams, Jr., Medical Center Clinic, P.A., Dept. of Internal Medicine, Pensacola, Fla.; contributions and review of this chapter by: Karen J. Smith, Head Athletic Trainer, University of West Florida and J. Laurence Day, Professor, Communication Arts, University of West Florida; Kay Antone for typing the many drafts of this manuscript.

REFERENCES
American Psychological Association. (December, 1992). *Ethical principles of psychologists and code of conduct.* Washington, DC: Author.

Ball, R.T., Robinson, R., & Narol, M.S. (1991). *Legal aspects.* (Audio Recording No. 5A, B). Orlando, FL: National Youth Sports Coaches Association.

Butler, J. (1873). *Sermons.* New York: Robert Carter & Brothers.

Derlega, V., & Chaikin, A. (1975). *Sharing intimacy.* Englewood Cliffs, NJ: Prentice-Hall.

Kane, B. (Fall, 1984). Trainer counseling to avoid three face-saving maneuvers. *Athlete Training,* 171-174.

McGuire, R. (1990). History and evolution of drugs in sport. In R. Tricker, & D.L. Cook (Eds.), *Athletes at risk: Drugs and sport* (p. 10).

Dubuque, IA: Wm. C. Brown.

National Athletic Trainers' Association. (1990). *Role delineation validation study for the entry-level athletic trainers' certification examination.* NATA Board of Certification.

Raths, L., Merrill, H., & Simon, S. (1966). *Values and teaching.* Columbus, OH: Charles E. Merrill.

Rotella, R.J., & Connelly, D. (1984). Individual ethics in the application of cognitive sport psychology. In W.F. Straub, & J.M. Williams (Eds.), *Cognitive sport psychology* (pp. 102-112). Lansing, NY: Sport Science Associates.

Shake racial stereotypes. (1991, December 19) *USA Today,* 12A.

Simon, S.B., Howe, L.W., & Kirschenbaum, H. (1974). *Value clarification.* New York: Hart.

Soloman, R. (1982). *The big question* (3rd ed.). New York: Harcourt Brace.

Thompson, A. (1983). *Ethical concerns in psychotherapy and their legal ramifications.* Lanham, MD: University Press of America.

Tricker, R., & Cook, D.L. (Eds.). (1990). *Athletes at risk: Drugs and sport.* Dubuque, IA: Wm. C. Brown.

Ungerleider, S., & Golding, J.M. (1992). *Beyond strength.* Dubuque, IA: Wm. C. Brown.

Van Hoose, W.H., & Kottler, J.A. (1985). *Ethical and legal issues in counseling and psychotherapy.* San Francisco: Jossey-Bass.

Voy, R. (1991). *Drugs, sport, and politics.* Champaign, IL: Leisure Press.

Zeigler, E.F. (1987). Rationale and suggested dimensions for a code of ethics for sport psychologists. *The Sport Psychologist, 1,* 138-150.

SECTION 2

Psychological Perspectives on Athletic Injury

Psychological Perspectives on Athletic Injury

In this section four psychological considerations relevant to sport injury rehabilitation are addressed. These chapters should be of value to those whose primary interests lie in the construction and implementation of such programs.

In the first chapter of this section, **Michael L. Sachs, Michael R. Sitler,** and **Gerry Schwille** emphasize the role of life stress, mood, anxiety, and personal coping skills in understanding and predicting athletic injury. They offer a model that incorporates these factors and thereby suggest that it may be useful in rehabilitative efforts of collegiate athletes.

The focus of this section's second chapter is the malingering athlete. **Robert J. Rotella, Bruce C. Ogilvie,** and **David H. Perrin** define and discuss the term *malingerer*, and indicate that some athletes seek out and derive gain from the "injured" status. Suggestions are made for dealing with this type of athlete.

J. Robert Grove writes about personological underpinnings of sport injury rehabilitation in this section's third chapter. He argues that rehabilitative approaches might vary according to dispositions of personality.

In the final chapter of this section, **Charles J. Hardy** and **R. Kelly Crace** address a frequently ignored dimension of athletic injury rehabilitation–social support. They urge that the role of friends, loved ones, and relatives cannot be overestimated in injury rehabilitation.

Chapter 5

Assessing and Monitoring Injuries and Psychological Characteristics In Intercollegiate Athletes: A Counseling/Prediction Model

Michael L. Sachs, Michael R. Sitler, and Gerry Schwille
Temple University

One of the consequences of participation in intercollegiate athletics for almost all athletes at some point during their careers is injuries. These injuries may be due to any number of factors, which include, but are not limited to, contact with another player or equipment, overuse, equipment failure, previous injury, exposure to injury, and conditioning. An additional important factor may be life stress, resulting from factors both within the athletic context and outside the athletic domain, which may negatively affect the person physically and psychologically. A counseling/prediction model is discussed that incorporates the development of a data base of key physical and psychological characteristics of the athlete to track changes in the athlete that

might alert the sport psychologist to potential stress, as well as encompass periodic monitoring and referral as needed. The prediction of athletic injuries and adherence to rehabilitation regimens may also be an outcome of use of the model.

One of the consequences of participation in intercollegiate athletics for almost all athletes at some point during their careers is injuries. Although not all athletes are injured severely enough to miss practices and/or games, virtually all intercollegiate athletes sustain injuries at least one or more times during their careers to the extent that medical treatment is required. These injuries may be due to any number of factors, which include, but are not limited to, contact with another player or equipment, overuse, equipment failure, previous injury, exposure to injury, and conditioning.

One area that has recently been examined more extensively is the effect of psychological factors on injuries. In particular, the area of life stress is one that applied sport psychologists find especially important. Although life stress may not lead directly to injuries in intercollegiate athletes, dealing with stress (or, more precisely, not dealing effectively with stress) may indirectly affect the athlete. Life stress resulting from factors both within the athletic context (concern about upcoming games, conflicts with teammates or coaches, pressure to perform, etc.) and, particularly, outside the athletic domain (family problems, difficulties with significant others–spouse, boyfriend/girlfriend, academic problems, etc.) may negatively affect the person physically (i.e., immune system responses, excessive fatigue) and psychologically (i.e., distraction–constant thinking about the problems faced).

A proactive approach to dealing with life stress would encompass periodic monitoring, through established psychological inventories, interviews, and other approaches, of the athlete's psychological well-being. Those athletes who offer evidence of some degree of psychological distress could be offered counseling to help them deal with the stress. Reducing/eliminating the stress would then facilitate restoration of psychological well-being and concomitant physical well-being, thereby reducing one key factor that may result in injuries. While injuries will occur during participation in the sporting environment, an important underlying, factor may be the stress experienced by the individual.

Athletic trainers are key individuals in the athletic environment, given their regular interaction with many athletes and their "front-line" contact and responsibilities for the care and well-being of the athletes. Although other medical professionals, such as physicians and nurses (Gregory & Van Valkenburgh, 1991), have roles to play with injured athletes, athletic trainers are, in many ways, potentially the staff most likely to hear about concerns of the athletes and/or spot physical and related mood changes in athletes. As part of a proactive model in dealing with stress, athletic trainers must be involved in a significant way. Recent work (Wiese, Weiss, & Yukelson, 1990) indicates that athletic trainers are aware of, and supportive of, the key role of sport psychology in athletics, particularly in the injury rehabilitation process.

Background
On first examination it appears reasonably clear from the literature that life stress has a significant impact on injuries in athletes. Kerr and Minden (1988) examined elite female gymnasts and found that stressful life events were significantly related to both frequency and severity of injuries. Hardy and Riehl (1988) found that total life change and negative life change significantly predicted frequency of athletic injury (although not severity) among noncontact-sport participants. Similar results with football players were found by Blackwell and McCullagh (1990). Injured players had higher scores on life stress factors and competitive anxiety, and lower scores on coping resources, than did uninjured players.

Recent work, however, suggests that the relationship of life stress to injuries may be more complicated than first thought. Smith, Smoll, and Ptacek (1990) found that, in considering the variables of life stress, social support, and coping skills, these factors must be considered together rather than separately. They describe this as conjunctive moderation, "in which multiple moderators must co-occur in a specific combination or pattern to maximize a relation between a predictor and an outcome variable," (p. 360) as opposed to disjunctive moderation "in which any one of a number of moderators maximizes the predictor-criterion relation" (p. 360). These authors found that, for adolescent sport injuries, social support and psychological coping skills acted in a conjunctive manner: A significant relationship between stress and injury was found only for athletes low in both coping skills and social support.

In attempting to clarify the life stress, coping skills, and social support interaction, a model of stress and athletic injury may be helpful. Andersen and Williams (1988) developed a theoretical model of stress and athletic injury that includes cognitive, attentional, behavioral, physiological, intrapersonal, social, and stress history variables. A comprehensive view of the stress-injury relationship requires this type of multivariate approach. Previous studies (with the exception of Smith, Smoll, and Ptacek, 1990) have tended to examine only components of this model with comparatively small groups of athletes. Advancement in theory, research, and practice (i.e., potential application) in this area would be aided by examining an array of factors within the model with a much larger group of athletes, across a variety of sports, for an extended period of time.

Monitoring

A basic component of a counseling/prediction model would be the development of a data base of key physical and psychological characteristics of the athlete, to track changes in the athlete that might alert the sport psychologist to potential stress. The physical (including demographic) components would include a number of factors. These would encompass age, gender, height, weight, percent body fat, years and level of participation in sport, and previous history of injuries.

A battery of psychological inventories (see Table 1 and discussion in the section on psychological tests) dealing with a number of different psychological states and traits suggested in the model - life stress, mood, anxiety, coping skills, etc.–would, in this model, be administered to all intercollegiate athletes at a given university during the period set aside for physical examinations at the start of the school year. This could also be done, of course, with interscholastic athletes at a high school, members of a club team, etc. These results would provide baseline data from which to work with athletes during the school year. Some of the tests could be scheduled for administration several times during the semester. The complete battery could also be administered again prior to the start of the spring semester, to increase the likelihood that psychological problems that might have arisen since the earlier testing points would be detected.

The information obtained would be used in three ways. First, if the results indicated a clinically significant level of psychological distress on one of the inventories, the athlete would be counseled to seek assistance, either at the university counseling center or with one of the sport psychologists (preferably a "clinical" sport psychologist, rather than an "educational" sport psychologist) working with athletes at the university. In some cases the model will be used within the context of a research study examining psychological factors and injuries. Although advising athletes to seek assistance would potentially confound the research component of such a study, it represents a proactive approach based on the desire to ensure maximum psychological mental health and well-being of the athlete and, concomitantly, readiness to practice and compete in intercollegiate athletics. In this case, ethical principles would suggest that applied concerns outweigh research considerations. Follow-up information would be obtained on each athlete to ascertain adherence to recommendations to seek counseling and readministration of appropriate psychological inventories to measure potential changes on the psychological measure of concern.

Second, the results could be used in a model to attempt to predict occurrence of athletic injuries during the course of the year. These injuries might be suffered as a result of practices or games, or in other settings (i.e., basketball players playing on their own before practice for the season can officially begin). This model might be useful at other universities as well, or may be found to be specific to the university where testing takes place (e.g., perhaps due to peculiarities in environmental conditions).

Third, it is possible that some of the psychological factors measured may allow prediction of which athletes will return to practice and competition most quickly. Delineation of factors related to adherence to a rehabilitation regimen and a return to participation may be an added outcome of this model, although not a primary focus.

It is important to emphasize that all information obtained through the testing procedures would be kept confidential. The information is designed to be used in an individual counseling/prediction approach by sport psychologists. Coaches and athletic administration personnel would not have access to the information unless written permission was obtained from the athlete. Indeed, one problem encountered is reluctance on the part of some athletes (and teams in general) to complete a battery of standardized inventories. One will most likely find that participation in the program will be considerably less than 100%. However, those motivated to participate will probably find the process useful, and this may "sell" the program to others who initially are hesitant to participate.

Injury Definition and Documentation/Guidelines

Important to psychological intervention studies in athletic settings is defining the term "injury." It is from this most fundamental level that the incidence of injury can be determined and interpretation of findings and comparison of results between studies can be made more reliably.

The most basic elements in the establishment of an injury definition encompass the need for detail, explicitness, and ease of interpretation

Injury Rate = $\dfrac{\text{Definition of Injury}}{\text{Population-at-risk}}$

Figure 1. Injury rate and determination of risk.

(Wallace & Clark, 1988). A set of inclusive and exclusive criteria are needed that allow for differentiation between those who have been injured and those who have not been injured. To date, however, no universally agreed upon definition of what constitutes an injury has been established, although three generally accepted classification criteria include (a) time loss from participation, (b) anatomical tissue diagnosis, and (c) medical consultation. Each of the definitions available has its own strengths and weaknesses and, as such, varies in its ability to meet research objectives.

One way we have found most helpful is to define an injury as (a) being sports related, (b) resulting in a player's inability to participate one day after injury, and (c) requiring medical attention (university athletic training staff, physician, emergency room), including concussions, nerve injuries (regardless of their time loss), eye injuries, and dental care (Noyes, Lindefeld, & Marshall, 1988). This definition has the advantage of comprising a multidimensional approach and is relatively sensitive to the broad spectrum of injuries encountered in the athletic setting. This does not include, however, occurrences of the flu, colds, and other related illnesses that would not be seen as sports related per se but could still be due, in part, to psychologically induced stress/depression resulting in a weakened and potentially more susceptible bodily state. Recent work on psychoneuroimmunology (Carlson & Seifert, 1991; Friedman, Specter, & Klein, 1991; Husband, 1992) supports this point of view and may lead to a change in how we define injury in the future.

Injury frequency is determined by the total number of occurrences encountered during the course of testing (e.g., a season, a year). Injury frequency can then be expressed as a function of the exposure to injury, resulting in determination of an injury rate. The injury rate (see Figure 1) comprises a numerator, the number of events (i.e., injuries) under study, and a denominator, the number of persons at risk of a specific occurrence or event, providing for a determination of risk. A useful way of expressing the denominator is to base it upon every 1,000 athlete-exposures. Athlete-exposures are defined as the frequency with which an athlete is exposed to the potential of injury, and every player at a practice or game is counted as one athlete-exposure. Although this determination involves a fair amount of record keeping, much of this information is already being kept by athletic training staff, and may require only a systematic organization of the record-keeping process.

Injury severity is defined by the significance of the injury sustained. Here again, no universal definition exists, although time-loss from activity has been used in several nationally based sports injury epidemiology studies (Alles, Powell, Buckley, & Hunt, 1979; Powell, 1988). The utility of a time-loss definition is that it is relatively easy to measure and is based on the functional consequences of participation (or not participating!) following the injury. When more objective criteria are needed, as is frequently necessary with ligamentous and muscle-related injuries, categorization in accordance with the injury severity index established by the American Medical Association's *Standard Nomenclature of Injuries* (1968) can be used.

Injury data can be prospectively collected by the medical staff assigned to the study. This includes the university's intercollegiate athletic training staff and student athletic trainers who are enrolled in the National Athletic Trainers' Association Approved Undergraduate Athletic Training Program.

Psychological Tests

There are numerous psychological inventories which can be administered to athletes. Ostrow (1990), for example, has a *Directory of Psychological Tests in the Sport and Exercise Sciences* with information on 175 psychological tests specifically related to sport and exercise. There are a number of inventories (see Table 1) that may be of particular interest in applying the counseling/prediction model.

Profile of Mood States (POMS). The POMS (McNair, Lorr, & Droppleman, 1971) is a 65-adjective rating scale, derived through factor analysis, which measures six dimensions of *mood states*: Tension-Anxiety, Depression-Dejection, Anger-Hostility, Vigor-Activity, Fatigue-Inertia, and Confusion-Bewilderment. The POMS has excellent psychometric properties (established validity and reliability). Instructions request respondents to indicate how they have been feeling during the past week, but it can be used to ask how respondents have been feeling for longer (i.e., past month) or shorter (i.e., daily) periods of time. Ideally, athletes would have comparatively high scores on Vigor-Activity and

Table 1. List of Psychological Inventories.

Profile of Mood States (POMS) (McNair, Lorr, & Droppleman, 1971)

Incredibly Short POMS (Dean, Whelan, & Meyers, 1990)

Sport Anxiety Scale (SAS) (Smith, Smoll, & Schutz, 1990)

Eating Disorders Inventory-2 (EDI-2) (Garner, 1991)

Health Attribution Test (HAT) (Lawlis & Lawlis, 1990)

Coping Resources Inventory (CRI) (Hammer & Marting, 1988)

Life Experiences Survey-Athletes (LES-A) (Hardy, 1989)

The Exercise Salience Scale (TESS) (Morrow & Harvey, 1990)

---

comparatively low scores on the other five factors, providing what has been termed an "iceberg profile" (Morgan & Pollock, 1977), with a peak of vigor and "submerged" levels on the other factors.

The POMS is an excellent means of regularly measuring mood and is used frequently in applied and research contexts, but can become burdensome if administered too frequently. Although 65 items is not a great number, too frequent administration may be undesirable. One way around this problem may be a "new" instrument termed the *Incredibly Short POMS* (Dean, Whelan, & Meyers, 1990), or ISP, which has reduced the 65-item POMS to six items. Concurrent validity appears acceptable, and this instrument has been used effectively in athletic contexts (Fritts, in preparation). One advantage found with administration of the ISP on a regular basis is that respondents develop the habit of completing the form at a regular time in their schedule in a matter of only 10-15 seconds, placing little burden on their time and energy. However, we have also found that coaches are hesitant to have athletes complete even the ISP on days when competition is scheduled, for fear of having the athletes focus too much on their mood states, particularly, of course, if the mood state is negative.

Sport Anxiety Scale (SAS). The SAS (Smith, Smoll, & Schutz, 1990) is a sport-specific measure of cognitive and somatic trait anxiety. Current thinking in sport psychology suggests the advisability of using sport-specific measures as well as instruments that address both cognitive and somatic components of anxiety, such as the SAS. Individual differences in somatic anxiety and two classes of cognitive anxiety, Worry and Concentration Disruption, are measured. The SAS has excellent psychometric properties.

Eating Disorders Inventory-2 (EDI-2). The EDI-2 (Garner, 1991) is a 91-item self-report inventory which assesses an array of *factors related to anorexia nervosa and bulimia nervosa*. Eleven subscales make up the EDI: Drive for Thinness, Bulimia, Body Dissatisfaction, Ineffectiveness, Perfectionism, Interpersonal Distrust, Interoceptive Awareness, Maturity Fears, Impulse Regulation, Social Insecurity, and Asceticism. The EDI-2 has excellent psychometric properties. A new symptom checklist provides additional information about the frequency and severity of symptoms important in considering a diagnosis of an eating disorder, a problem area particularly prevalent in some athletic populations (e.g., gymnasts, runners, divers, wrestlers).

Health Attribution Test (HAT). The HAT (Lawlis & Lawlis, 1990) is a 22-item test that evaluates an individual's *health locus of control*. Attributions for control of one's health may be made to internal factors, powerful others, and chance. The HAT has excellent psychometric properties. This scale provides an excellent measure for attempting to develop a predictive profile for recovery time for individuals who are injured.

Coping Resources Inventory (CRI). The CRI (Hammer & Marting, 1988) is a 60-item inventory that assesses one's *resources for coping with situations*. Coping resources can be defined as "those resources inherent in individuals that enable them to handle stressors more effectively, to experience fewer or less intense symptoms upon exposure to a stressor, or to recover faster from exposure" (Hammer & Marting, 1988, p. 2). The CRI measures resources in five domains: cognitive, social, emotional, spiritual/philosophical, and physical. Hammer and Marting identify seven uses for the CRI, two of which are particularly relevant to this study: "as a research instrument to investigate coping resources in various populations" and "as a tool for identifying individuals who might be at-risk, in need of counseling, or in need of medical intervention" (p. 2). The CRI has excellent psychometric properties.

Life Experiences Survey-Athletes (LES-A). The LES-A (Hardy, 1989) is an 80-item survey that attempts to determine if any of a variety of *life experiences* have occurred to the athlete within the past 12 months *and* what the perceived impact of the event on the person was at the time the event occurred. The survey provides a framework within which to potentially understand moderate to high levels of stress that athletes might be experiencing.

The Exercise Salience Scale (TESS). The TESS (Morrow & Harvey, 1990) measures a number of factors which determine dependence upon exercise. Athletes who are more dependent upon exercise may be more likely to persist in participating in athletics in spite of negative life stress. The TESS has strong psychometric properties.

It is important to emphasize that these are not the only psychological inventories, nor the only psychological constructs, that can be used. Different researchers/practitioners have other areas and other tests they have found meet their needs more effectively. For example, Bergandi and Wittig (1991) found that attentional style was related to frequency of athletic injury with some athletes (in one sport, women's softball), but not others. The *Test of Attentional and Interpersonal Style (TAIS)* (Nideffer, 1976) could, therefore, be used to measure this construct, particularly if one considers sport-specific versions of the TAIS. Other approaches, looking at other variables (Nideffer, 1989), may prove attractive for different needs in different athletic settings.

Model Application

As noted earlier, the battery of inventories would be administered before the fall semester begins or before the first practice in the case of sports (i.e., football) which begin their season before school is in session. This initial baseline also provides an indication of psychological problems that may have arisen during the summer, when contact with athletes may have been minimal. Intervention can then occur if the sport psychologist feels that the test scores indicate this course of action.

Injury data are then collected throughout the course of the year, through the competitive season and practices, as well as recreational periods (i.e., basketball before the "official" practice date). Some inventories may be readministered on a regular basis to monitor potential changes. This is particularly important for those measures addressing issues that are state, rather than trait, in nature. Trait measures will tend to remain stable over time, and administering such measures twice a year may be sufficient. State measures, however, by definition, will change, even on a daily basis. Administering these measures, such as the ISP, on a more frequent basis is therefore desirable. Of course, scoring of these inventories must be done quickly to ensure opportunities for intervention if this is so desired.

At the end of the year data from the psychological inventories and the injury data can be analyzed to assess potential relationships of theoretical and applied importance, as well as to detect changes over time if this is an ongoing process. It is important to note that the process of administering the psychological inventories must have the cooperation of the coach and the athletes. As noted, there will be coaches and athletes who choose not to participate (and human subjects guidelines at universities require that this nonparticipation option be present), and this must be respected.

In applying the model, there are a number of potential uses, as noted earlier. Perhaps the most important, from a clinical/ proactive perspective, is the case wherein the results indicate a clinically significant level of psychological distress on one of the inventories. For example, Jane Doe, athlete on team sport x, provides a POMS with a "negative" or inverted iceberg profile, with high scores on tension, depression, anger, fatigue, and confusion, and a low score on vigor. This suggests that something may be going on in Jane's life; this something could "simply" be overtraining (Morgan, Costill, Flynn, Raglin, & O'Connor, 1988) or could reflect some other problems, such as interpersonal relationships, academic difficulties, or family matters. The athlete would be counseled to seek assistance, either at the university counseling center or with one of the sport psychologists working with athletes at the university. Providing the athlete with a choice and maintaining confidentiality are important elements in this process.

In Jane's case, the POMS, as well as the ISP, could be used to follow up progress in the weeks following the beginning of counseling. Some of the inventories, such as the POMS, may prove quite useful as well in working with athletes who are recovering from an injury (Smith, Scott, O'Fallon, & Young, 1990) and "facilitate the athlete's optimal rehabilitation and a safe return to participation in sports" (p. 38).

This approach provides for a unique partnership of the sport psychologist and athletic trainer. Both groups of individuals have the physical and psychological well-being of the athlete as their greatest concern. Interventions as described in the above model provide a means for facilitating the help we give our athletes in achieving their goals as individuals, students, and athletes.

SUMMARY

Although injuries are a "fact of life" in intercollegiate athletics, it is extremely desirable to minimize injury frequency and severity. The impact of physical and psychological factors on the frequency and severity of injuries is critical and is worthy of in-depth investigation. A counseling/ prediction model is proposed as an effective means of working with athletes and providing important information for theory and research in this critical area of study.

REFERENCES

Alles, W., Powell, J., Buckley, H., & Hunt, E. (1979). The national athletic injury/illness reporting system: 3-year findings of high school and college football injuries. *Journal of Orthopedic and Sports Physical Therapy, 11*, 103-108.

American Medical Association. (1968). *Standard nomenclature of injuries*. Chicago, IL: Author.

Andersen, M.B., & Williams, J.M. (1988). A model of stress and athletic injury: Prediction and prevention. *Journal of Sport & Exercise Psychology, 10*, 294-306.

Bergandi, T.A., & Wittig, A.F. (1991). *Attentional style as a predictor of athletic injury*. Unpublished manuscript. Spalding University, Louisville, KY.

Blackwell, B., & McCullagh, P. (1990, Spring). The relationship of athletic injury to life stress, competitive anxiety and coping resources. *Athletic Training, 25*, 23-27.

Carlson, J.G., & Seifert, A.R. (Eds.) (1991). *International perspectives on self-regulation and health*. New York: Plenum Press.

Dean, J.E., Whelan, J.P., & Meyers, A.W. (1990, September). *An incredibly quick way to assess mood states: The Incredibly Short POMS*. Paper presented at the annual meeting of the Association for the Advancement of Applied Sport Psychology, San Antonio, TX.

Friedman, H., Specter, S., & Klein, T.W. (Eds.) (1991). *Drugs of abuse, immunity, and immunodeficiency*. New York: Plenum Press.

Fritts, S.M. (1992). *Psychologial factors that predispose athletes to injuries*. Unpublished Master's Thesis, Temple University, Philadelphia, PA.

Garner, D. M. (1991). *Eating Disorder Inventory-2 manual*. Odessa, FL: Psychological Assessment Resources, Inc.

Gregory, B., & Van Valkenburgh, J. (1991). Psychology of the injured athlete. *Journal of Post Anesthesia Nursing, 6*(2), 108-110.

Hammer, A.L., & Marting, M.S. (1988). *Manual for the Coping Re-*

sources Inventory (research edition). Palo Alto, CA: Consulting Psychologists Press.

Hardy, C.J. (1989). *Life Experiences Survey-Athletes.* Chapel Hill, NC: Department of Physical Education, University of North Carolina.

Hardy, C.J., & Riehl, R.E. (1988). An examination of the life stress-injury relationship among noncontact sport participants. *Behavioral Medicine, 14,* 113-118.

Husband, A.J. (Ed.) (1992). *Behavior and immunity.* Boca Raton, FL: CRC Press.

Kerr, G., & Minden, H. (1988). Psychological factors related to the occurrence of athletic injuries. *Journal of Sport & Exercise Psychology, 10,* 167-173.

Lawlis, J., & Lawlis, G.F. (1990). *Health Attribution Test manual.* Champaign, IL: Institute for Personality and Ability Testing.

McNair, D.M., Lorr, M., & Droppleman, L.F. (1971). *Manual: Profile of mood states.* San Diego, CA: Educational and Industrial Testing Service.

Morgan, W.P., Costill, D.L., Flynn, M.G., Raglin, J.S., & O'Connor, P. H. (1988). Psychological monitoring of overtraining and performance. *British Journal of Sports Medicine, 21,* 107-114.

Morgan, W.P., & Pollock, M.L. (1977). Psychologic characterization of the elite distance runner. *Annals of the New York Academy of Sciences, 301,* 382-402.

Morrow, J., & Harvey, P. (1990). *The exercise salience scale.* Unpublished manuscript.

Nideffer, R.M. (1976). Test of Attentional and Interpersonal Style (TAIS). *Journal of Personality and Social Psychology, 34,* 397-404.

Nideffer, R.M. (1989). Psychological aspects of sports injuries: Issues in prevention and treatment. *International Journal of Sport Psychology, 20,* 241-255.

Noyes, R., Lindefeld, T., & Marshall, M. (1988). What determines an athletic injury (definition): Who determines an injury (occurrence)? *American Journal of Sports Medicine, 16* (Suppl.), 134-135.

Ostrow, A.C. (1990). *Directory of psychological tests in the sport and exercise sciences.* Morgantown, WV: Fitness Information Technology, Inc.

Powell, J. (1988). National high school athletic injury registry. *American Journal of Sports Medicine, 16*(Suppl. 1), 55-56.

Smith, A.M., Scott, S.G., O'Fallon, W.M., & Young, M.L. (1990).

Emotional responses of athletes to injury. *Mayo Clinic Proceedings,* *65*, 38-50.

Smith, R.E., Smoll, F.L., & Ptacek, J.T. (1990). Conjunctive moderator variables in vulnerability and resiliency research: Life stress, social support, and coping skills, and adolescent sport injuries. *Journal of Personality and Social Psychology, 58,* 360-370.

Smith, R.E., Smoll, F.L., & Schutz, R.W. (1990). Measurement and correlates of sport-specific cognitive and somatic trait anxiety: The sport anxiety scale. *Anxiety Research, 2,* 263-280.

Wallace, R., & Clark, W. (1988). The numerator, denominator, and the population-at-risk. *American Journal of Sports Medicine, 16*(Suppl. 1), 55-56.

Wiese, D.M., Weiss, M.R., & Yukelson, D.P. (1990). *Sport psychology in the training room: A survey of athletic trainers.* Paper presented at the annual meeting of the American Alliance for Health, Physical Education, Recreation, and Dance, New Orleans, LA.

Chapter 6

The Malingering Athlete: Psychological Considerations

Robert J. Rotella
University of Virginia
Bruce C. Ogilvie
Professor Emeritus
San Jose State University
David H.Perrin
University of Virginia

This chapter describes malingering in general terms and discusses the causes or origins of malingering in sports. Although it is impossible to know with certainty that an athlete is a malingerer, certain persistent characteristics and/or causal factors related to malingering are identified. Several strategies for changing malingering are also presented. It is recommended that these strategies be considered with respect to the individual athlete and that the entire rehabilitation team be involved in the development of an effective treatment plan.

The malingering athlete is of interest to coaches, trainers and sport psychology counselors alike. Individual as well as team underachievement and unfulfilled sport careers may be attributed to malingering. In particular, athletic trainers who interact regularly with injured athletes should be familiar with characteristics, ploys and practices of malingerers (Kane, 1984; Nack, 1980).

Although malingering has been discussed in the sport psychology literature since 1966, it is still not completely understood (Rogers, 1990). In fact, it is very difficult to know with certainty when an individual is a malingering. This contributes to the behavior's intrigue, confusion and controversy. This chapter combines the perspectives of specialists in sport psychology, and sport medicine/athletic training, in an effort to provide insights into the motives and behaviors of sport malingerers. In addition, the chapter includes selected strategies for helping such individuals disengage from malingering behaviors (Ogilvie & Tutko, 1966; Rotella, 1988; Shank, 1989). However, considerably more sound empirical research is needed before the psychological underpinnings of malingering motives and behaviors are completely understood.

Prior to discussing the "whys" of malingering, it is crucial that rehabilitation team members believe that athletes are truthful in describing the condition of their bodies. It is a serious mistake to quickly and irresponsibly judge an athlete to be a malingerer (Kane, 1984; Nack, 1980). Caution should be exercised when making such a diagnosis and the athlete should receive benefit of doubt about his or her alleged inability to perform optimally due to injury. Rehabilitation team members should believe in the athlete's claim and not be influenced by past experiences with the same or other athletes. Mental health practitioners can never be certain of the accuracy and reliability of their diagnosis of malingering since no completely reliable way of arriving at such a conclusion is available. However, through careful observation of behavior patterns, insightful professionals may find support for such a diagnosis.

Understanding Malingering

Some reasons for malingering may be justifiable, at least in the mind of a particular athlete; and some reasons may lead to a short-term problem that will only surface in certain predictable situations. In some cases, underlying motives may lead to continued and repeated malingering if effective intervention is not provided. The primary focus for the remainder of this chapter will be on athletes who have a serious, recurring problem with malingering.

Table 1 provides some common reasons for sport malingering that derive from the experiences of this chapter's authors.

Malingering is not restricted to the world of sport. For instance, in industrial medicine, it has proven to be an extremely costly psychological and behavioral problem (Brink, 1989; Labbate & Miller, 1990; Lees-

Table 1. Reasons for Malingering in Sport

- Using an insignificant injury to rationalize loss of starting status, reduction in playing time and poor competitive performance.
- Using injury-related disability to prevent loss of athletic scholarship.
- Using injury to account for apparent decrease or change in motivation for participation.
- Using injury to offset the personal realization of insufficient ability (talent) to compete successfully.
- Using injury to attract needed or desired attention from others that has not been forthcoming elsewhere.
- Using injury to demonstrate personal courage by "playing hurt."
- Using injury to offset expectations of coaches, teammates and parents.
- Using injury as a reason to desist from performing thereby not contributing skill, talent and ability to the team's effort, and thus expressing hostility or anger towards coaches, teammates or parents.
- Using injury to avoid the rigors of practice but still be able to compete since the coach may need the athlete's services on game day. (The athlete does not wish to "waste" his or her body.)
- Using minor injury as a reason not to play in order to save the body for intercollegiate or professional competition where the material rewards are greater than those at the present level.
- Using injury as a way of disengaging from a dimension of life that heretofore has proven to be undesirable but also unavoidable. (All males in the family traditionally play football.)

Haley, 1986a). The difficulties range from the assessment and identification of malingerers to the provision of effective treatments for modifying behavior patterns, to making legal decisions regarding workers' compensation (Brink, 1989).

Malingerers, casually labelled by coaches and athletes as those who intentionally lie about an injury in order to avoid practice or competition, have been studied (Kane, 1984; Ogilvie & Tutko, 1966). "One major cue to malingering is the potential for gain or loss as a consequence of having problems" (Lees-Haley, 1986b, p.68). The presence of a clearly definable goal differentiates malingerers from persons with other forms of fictitious illness (Swanson, 1984). Assessment, although plagued with uncertainty even today, has included the Minnesota Multiphasic Personality Inventory (MMPI), the Bender-Gestalt Test, the Wechsler Adult Intelligence Scale (WAIS) (Lees-Haley, 1986a), the Rorschach, and the Structural Interview of Reported Symptoms (SIRS) (Rogers, Gillis, & Bagby, 1990). Beal (1989) has argued that other scales are more appropriate and sensitive depending upon the specific kind of malingering in question.

Recent models of malingering portray it as a result of adaptive responses to adverse circumstances. It has been suggested that malingering may be understood by examining the underlying psychopathology or criminal backgrounds of malingerers (Rogers, 1990). However, within the context of sport it seems more helpful to consider this behavior as an adaptive response to adverse circumstances requiring the presence of an external incentive for being injured (Labbate & Miller, 1990). Travin and Protter (1984) attempted to reconceptualize malingering along a continuum ranging from other-deceptive to self-deceptive, depending upon the degree of one's self-awareness.

Historically, attempts have been made to distinguish between malingering and other forms of pathological avoidance behavior. Much clinical insight derives from the comparisons with mentally aberrant avoidance reactions such as those found in conversion hysteria. Such a comparison can contribute greatly to our understanding of malingering. Malingerers may present a considerable challenge to the clinical psychologist since there is no foolproof way to confirm that a person is consciously faking symptoms of discomfort or physical distress. This is especially true when such individuals seem to cling to their symptoms or disability in the absence of physiological support for such behavior. When the various categories of the hysterical disorders are examined, it is found that it is possible to mimic almost every known disease and physical disorder. Malingerers may mimic disorders of entire systems such as hysterical blindness, or aphonia, a loss of speech, and a wide range of other motor systems. The range of visceral symptoms also covers the entire range of possible somatic disorders (Overholser, 1990).

In view of the manifold opportunities for deception, it is a formidable challenge indeed to determine the presence of malingering. Critical to such a determination is the unique way in which the individual communicates the nature of the disability and how such is expressed in terms of pain or state of recovery. Extremely subtle forms of communication are necessary in order for a rehabilitation team to find support for a malingering diagnosis. As has been outlined, experience suggests that identifiable behavior patterns may indicate malingering. What becomes apparent in the face of an unsuccessful treatment program is the issue of intentionality. The athlete who fails to respond to treatment or to a physician's assurance as to his or her state of physical recovery may be driven by unconscious as well as conscious motives. Some athletes are content to continue expressing their symptoms and receive consequential attention. They tend to be highly verbal and their descriptions of personal physical limitations are presented in considerable detail. Malingerers appear to be emotionally detached from even the most disabling symptoms.

Malingerers will be characterized by their guile and deceit as they seek to manipulate others with their verbal skills. To avoid expectations that require them to behave maturely and confront their personal responsibility to the team, teammates, treatment staff, and coaches, malingerers engage in various forms of deception (Ogilvie & Tutko, 1966).

Treatment for malingering is always confounded by the issue of secondary gain. In the workplace, when workers fake disability, the secondary gain becomes a financial settlement or material support for life. Athletes who fabricate or maintain symptoms are provided with an escape route from any appropriate demand that may be placed upon them. Experience in a military rehabilitation center enables one of this chapter's authors to suggest "that you have to outcon the conman" in order to force such individuals to expose their own preferred form of deceit. In World War II, it seemed that the number one symptom for the malingerer was low back pain. This remains one of the most difficult differential diagnoses for the physician to make.

Based on the present knowledge of the available literature and experience in the athletic environment, most athletes who have a repeated habit of malingering do so primarily as a result of (a) a need for attention or (b) fears.

The need for attention is typically at the top of the list of causes for malingering (Ogilvie & Tutko, 1966). For a variety of reasons the need for attention becomes a more important priority than the need to perform (practice and/or compete).

The malingerer presents a problem to many persons in the sport environment. For instance, the team suffers the loss of a potential contributor to its collective effort; coaches and athletic trainers may feel frustrated, helpless, and discouraged by their inability to help. The malingerer's behavior, attitude and general approach to participation is in stark contrast to the response of most other athletes who feel guilt when injured since injury inhibits their ability to contribute to the team's efforts. The non malingering but injured athlete usually attends every practice and game if allowed to do so and receives treatment before and after every practice session. His or her goal is to return as soon as possible to physical activity. In contrast, the malingerer is completely guilt free and seeks treatment with the goal of avoiding practice and/or competition while still receiving attention and sympathy.

The true malingerer is plainly and simply a fraud, or a skillful actor. When attempting to deceive coaches, athletic trainers, and teammates, the malingerer can show pain and suffering upon a moment's notice. That which often reveals malingering is *the degree to which the drama is exaggerated*. The malingerer, while demonstrating a lack of commitment to rehabilitation, wants everyone to know he or she is hurt in order to obtain the desired attention. If such an athlete in any way becomes concerned about getting caught in the lie, expression of the severity of the injury and the anguish he or she experiences is further exaggerated. *For the typical malingering athlete the greatest need is attention, and the greatest fear is getting caught.* In essence, dishonesty is the malingerer's most salient attribution. It is the malingerer's response that often accounts for him or her being identified and distinguished from others with low pain threshold and/or low pain tolerance. However, it is necessary to again emphasize that even experts cannot know for certain if an athlete is faking or truly experiencing pain.

Background

What factors explain the causes or origins of malingering? In this section an attempt is made to provide answers to this question by way of exemplifying childhood experiences that may have contributed to the tendency to malinger. An important realization is that athletes learn to malinger from personal experiences; observation of models such as parents, coaches, or older athletes. Malingering techniques may also be taught directly to athletes by older athletes. However it occurs, malingering is a behavior that has been ∤earned, *adopted as acceptable, rewarded,* and then done *willfully* and *intentionally* or *habitually* (Ogilvie & Tutko, 1966).

The typical malingering athlete was often spoiled in his or her early years. Regardless of the reasons for being spoiled, lying and deception were allowed. Quite commonly as a child (or in one's early sport ex-periences), the malingerer perceived that lying was acceptable and justifiable in order to get one's way. It is likely that the malingerer's own devious behavior was at some point directly reinforced or learned indirectly by observing parents, teachers, coaches, or older athletes being reinforced for dishonest behavior. The athlete may have simply observed others behaving in ways that belied what they expressed as a personal philosophy. Such hypocrisy in others whom the athlete considered models may have contributed to the malingering tendencies he or she now demonstrates.

Typically, malingerers learn at an early age that family members always intervene and rescue them from trouble. Moreover, they learn that if caught, the result is a simple reprimand or lecture. Thus, behaving improperly and yet avoiding due punishment becomes a frivolous and almost pleasant, game-like experience. Talented athletes from such backgrounds tend to enjoy knowing the team's success depends on them. Such athletes typically enjoy the potential for exercising control, the attention received, and the disturbances they may cause to their team.

Some gifted athletes do not become malingerers because of home- or family-related conditioning. For instance, when their athletic talents are first recognized in middle school or junior high school, they discover that many adults hold their abilities in very high esteem. Soon the young, elite athletes learn that unacceptable behaviors such as skipping class, cheating or stealing are overlooked. They revel in their immunity from punishment and enjoy very special attention. Later, they are likely to acknowledge their dishonesty, but assert that it has in part been fueled by adult hypocrisy.

Before the more persistent characteristics and/or causal factors related to malingerers are discussed, three factors should be emphasized. As stated previously, the condition labeled here as malingering is typically a *manifestation of complex motives*. Social and family influences that undermine the maturity of malingerers vary considerably; however, these influences seem to produce individuals with a *shallow conscience*. This, in turn, tends to result in the shirking of responsibility to others. Avoidance reactions then become the standard response when such persons are confronted with the demands of reality. Malingering is a consequence of faking, deceit, or selfish manipulation that is related in some way to underlying forms of *inadequacy*.

A malingerer is usually fearful of being exposed as such, and is therefore always on guard. However, self-confrontation of the inclination to be deceitful is unlikely since admission of such behavior is frightening. A malingerer therefore tends to cling to the strategy of dishonesty at all cost, making it very difficult to provide help. It must be emphasized that in describing malingerers in this chapter a variety of underlying factors, some of which may be referred to as character disorders, are identified. If some of these should involve sociopathic tendencies, treatment teams are likely to be faced with an unusual challenge since such athletes will be extremely skilled at rationalization, denial, and projection of responsibility. They will tend to have a history of manipulating and exploiting others. Having been in confrontations with authority figures most of their lives, they have become skilled at avoiding responsibility.

Helping Malingerers

Becoming involved in a battle of wills in order to salvage an athlete who exhibits the foregoing traits may place too many demands upon members of the treatment team. Knowledge may be most effectively used when it prevents the treatment team from being exploited by such athletes. At some point, cost effectiveness must be evaluated and a decision made as to whether or not the time and energy required for changing the behavior or behavioral tendencies of a particular athlete is worth the effort. It is appropriate at some point to conclude that an athlete may be too immature to be helped. It is preferable, however, that such a decision be postponed as long as possible and not be reached at the initial level of interaction with the athlete.

The following generalizations about the malingerer may provide members of the treatment team with insight that enables them to feel empowered to be positive service providers. During interviews, verbal communication, and treatment sessions, it will be helpful to observe the following (Lees-Haley, 1986b; Ogilvie & Tutko, 1966; Overholser, 1990; Swanson, 1984):

1. The extent to which the athlete exhibits narcissistic behavior patterns: that is, the athlete is self-centered and demanding, displays low interest in other people's pain or disabilities, complains that he or she never receives the same care as others, and tends to rationalize his or her responsibility for following the treatment program.
2. The tendency to want to avoid talking about his or her real or imagined disability. Members of the treatment team should watch eye contact, avoidance of personnel, failure to keep appointments, criticisms of treatment program.
3. The extent to which the athlete senses any responsibility with regard to supporting the team or coach and the effect his or her absence might be having on the team.
4. Consistency or inconsistency in the athlete's behavior as observed in unguarded moments.

5. A lack of true emotional involvement in the injury. Athletes who are genuinely injured tend to grieve and deny loss.
6. A lack of cooperation with diagnostic and/or therapeutic regimes.
7. The presence of external incentives that are greater for being injured than for being healthy.

Because athletes malinger for a variety of reasons, there are many different strategies for changing their behavior (Kane, 1984; Ogilvie & Tutko, 1966; Olmstead, 1976; Shank, 1989). Athletic trainers, coaches, and sport psychologists may find one or all of the following to be useful. It is recommended that each suggestion be considered in terms of individual athletes and that the entire rehabilitation team be involved in developing an effective strategy.

1. As a first step, attempts should be made to understand the individual athlete's problems and the underlying reason for malingering. This will require taking the time to develop a trusting relationship with an athlete whom it may initially be difficult to like, respect, and admire. *Listening* to the athlete is a necessary second step, but the coach, sport psychologist, or athletic trainer must go beyond listening. It is important to show care, concern, and interest in the athlete. Yet, it is crucial not to let such athletes use the discussion or counselling session as another opportunity to lie and manipulate. The treatment team should expect that a malingering athlete will likely try these strategies, but the treatment team should attempt not to take such ploys personally. These are simply well-learned habits. Listening must be combined with straight-forward feedback to the athlete.

2. If, after in-depth observation and thoughtful evaluation, it is difficult to ascertain that the athlete is faking, it is important to sit with the athlete and confront the issue honestly and directly. The treatment team must not attack or accuse the athlete of lying, and should be sure to display empathy for the possibility of an undetected injury. It should be made clear that the best interests of the athlete and the team are the only concern. The athlete should be allowed to express thoughts and concerns. Honesty and openness should be encouraged, and the athlete should be questioned about statements that seem inconsistent with behavior.

3. Empathy and understanding of the athlete's situation promotes growth and positive development, whereas sympathy breeds weakness, stagnation, and self-pity.

4. Malingering is done only if it produces gain for the athlete. It will not occur in the absence of perceived gain.

5. The treatment team should attempt to determine if the athlete malingers due to fear of playing, need of help in managing stress or fear, need to reduce internally or externally imposed pressure, or need for attention.

6. It should be honestly explained to the malingering athlete that both the athletic trainer and coach are very frustrated and are either lost or still searching for answers. The athlete should be asked for suggestions and the members of the treatment team may admit that their patience is running thin. The athlete should be advised that he or she seems to defy getting well, and that the treatment team wonders if the athlete really wants to get well or if the treatment team is failing to do something that might help. It should be made clear that no one is trying to assign blame. The goal is to solve the problem because that is the responsibility of the treatment team, and its members care about the athlete.

7. At some point, malingering athletes must be given strictly defined boundaries for behavior and detailed consequences of stepping outside those boundaries. They should be advised that these steps are being taken in their best interest. Members of the treatment team must establish and maintain their authority over the team of athletes. In the preseason it is ideal to establish team rules that make expectations and consequences perfectly clear. A simple rule stating that athletes who cannot practice for two days prior to a game will not play in the game regardless of the athlete's talent often works wonders in eliminating malingering in a sport such as football. Doing this makes a definite statement that the team will not rely on any one athlete for its success and that no athlete will be permitted to manipulate the coach, sport psychologist, or athletic trainer. Thus malingerers will not get the attention they desire–if they can't practice they can't play. Nothing personal is implied by this strategy. It is simply a team rule. (Table 2 lists several other techniques important to the prevention of malingering.)

8. With the athlete's agreement specific rehabilitation goals should be established and recorded. Athlete, counselor, and athletic trainer should agree on times for treatments, length of program, and exact individual responsibilities. The date and time for the next appointment should be determined.

9. The athlete should be required to talk with other athletes who have

Table 2. Recommendations for Preventing or Reducing Malingering in Sport

- Practice sessions should include as much "fun" as possible, while being challenging and stimulating.
- Privately and publicly reinforce participation (practice as well as competition) despite relatively minor pain, soreness and discomfort while being careful not to encourage athletes to risk additional or serious injury.
- Do everything possible to give starters and nonstarters equal attention.
- Be alert to signs of high levels of fatigue in athletes, give the team a day off when necessary or assign reduced work loads to those who are particularly overtired.
- Enable elite performers (especially able athletes on the team) to appreciate their special responsibilities and the ways in which they may influence other team players.
- Be sure that members of the coaching staff and athletic trainers adhere to guidelines set in the preseason.
- Emphasize that game and practice rules are intended to benefit and protect athletes.
- After an athlete is injured help him or her establish short- and long-term goals for rehabilitation. Whenever possible indicate and reinforce progress toward achieving goals.
- Be tolerant of short-lived (a day or two) malingering attributable to fatigue, or personal or family problems.
- Be supportive, understanding and sensitive to the feelings of athletes after they sustain a competitive loss or are mired in a streak of losses.

successfully recovered from a similar injury and who have returned to a preinjury level of performance.

10. Rewards (etc.) should be provided for desired behavior or retracted for malingering. Initially it is useful to give malingerers rewards for desired behaviors and withdraw rewards for unwanted behaviors. In the early stages, continuous reinforcement or praise and attention should be provided every time the desired behavior occurs, but as behavior shaping continues, feedback should be provided on a variable schedule (e.g., every 4th, 7th time the desired behavior occurs). Finally, one must be sure that what is offered as a reward is indeed viewed as such by the athlete.

11. In most cases, it is best to avoid using a word like "malingerer" when speaking to the athlete, as it will most likely serve only to raise defenses

and further hinder honest communication. On the other hand, the term may be applied strategically when the athletic trainer's, coach's, or sport psychologist's patience, care, and concern have been provided to no avail.

CONCLUSIONS

Although data depicting the actual incidence of malingering in sport are not available, it is likely that although real and prevalent, the problem is not overwhelming. Nonetheless, for obvious reasons pertaining to the athlete, the team, and its management, malingering should be eradicated whenever possible. To this end, this chapter attempts to clarify reasons for such behavior in sport as well as to recommend strategies for its elimination or reduction. Also important is the establishment of a trusting and respectful relationship with the malingering athlete. The athletic trainer, coach, and counselor may demonstrate caring by setting and enforcing rules for their athlete's practice and on-the-field behaviors. Helping malingerers requires tremendous patience, but the long-term benefits of doing so are enormous. Finally, athletic trainers and coaches must remember that some injuries may have unusual or subtle signs and symptoms. Thus, although malingering may be suspected, the potential always exists that the athlete is in fact injured.

REFERENCES

Bandura, A. (1977). Self-efficacy: Toward a unifying theory of behavioral change. *Psychological Review, 84,* 191-215.

Beal, D.C. (1989). Assessment of malingering in personal injury cases. *American Journal of Forensic Psychology, 7,* 59-65.

Brink, N. E. (1989). The power struggle of Workers Compensation: Strategies for intervention. *Journal of Applied Rehabilitation Counseling, 20,* 25-28.

Dishman, R.K. (1982). Compliance/adherence in health-related exercise. *Health Psychology, 1,* 237-267.

Kane, B. (1984). Trainer counseling to avoid three face-saving maneuvers. *Athletic Training, 19,* 171-174.

Labbate, L.A., & Miller, R.W. (1990). A case of malingering. *American Journal of Psychiatry, 47,* 257-258.

Lees-Haley, P.R. (1986a). How to detect malingerers in the workplace. *Personnel Journal, 65,* 106-110.

Lees-Haley, P.R. (1986b). Psychological malingerers. *Trial, 21,* 68-69.

Locke, E.A., Shaw, K.N., Saari, Z.M., & Latham, G.P. (1981). Goal setting and task performance: 1969-1980. *Psychological Bulletin, 90,* 125-152.

Nack, W. (1980). Now everyone believes him. *Sports Illustrated, 53,* 12-17.

Ogilvie, B., & Tutko, T. (1966). *Problem athletes and how to handle them.* London: Pelham Books.

Olmstead, A.E. (1976). Malingering and stroking. *Transactional Analyses Journal, 6,* 268-269.

Overholser, J.C. (1990). Differential diagnoses of malingering and fictitious disorders with physical symptoms. Special issue: Malingering and deception: An update. *Behavioral Science and the Law, 8,* 55-65.

Rogers, R. (1990). Development of a new classification model of malingering. *Bulletin of the American Academy of Psychiatry and the Law, 18,* 323-333.

Rogers, R., & Cavanaugh, J.L. (1983). "Nothing but the truth"...a reexamination of malingering. *Journal of Psychiatry and the Law, 11,* 443-459.

Rogers, R., Gillis, J., & Bagby, R. (1990). The SIRS as a measure of malingering. *Behavioral Sciences and the Law, 8,* 85-92.

Rotella, R. (1988). Psychological care of the injured athlete. In D.N. Kuland (Ed.), *The injured athlete* (pp. 213-224). Philadelphia: J.P. Lippincott.

Shank, R.H. (1989). Academic and athletic factors related to predicting compliance by athletes to treatments. *Athletic Training, 24,* 125.

Stuart, R.B. (1982). *Adherence, compliance, and generalization in behavioral medicine.* Brunner/Magel: New York.

Swanson, D.A. (1984). Malingering and associated syndromes. *Psychiatric-Medicine, 2,* 287-293.

Travin, S., & Protter, B. (1984). Malingering and malingering-like behavior: Some denial and conceptual issues. *Psychiatry-Quarterly, 56,* 189-197.

Chapter 7

Personality and Injury Rehabilitation Among Sport Performers

J. Robert Grove
The University of Western Australia

Personality is one of several factors that influence the thoughts, feelings, and behaviors of athletes during rehabilitation. Research indicates that explanatory pessimism, dispositional optimism, and hardiness have health-related consequences, and it has been suggested that these traits might also affect psychophysiological processes during recovery from injury. Preliminary data collected from athletes in the three months following knee surgery suggest that mood states are, indeed, influenced by these personality factors.

Knowledge of an athlete's personality may help sports medicine personnel to anticipate, understand, and deal with undesirable rehabilitation responses. For that reason, formal and informal approaches to personality assessment are examined, and potential problems are discussed with reference to specific personality characteristics. Effective resolution of these problematic responses will require knowledge, awareness, compassion, and creativity on the part of the practitioner.

Sport scientists have devoted considerable attention to psychological factors that might be associated with injury occurrence among athletes. In summarizing this research, Andersen and Williams (1988) implicated the stress response as an important mediator of injury occurrence and identified a number of factors that may contribute to both athletic stress and injury. These factors include the athlete's stress history (e.g., general life stress or prior injury), coping resources (e.g., social support networks), and personality.

Grove and colleagues have suggested that a modified form of the Andersen and Williams model is a useful framework for thinking about psychological factors in injury rehabilitation (Grove & Gordon, 1991; Grove, Hanrahan, & Stewart, 1990). A diagram of this modified model is presented in Figure 1.

Certain aspects of the model in Figure 1 deserve comment. First, although injury is the end-point of the original Andersen and Williams (1988) model, it is the starting point in this model. Thus, our framework can be viewed as a simple extension of the Andersen and Williams framework, with the athlete's return to competition as an end-point. Second, our extended model considers the stress response to be one manifestation of the interplay among cognitions, physiological reactions, and behaviors during rehabilitation. A variety of other positive and negative manifestations may also occur (e.g., increased self-awareness or noncompliance to treatment regimes). Finally, we have included "injury-related factors" and "treatment-related factors" as general influences on psychophysiological aspects of the rehabilitation response. This modification is consistent with statements made by athletes and sports medicine personnel about factors that affect progress during rehabilitation (Brewer, Van Raalte, & Linder, 1991; Gordon, Milios, & Grove, 1991a; Grove, Hanrahan, & Stewart, 1990; Wiese, Weiss, & Yukelson, 1991).

Although any of the general factors shown in Figure 1 is a legitimate area of concern for those who deal directly with injured athletes, a detailed description of all these factors is beyond the scope of this chapter. Instead, attention will be directed specifically to personality variables that may be related to the athlete's thoughts, feelings, and behaviors during rehabilitation. Research related to selected personality factors will be reviewed, alternative ways of assessing relevant dispositions will be discussed, and potential uses for this information will be examined.

What Personality Variables Might Be Important?

Recent reviews suggest that a number of personality variables may have health-related consequences (Carson, 1989; Friedman & Booth-

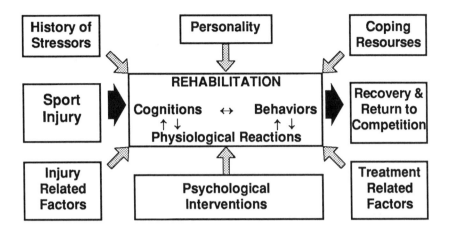

Figure 1. An extension of the Andersen and Williams (1988) model to rehabilitation from sport injury.

Kewley, 1987; Rodin & Salovey, 1989; Taylor, 1990). It is reasonable to assume that some of these same variables will also affect the athlete's thoughts, physical reactions, and/or behaviors during injury rehabilitation. Three of these personality factors (explanatory style, dispositional optimism, and hardiness) are described below. These particular factors have been selected because they are prominent in the health psychology literature, and because my colleagues and I have recently examined them in relation to injury recovery among sport performers.

Explanatory Style
Explanatory style is the way an individual typically accounts for significant events in his or her life. In other words, it is a relatively permanent tendency to explain things in a certain way. Individuals who exhibit a "pessimistic explanatory style" tend to explain negative events as personally caused ("It's my own fault I got injured"), stable over time ("I'm going to be out of commission for a long time"), and global in nature ("It's going to disrupt my entire life"). At the same time, these individuals tend to explain positive events as externally caused ("Healing just takes time"), unstable over time ("My progress is likely to be up and down"), and specific in nature ("My recovery depends on this particular therapist/ treatment").

There is a growing body of literature connecting various components of pessimistic explanatory style with undesirable health consequences. Peterson and Seligman (1987) reported data from three such studies. In the first study, quotes made by Hall of Fame baseball players were content analyzed for their degree of internality, stability, and globality. Scores based on these explanatory dimensions were then correlated with the life span of the player who made the statements. Results indicated that shorter life spans were associated with pessimistic explanations for both good ($r = .45; p < .02$) and bad events ($r = .26; p < .08$). In a second study, Peterson and colleagues content analyzed accounts of World War II experiences supplied by 18 outstanding university graduates. An index of pessimistic explanatory style was calculated from statements made in 1946 for bad events during the war. This index correlated positively ($r = .40; p < .10$) with health status in 1980.

The third study reported by Peterson and Seligman (1987) dealt with the health status of university students over a one-year period. The students were asked to imagine that they had experienced a variety of hypothetical negative events and to state the most likely cause for each event. They were also asked to rate each cause in terms of its internality, stability, and globality. A composite measure of pessimistic explanatory style was obtained by summing the ratings for these negative events. This score was then correlated with reports of illness and number of visits to the doctor at one month and at one year. Significant correlations were observed for number of illnesses at one month ($r = .21; p < .05$), and the vast majority of these illnesses were infectious in nature. Pessimistic explanatory style also correlated significantly with number of doctor visits at one month and one year ($rs = .22$ and $.23$, respectively).

Although the correlations obtained by Peterson and colleagues between explanatory style and various health measures are rather small, they are consistent in their direction. The tendency to explain life events in a pessimistic manner does appear to be associated with poor health.

Peterson and Seligman (1987) suggest that a number of mechanisms may be responsible for this relationship. It is possible that the fatalistic outlook of pessimists causes them to experience more negative life events, neglect the basics of health care, and/or become passive in the face of illness or injury. It is also possible that pessimistic explanatory style increases the chances of social isolation, loneliness, and/or depression. Interestingly, all three of these factors have been noted as negative indicators of psychological adjustment to injury among athletes (Gordon, Milios, & Grove, 1991a). Finally, recent evidence indicates that the health consequences of pessimistic explanatory style could also be mediated by a suppression of immunity (Kamen-Siegel, Rodin, Seligman, & Dwyer, 1991).

Dispositional Optimism

Scheier and Carver (1985, 1987, in press) have discussed the health-related consequences of a personality variable that bears some resemblance to explanatory style. They call this variable "dispositional optimism" and define it simply as a general expectancy for good rather than bad outcomes to occur. Such general expectancies are believed to influence health because they determine the extent to which an individual is willing to initiate health-oriented behaviors and persist with them in the face of difficulties.

Dispositional optimism has been linked to self-reports of physical symptoms among the elderly and among university students. Reker and Wong (1985), for example, found optimism to be negatively correlated with physical symptoms and positively correlated with ratings of physical, psychological, and general well-being in a group of elderly persons. Similar findings were reported for university students in a study by Scheier and Carver (1985). They asked the students to complete a measure of optimism and a physical symptom checklist on two occasions: one month before the end of semester and immediately after end-of-semester exams. Number of physical symptoms experienced during the stressful exam period showed a significant negative correlation ($r = -.27$) with optimism scores.

More compelling evidence for the link between optimism and health was obtained in a study of recovery from coronary artery bypass surgery conducted by Scheier and colleagues (Scheier et al., 1989). They assessed mood and coping strategies before surgery, physiological reactions during surgery, and progress after surgery among optimists and pessimists. The findings indicated that optimism had positive consequences before, during, and after surgery. More specifically, optimists reported less hostility and depression than did pessimists immediately prior to surgery. Optimists also made plans and set goals for recovery prior to the operation to a greater extent than did pessimists. Measures taken during surgery showed fewer adverse physiological reactions on the part of optimists. In addition, there was a general tendency for optimists to recover faster than pessimists, both in terms of objective "recovery milestones" and in terms of subjective ratings of improvement by members of the rehabilitation team. Finally, there was a strong correlation ($r = .60$; $p < .001$) between resurgery optimism and self-reported quality of life six months after the operation.

Scheier and Carver (1987) suggest that both behavioral and physiological mechanisms could be responsible for the apparent connection between optimism and health. From a behavioral perspective, optimists seem to cope with stress differently, perhaps more effectively, than pessimists. Specifically, optimists show a tendency to accept the reality of negative situations; engage in direct, problem-focused coping; use positive reinterpretation; and seek social support. At the same time, they show less of a tendency to deny the reality of negative situations, disengage from their coping efforts, and become preoccupied with their emotional distress.

From a physiological perspective, both cardiovascular reactivity and immunological functioning could contribute to the effects of optimism on health. Data collected by Van Treuren and Hull (1986) suggest that optimists and pessimists exhibit differential changes in blood pressure and pulse rate when exposed to success and failure feedback. In general, optimists appear to be less reactive than pessimists (Scheier & Carver, 1987). In addition, there is evidence that an optimistic orientation may be positively related to natural killer cell activity (Levy & Wise, 1987), whereas a pessimistic orientation may be associated with progression from precancerous to cancerous states (Goodkin, Antoni, & Blaney, 1986). Both of these findings imply that immunological functioning may be related to dispositional optimism (Scheier & Carver, 1987).

Hardiness

Kobasa (1979) noted that the general relationship between stress and illness was rather weak and suggested that certain personality factors might mediate this relationship. Of particular interest to her was a constellation of personality characteristics that she believed could act as a "resistance resource" when an individual was faced with stressful life events. She referred to this general personality disposition as "hardiness" and proposed that it consisted of three component traits: commitment, challenge, and control.

Commitment entails a strong belief in one's own value and self-worth as well as a sense of purpose and involvement in whatever one is doing. *Challenge* refers to a tendency to view difficulties and change as problems to be overcome rather than threats to one's personal security. Individuals scoring high in challenge exhibit a high degree of cognitive flexibliity that permits effective appraisal of potentially threatening events. *Control* involves a sense of personal power over the events in one's life. Individuals with a strong sense of control assume responsibility for their actions and are able to avert feelings of helplessness through the use of effective thinking, decision-making, and coping strategies.

Research conducted by Kobasa and colleagues has linked hardiness to physical health both retrospectively and prospectively. Kobasa (1979), for example, measured various elements of the hardiness construct and self-reported illness among executives from a utility company. Groups of executives experiencing low rather than high levels of illness over the previous three years were characterized by the following traits: self-commitment (vs. self-alienation), active seeking of environmental stimulation, a sense of meaningfulness in their activities, and an internal locus of control. These findings were viewed as consistent with the model of hardiness outlined above.

In a second study, Kobasa, Maddi, and Kahn (1982) collected data on personality and previous illness from a group of middle-aged male executives. The researchers then followed these individuals for two years, with illness data recorded at the end of each 12-month period. Hardiness showed a significant relationship to illness among executives exposed to high-stress conditions, even after the effects of prior illness were taken into account. Specifically, executives low in hardiness experienced high levels of illness when exposed to stressful environments. Executives high in hardiness, on the other hand, had self-reported illness scores that were close to baseline under these conditions.

Hull, Van Treuren, and Virnelli (1987) have taken issue with Kobasa's claim that hardiness is a higher order personality factor composed of three lower order traits. They note that the commitment and control dimensions show reasonably consistent relationships to health, but that the challenge dimension does not exhibit such a relationship. They recommend that the commitment and control aspects of hardiness continue to be examined, but that these dimensions be dealt with separately rather than in combination as a global index. These researchers also suggest that the mechanism by which commitment and control influence health is direct rather than indirect. In other words, *absence* of commitment and control may themselves be stressful and may, therefore, increase the chances of illness. If this is the case, it is possible that a lack of commitment and/or a lack of control could also delay injury recovery by creating psychophysiological

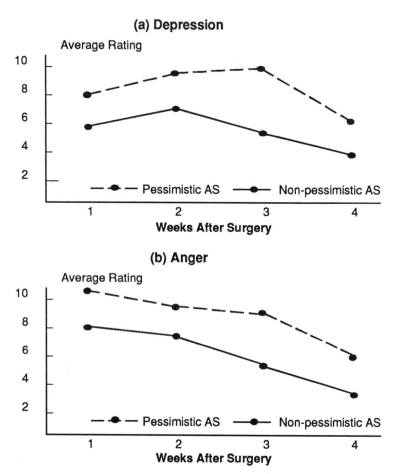

Figure 2. Depression and anger in the first month after knee surgery for athletes with pessimistic and non-pessimistic attributional styles.

stress during rehabilitation (see Figure 1).

Do These Variables Affect Athletes During Injury Recovery?

How do explanatory style, dispositional optimism, and hardiness influence the way athletes respond to rehabilitation? Grove, Stewart, and Gordon (1990) explored this question in a sample of 21 sport performers who required knee surgery because of anterior cruciate ligament damage. The athletes completed several personality scales and responded to a mood

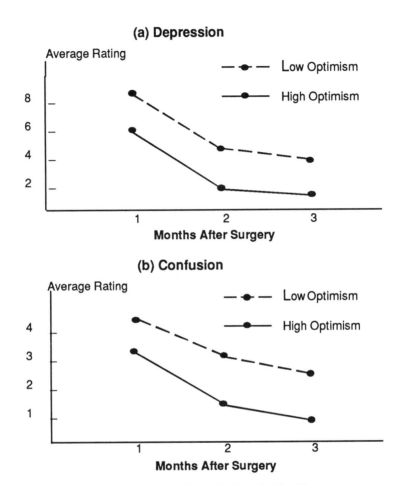

Figure 3. Depression and confusion in the three months after knee surgery for athletes high and low in dispositional optimisim

state inventory once a week for three months following surgery. Periodic explanations for rehabilitation progress were also obtained and transformed into an index of explanatory style. Athletes scoring high or low on explanatory pessimism, dispositional optimism, commitment, and control were then compared in terms of their emotional states during rehabilitation.

The findings from this investigation suggested that personality did affect certain mood states during recovery from knee surgery. Specifically, depression ($p < .05$) and anger ($p < .05$) were greater during the first month of rehabilitation for athletes with a pessimistic explanatory style than for those with a nonpessimistic style (see Figure 2). Dispositional optimism also tended to influence mood, but its impact extended across the full 12-week period of the study rather than being restricted to just the first month. As shown in Figure 3, injured athletes with high optimism scores displayed a tendency toward less depression ($p < .12$) and lower levels of confusion ($p < .15$) than did athletes with low optimism scores. No differences in mood disturbances were were evident when the commitment and control dimensions of hardiness were examined separately, but athletes with high total hardiness scores did report less overall mood disturbance than did those low in total hardiness ($p < .05$).

We are encouraged by these findings because they are generally consistent with expectations and because they relate specifically to the rehabilitation responses of injured athletes. Moreover, the number of participants in this study was rather small which meant that "high" and "low" scores on the various personality factors had to be defined relative to other athletes in the sample rather than in absolute terms. Observations of larger numbers of athletes will permit a comparison of more extreme personality groups and may reveal stronger and/or additional effects of personality during rehabilitation. Since sports medicine personnel are in the best position to make such observations and to benefit from them, we believe they should become familiar with the assessment and interpretation of potentially relevant personality variables.

How Can Practitioners Obtain Personality Information?

There are basically two ways that personality information can be collected by practitioners. These two procedures are best used in a complementary fashion, but they will be discussed separately here for ease of exposition. A "formal" approach to personality assessment involves the use of written scales. The advantage of this approach is that it is time efficient and quantifiable. At the same time, however, it can sometimes be perceived as impersonal by the athlete. The alternative method, "informal" personality assessment, involves an analysis of statements and behaviors that arise spontaneously or in face-to-face discussions. This approach is less directive and allows the therapist considerable lattitude to pursue issues that she or he thinks are meaningful. This method does tend to be less precise than the formal approach, however, and, for that reason, may require more experience on the part of the therapist.

Table 1. Items Comprising the Short Form
of the Sport Attributional Style Scale (SASS)

1. You have *no* difficulty withstanding a demanding training session.

2. You are *not* selected for the starting team in an important competition.

3. Your teammates claim that you *are* a very good performer.

4. You perform very *poorly* in a competition.

5. The coach *compliments* your performance.

6. You have *great* difficulty withstanding a demanding training session.

7. You *are* selected for the starting team in an important competition.

8. Your teammates claim that you are *not* a very good performer.

9. You perform very *well* in a competition.

10. The coach *criticizes* your performance.

Formal Assessment Procedures

Because most of the personality factors discussed in this chapter can be measured with relatively short pen-and-paper scales, sports medicine personnel can obtain written information on these traits with very little inconvenience to the athlete. Relevant scales can be administered in the waiting area prior to treatment, during periods of passive treatment (e.g., icing), or as part of a posttreatment debriefing. If the athlete is presented with one scale per session, practitioners can obtain a reasonably comprehensive personality profile in just three or four treatment sessions.

Explanatory style. A number of scales could be employed to measure explanatory style among injured athletes. Perhaps the most relevant one for sports medicine practitioners, however, is the short form of the Sport Attributional Style Scale (SASS); (Hanrahan & Grove, 1990; Hanrahan, Grove, & Hattie, 1989). This scale asks athletes to imagine that they have experienced five positive and five negative sport-related events and to generate "the most likely cause of the event." The specific situations used in this questionnaire are shown in Table 1.

After writing down the most likely cause of a given event, the athlete analyzes this causal explanation for its degree of internality, stability, and globality. All ratings are made on 7-point scales, with the extremes of each scale labeled with appropriate phases. The internality scale, for example,

Table 2. Steps in Calculating a Numerical Index of Explanatory Pessimism from Items in the Short Form of the SASS.

1. Determine the degree of internality, stability, and globality for negative event explanations.

   This is accomplished by summing the raw numerical ratings for all three dimensions across items 2, 4, 6, 8, and 10. The summation involves 15 separate numbers (5 items x 3 dimensional ratings per item) and produces a composite score for negative event pessimism.

2. Determine the degree of externality, instability, and specificity for positive event explanations.

   To calculate this score, it is necessary to recode (reverse) the numerical ratings provided for the five positive items. Recoding is accomplished by setting 7=1, 6=2, 5=3, 4=4, 3=5, 2=6, and 1=7 for all ratings on items 1, 3, 5, 7, and 9. Summation of the recoded values produces a composite score for positive event pessimism.

3. Determine an overall score for explanatory pessimism by adding the value obtained in step #1 to the value obtained in step #2. This score can range from 10 to 70, with higher values indicating greater pessimism.

---

extends from *totally due to other people or circumstances* (1) to *totally due to me* (7). Similarly, the stability scale is labeled by the phrases *will never again be present* (1) and *will always be present* (7). The extremes of the globality scale contain the phrases *influences just this particular event* (1) and *influences many events in my life* (7).

When causal explanations and dimensional ratings have been generated for all 10 items in the SASS, a numerical score can be calculated that represents the degree to which the athlete exhibits a pessimistic explanatory style. Since a pessimistic style involves internal, stable, and global explanations for negative events as well as external, unstable, and specific explanations for positive events, some recoding of numerical responses is necessary in order to calculate this score. Specific instructions for calculating a composite index of pessimistic explanatory style from the items in the short form of the SASS are given in Table 2.

Dispositional optimism. This personality variable is measured with the Life Orientation Test (LOT); (Scheier & Carver, 1985). The LOT contains 12 statements, with 4 of them worded in an optimistic direction and 4 of them worded in a negative direction. The remaining 4 statements

Table 3. Items from the Life Orientation Test
(LOT; Scheier & Carver, 1985)

1. In uncertain times, I usually expect the best.

2. It's easy for me to relax. [not scored]

3. If something can go wrong for me, it will.˙

4. I always look on the bright side of things.

5. I'm always optimistic about my future.

6. I enjoy my friends a lot. [not scored]

7. It's important for me to keep busy. [not scored]

8. I hardly ever expect things to go my way.˙

9. Things never work-out the way I want them to.˙

10. I don't get upset too easily. [not scored]

11. I believe that "every cloud has a silver lining."

12. I rarely count on good things happening to me.˙

˙ These items are reverse scored. Prior to calculation of the total score, set 4
  = 0, 3 = 1, 2 = 2, 1 = 3, and 0 = 4 for these items.

are filler items and do not contribute to the score on the scale (see Table 3). Respondents are simply asked to indicate the extent to which they agree or disagree with each of the 12 statements. Response categories and their numerical equivalents are as follows: "strongly agree" (4); "agree" (3); "neutral" (2); "disagree" (1); "strongly disagree" (0). A total score for dispositional optimism is obtained by first recoding the answers to the negatively worded items (4 = 0, 3 = 1, 2 = 2, 1 = 3, 0 = 4) and then totalling the numerical values for the 8 scale items. Higher scores indicate more optimsim on the part of the athlete.

Hardiness components. Hull et al. (1987) have noted that the commitment and control dimensions of hardiness appear to have the strongest impact on health outcomes, and they have made recommendations about the assessment of these dimensions. They believe that commitment can be accurately measured with 12 items developed by Kobasa and Maddi (1982). These items are shown in Table 4. The athlete is asked to indicate

Table 4. Items Used to Assess the Commitment Dimension of Hardiness (Based on Kobasa & Maddi, 1982)

1. I often wonder why I work at all.

2. The ability to think is not really such an advantage.

3. Much of life is wasted in meaningless activity.

4. Attempting to know yourself is a waste of time.

5. If you have to work, it might as well be a job where you deal with matters of life and death.

6. I am interested in the possibility of expanding my consciousness through the use of certain drugs.

7. Regardless of how hard I try, my efforts will accomplish very little.

8. Life often seems empty and without meaning for me.

9. I find it difficult to become enthusiastic about work.

10. I would like a simple life that didn't require decisionsto be made.

11. I don't understand people who say that the work they perform is of value to society.

12. My own fantasies are the most exciting thing in my life.

the extent to which he or she thinks each statement is true by selecting one of four categories: "not at all true" (4); "a little true" (3); "quite true" (2); "completely true" (1). Numerical values associated with each category are then summed across the 12 items to obtain a total score, with higher scores indicative of greater commitment.

Hull and colleagues (1987) suggest that the control dimension of hardiness should be assessed using Rotter's External Locus of Control Scale (Rotter, 1966; Rotter, Seeman, & Liverant, 1962). This scale contains 23 items, with each item consisting of two statements. One statement emphasizes external control while the other statement emphasizes personal control. The athlete is asked to choose the statement from each pair that she or he believes is most true. Scoring involves counting the number of external statements chosen, so low scores indicate a stronger belief in one's own ability to control the events in one's life. Research by Hull et al. (1987) suggests that the 12 items shown in Table 5 could be useful as an abbreviated measure of perceived control.

Table 5. Selected items from the External Locus of Control Scale (Rotter et al., 1962)

1. a. Many of the unhappy things in people's lives are partly due to bad luck.˙

    b. People's misfortunes result from the mistakes they make.

2. a. In the long run people get the respect they deservin this world.

    b. Unfortunately, an individual's worth often passes unrecognized no matter how hard he or she tries.˙

3. a. Without the right breaks, one cannot be an effective leader.˙

    b. Capable people who fail to become leaders have not taken advantage of their opportunities.

4. a. In the case of a well-prepared student, there is rarely (if ever) such a thing as an unfair test.

    b. Many times exam questions tend to be so unrelated to course work that studying is really useless.˙

5. a. Becoming a success is a matter of hard work, luck has little or nothing to do with it.

    b. Getting a good job depends mainly on being in the right place at the right time. ˙

6. a. In my case, getting what I want has little or nothing to do with luck.

    b. Many times, we might just as well decide what to do by flipping a coin.˙

7. a. Getting to be the boss often depends on who was lucky enough to be in the right place first. ˙

    b. Getting people to do the right thing depends upon ability; luck has little or nothing to do with it.

Informal Assessment

Some sports medicine personnel may decide that informal assessment procedures are more appropriate than formal ones. This decision could arise because the desired personality scales are unavailable, because the practitioner is uncomfortable with written scales, or because the athlete indicates that she or he is uncomfortable with such scales. For purposes of this discussion, adopting an informal approach to personality assessment means (a) talking to the injured athlete on a one-to-one basis in an

Table 5 (cont'd.) Selected items from the External Locus of Control Scale (Rotter et al., 1962)

8.   a. Most people don't realize the extent to which their lives are controlled by accidental happenings.*

        b. There really is no such thing as "luck".

9.   a. With enough effort, we can wipe out political corruption.

        b. It is difficult for people to have much control over the things politicians do in office.*

10.   a. Sometimes I can't understand how teachers arrive at the grades they give.*

        b. There is a direct connection between how hard I study and the grades I get.

11.   a. Many times I feel that I have little influence over the things that happen to me. *

        b. It is impossible for me to believe that chance or luck plays an important role in my life.

12.   a. What happens to me is my own doing.

        b. Sometimes I feel that I don't have enough control over the direction my life is taking.*

* These choices reflect a belief in external control. The total score for the scale is the number of external choices made.

effort to gain insight into the individual's character and (b) paying attention to comments made by the athlete either spontaneously or in response to others in the rehabilitation setting (including other injured athletes). Effective use of this approach requires a thorough understanding of the personality factors that may influence rehabilitation behavior and good communication skills. The practitioner must be able to establish trust and rapport with the athlete, ask appropriate questions at appropriate times, listen attentively to statements made by the athlete, and draw inferences about the athlete's character and likely behavior based on these statements.

Insight into the athlete's explanatory style will be obtained most directly by paying attention to "why" statements. These statements might refer to events that have actually occurred or to hypothetical events. For example, if actual recovery has been either slower than expected or faster than expected, the athlete could be asked why he or she believes this has occurred. Similarly, the athlete could be asked to generate a likely cause for a hypothetical setback during rehabilitation. If explanations for positive rehabilitation events tend to be external, unstable, and specific (e.g., "I had a different therapist for those two weeks where I did really well") and/or explanations for negative events tend to be internal, stable, and global (e.g., "I never have been able to handle pain and discomfort too well"), then a pessimistic explanatory style may be indicated. In order to confirm such an impression, it is essential that the practitioner obtain *several* explanations (across at least several days) and carefully consider both their dimensional properties and their legitimacy. If, for example, one of the therapists really *is* much better than the others, then such an attribution may reflect accurate perception more than pessimistic style.

Dispositional optimism could be assessed informally by asking questions similar to those in Table 3 at an opportune time during treatment. An athlete who is handling a particular phase of treatment in a positive manner could be asked something like "Are you always so positive about things?" or "Do you approach everything with such a bright outlook?" Similarly, an athlete who has experienced a setback could be asked "I tend to believe that every cloud has a silver lining; how do you feel about that?" If responses to several of these questions and/or other comments made by the athlete indicate a consistently positive or negative outlook, then the practitioner may be able to make an inference about the degree of general optimism possessed by the individual.

The items in Tables 4 and 5 suggest potential areas of consideration for the informal assessment of commitment and control, respectively. Commitment essentially involves finding meaning in what one does as opposed to having a sense of alienation and detachment. Statements about lack of enthusiasm for studies, sport, work, or life in general may indicate low levels of commitment, and, if pronounced, could suggest the need for psychological intervention. The therapist should note such comments and discuss them with other members of the rehabilitation team. Statements or behaviors that reflect a denial of personal responsibility and control during rehabilitation are also noteworthy. Refusing to set recovery goals or blaming the therapist and/or rehabilitation program for lack of progress may reflect such an attitude. Placing responsibility for recovery primarily in the hands of an external spiritual entity could also indicate a low level of perceived control.

How Can Sports Medicine Personnel
Use Personality Information?

Knowledge of an individual's personality will be useful to the extent
that it helps practitioners anticipate and deal with the athlete's thoughts,
emotions, and behaviors during rehabilitation. Although we know very
little about the specific effects of explanatory style, dispositional optimism, or hardiness on the thoughts, emotions, and behaviors of *injured
athletes*, the research literature does offer some clues about what we can
generally expect from individuals who differ on these traits. Because
negative rehabilitation responses are likely to concern sports medicine
personnel more than are positive ones, a summary of responses likely
among individuals at the negative extremes of these traits will be presented.

Athletes with a highly pessimistic attributional style may be predis-
posed to feelings of helplessness and depression. Therefore, they may tend
to isolate themselves from coaches and teammates and/or become overwhelmed by the adjustments required because of their injury. These
adjustments could include such things as retaining a job during convales-
cence, scheduling time for treatments, depending on others for transportation, and handling unexpected medical expenses (Gordon et al., 1991b).
Athletes who feel helpless may also fail to follow recommended treatment
programs (especially the unsupervised aspects of their programs) and may
exhibit a lack of persistence in the face of poor progress or setbacks.
Therapists should take steps to short-circuit such responses if they detect
a highly pessimistic orientation on the part of the athlete. Encouraging
continued attendance at team practices and offering suggestions about
how to cope with the extra demands of injury may prevent the athlete from
feeling isolated and overwhelmed. The use of daily and weekly rehabilitation goals may also be helpful on occasions when progress is slow.

Scheier and Carver (1987, in press) have noted a number of similarities
between the concepts of explanatory pessimism and dispositional optimism. They go on to say that pessimistic attributions may influence
behavior primarily through their effect on generalized expectancies (i.e.,
optimism). Thus, therapists might expect to see many of the same
reactions from athletes high in explanatory pessimism and those low in
dispositional optimism. This similarity would seem especially relevant for
depressive emotions, absence of self-initiated behavior change, and lack
of persistence in times of difficulty. Because individuals low in dispositional optimism tend to use denial and venting of emotions as coping

strategies, therapists might also expect athletes low in optimism to deny the seriousness of their injury and/or express anger during the course of rehabilitation. Denial tendencies might be diminished somewhat by providing the athlete with objective evidence about the extent of damage. Anger may be diffused by listening empathetically, confronting the athlete in a calm and rational manner if expressions of anger become disruptive, and/or providing information on thought management techniques (Novaco, 1979). Since anger often results from rumination about past events, it may occasionally be necessary to challenge the athlete to redirect emotional energy into present events such as rehabilitation and recovery (Gordon et al., 1991a, 1991b).

Research by Hull et al.(1987) indicates that individuals low in commitment and control share several common tendencies. Specifically, these individuals tend to worry about their public image, overgeneralize negative aspects of their character, and experience depressive moods. They also tend to make infrequent use of social support resources and to suffer high levels of anxiety and apprehension in distressing situations. Thus, practitioners might expect injured athletes who are low in commitment and/or control to ruminate about the way others view them and their injury, to become nervous and tense when faced with stressful treatment procedures, and perhaps, to get depressed about their incapacities. In addition, they might be inclined to isolate themselves from coaches and teammates and fail to adhere to recommended treatment regimes. Therapists should take care to communicate clearly with these athletes about the severity of the injury and should consider the need for supplying information on stress management (e.g., Greenberg, 1983). Contacts with coaches, teammates, and other recovering athletes should be actively encouraged, and steps should be taken to reinforce personal initiative/effort in relation to rehabilitation. Objective information about progress in the form of charts or graphs may also be desirable for these athletes in order to enhance feelings of involvement and personal control.

REFERENCES

Andersen, M.B., & Williams, J.M. (1988). A model of stress and athletic injury: Prediction and prevention. *Journal of Sport and Exercise Psychology, 10*, 294-306.

Brewer, B.W., Van Raalte, J.L., & Linder, D.E. (1991). Role of the sport psychologist in treating injured athletes: A survey of sports medicine providers. *Journal of Applied Sport Psychology, 3*, 183-190.

Carson, R.C. (1989). Personality. *Annual Review of Psychology, 40,* 227-248.

Friedman, H.S., & Booth-Kewley, S. (1987). The "disease-prone personality:" A meta-analytic view of the construct. *American Psychologist, 42,* 539-555.

Goodkin, K., Antoni, M.H., & Blaney, P.H. (1986). Stress and helplessness in the promotion of cervical intraepithelial neoplasia to invasive squamous cell carcinoma of the cervix. *Journal of Psychosomatic Research, 50,* 67-76.

Gordon, S., Milios, D., & Grove, R. (1991a). Psychological adjustment to sports injuries: Implications for athletes, coaches, and family members. *Sports Coach, 14*(2), 40-44.

Gordon, S., Milios, D., & Grove, J.R. (1991b). Psychological aspects of the recovery process from sport injury: The perspective of sport physiotherapists. *Australian Journal of Science and Medicine in Sport, 23,* 53-60.

Greenberg, J.S. (1983). *Comprehensive stress management.* Dubuque, IA: Wm. C. Brown.

Grove, J.R., & Gordon, S. (1991). The psychological aspects of injury in sport. In J. Bloomfield, P.A. Fricker, & K.D. Fitch (Eds.), *Textbook of science and medicine in sport* (pp. 176-186). London: Blackwell.

Grove, J.R., Hanrahan, S.J., & Stewart, R.M.L. (1990). Attributions for rapid or slow recovery from sports injury. *Canadian Journal of Sport Sciences, 15,* 107-114.

Grove, J.R., Stewart, R.M.L., & Gordon, S. (1990, October). *Emotional reactions of athletes to knee rehabilitation.* Paper presented at the annual meeting of the Australian Sports Medicine Federation, Alice Springs.

Hanrahan, S.J., & Grove, J.R. (1990). A short form of the Sport Attributional Style Scale. *Australian Journal of Science and Medicine in Sport, 22,* 97-101.

Hanrahan, S.J., Grove, J.R., & Hattie, J.A. (1989). Development of a questionnaire measure of sport-related attributional style. *International Journal of Sport Psychology, 20,* 114-134.

Hull, J.G., Van Treuren, R.R., & Virnelli, S. (1987). Hardiness and health: A critique and alternative approach. *Journal of Personality and Social Psychology, 53,* 518-530.

Kamen-Siegel, L., Rodin, J., Seligman, M.E.P., & Dwyer, J. (1991). Explanatory style and cell-mediated immunity in elderly men and women. *Health Psychology, 10,* 229-235.

Kobasa, S.C. (1979). Stressful life events, personality, and health: An inquiry into hardiness. *Journal of Personality and Social Psychology, 37,* 1-11.

Kobasa, S.C., & Maddi, S.R. (1982). Hardiness measurement. Unpublished manuscript, Department of Behavioral Sciences, University of Chicago.

Kobasa, S.C., Maddi, S.R., & Kahn, S. (1982). Hardiness and health: A prospective study. *Journal of Personality and Social Psychology, 42,* 168-177.

Levy, S.M., & Wise, B.D. (1987). Psychosocial risk factors, natural immunity, and cancer progression: Implications for intervention. *Current Psychological Research and Reviews, 6,* 229-243.

Novaco, R.W. (1979). The cognitive regulation of anger and stress. In P.C. Kendall & S.D. Hollon (Eds.), *Cognitive-behavioral interventions: Theory, research, and procedures* (pp. 241-286). New York: Academic.

Peterson, C., & Seligman, M.E.P. (1987). Explanatory style and illness. *Journal of Personality, 55,* 237-266.

Reker, G.T., & Wong, P.T.P. (1985). Personal optimism, physical and mental health: The triumph of successful aging. In J.E. Birren & J. Livingston (Eds.), *Cognition, stress and aging* (pp. 134-173). New York: Prentice-Hall.

Rodin, J., & Salovey, P. (1989). Health psychology. *Annual Review of Psychology, 40,* 533-579.

Rotter, J.B. (1966). Generalized expectancies for internal versus external control of reinforcement. *Psychological Monographs, 80* (1, Whole No. 609).

Rotter, J.B., Seeman, M., & Liverant, S. (1962). Internal vs. external control of reinforcement: A major variable in behavior therapy. In N.F. Washburne (Ed.), *Decisions, values, and groups* (pp. 473-516). London: Pergamon.

Scheier, M.F., & Carver, C.S. (1985). Optimism, coping, and health: Assessment and implications of generalized outcome expectancies. *Health Psychology, 4,* 219-248.

Scheier, M.F., & Carver, C.S. (1987). Dispositional optimism and physical well-being: The influence of generalized outcome expectancies on health. *Journal of Personality, 55,* 169-210.

Scheier, M.F., & Carver, C.S. (in press). Effects of optimism on psychological and physical well-being: Theoretical overview and empirical update. *Cognitive Therapy and Research.*

Scheier, M.F., Matthews, K.A., Owens, J.F., Magovern, G.J., Lefebvre, R.C., Abbott, R.A., & Carver, C.S. (1989). Dispositional optimism and recovery from coronary artery bypass surgery: The beneficial effects on physical and psychological well-being. *Journal of Personality and Social Psychology, 57,* 1024-1040.

Taylor, S.E. (1990). Health psychology: The science and the field. *American Psychologist, 45,* 40-50.

Van Treuren, R.R., & Hull, J.G. (1986, October). *Health and stress: Dispositional optimism and psychophysiological responses.* Paper presented at the annual meeting of the Society for Psychophysiological Research, Montreal, Canada.

Wiese, D.M., Weiss, M.R., & Yukelson, D.P. (1991). Sport psychology in the training room: A survey of athletic trainers. *The Sport Psychologist, 5,* 15-24.

Chapter 8

The Dimensions Of Social Support When Dealing With Sport Injuries

Charles J. Hardy
The University of North Carolina at Chapel Hill
R. Kelly Crace
College of William & Mary

Social support has far-reaching implications for dealing with sport injuries. This chapter reviews the research literature on social support, with particular emphasis given to an understanding of the role that social support can play in facilitating recovery from sport injuries. The chapter has two major components: (a) definitional, conceptual, and empirical information on the social support construct and (b) strategies for providing the different dimensions of social support and for creating and maintaining the injured athlete's social support network.

> After stressful events people turn to those closest to them as a source of strength. It is those closest to us who carry our burdens when we are incapable; who offer a shoulder on which to cry, shelter from adversity, and solace from grief. Significant others share their resources to help those for whom they care through these most difficult periods of life. (Hobfoll & Stephens, 1990, p. 459)

The Stress of Injury

Although athletes confront numerous challenges within the competitive environment, one of the most common and most stressful is dealing with injury. Danish (1986) stated that injury can be highly stressful because it threatens not only physical well-being, "but acts as a threat to the athlete's self-concept, belief system, social and occupational functioning, values, commitments, and emotional equilibrium" (p. 346). Injury can force athletes to (a) accept a new definition of their abilities; (b) redefine their role on the team; (c) withdraw from or change one's current level of involvement; and (d) redirect future career opportunities, both within and outside of sport (Hardy & Crace, 1990; Silva & Hardy, 1991).

Even though athletes react to injury in many different ways, Gordon (1991) argued that "every athlete who experiences an injury that renders him or her even temporarily inactive or disabled will experience a painful loss, and the subsequent physical and emotional significance of this loss is likely to be equivalently great" (p. 15). Hobfoll (1988, 1989) suggested that psychological stress occurs (a) when there is a threat of a net loss of resources, (b) when there is an actual loss of net resources, or (c) when coping strategies, the investment of resources, yield no net resource gain. Hobfoll (1989) defined resources as "those objects, personal characteristics, conditions, or energies that are valued by the individual or group or that serve as a means for attaining these objects, personal characteristics, conditions, or energies" (p. 516). For the injured athlete, the loss can involve a loss of independence, social mobility, capacity to perform, exposure to pain, and the threat of disfigurement, permanent disability, and death (Hobfoll & Stephens, 1990). Thus, dealing with injury involves coping with the stress of perceived losses in personal resources (McDonald & Hardy, 1990) and is one of the toughest opponents an athlete may have to face (Silva & Hardy, 1991).

The Role of Social Support in Dealing with the Stress of Injury

When confronted with the stress of injury, athletes will attempt to minimize net resource losses. In order to offset this loss athletes will employ their personal resources. When an athlete is injured, a loss in personal resources can be experienced. In the absence of effective personal resourses, athletes will seek the support of others to help them cope with the injury, thereby extending their resource pool (Hobfoll & Stokes, 1988). Social support provides resources that can assist in dealing with the stress of injury by (a) providing a feeling of attachment to others,

(b) directly preventing or limiting resource loss, (c) providing for re-sources that are lost, and/or (d) activating latent resources (Hobfoll & Stephens, 1990).

Research has demonstrated that support provided by others is helpful in coping with life stress, crisis, mental and physical illness, unemployment, job stress, bereavement, childbirth, mortality risk, and other stressors (cf., Albrecht & Adelman, 1984; Billings & Moos, 1981; Broadhead et al., 1983; Caplan, 1976; Cobb, 1976; Cohen, 1988; Cohen & Syme, 1985; Ganster & Victor, 1988; Gore, 1978; Hammer, 1981; House, 1981; Leavy, 1983; Schaefer, Coyne, & Lazarus, 1981). Supported individuals are generally more mentally and physically healthy than are unsupported individuals, perhaps due to the health-sustaining and stress-reducing functions of social support (Shumaker & Brownell, 1984). Moreover, it is reported that the treatment and recovery process is often enhanced by social support (Wallston, Alagna, DeVellis, & DeVellis, 1983), an effect recently extended to injured athletes (Gordon & Lindgren, 1990; Ievleva & Orlick, 1991; Silva & Hardy, 1991; Weiss & Troxel, 1986; Wiese & Weiss, 1987).

It appears, therefore, that there is ample evidence for the use of social support-based interventions in dealing with sport injury. Rotella and Heyman (1986) and Silva and Hardy (1991) have argued that social support is critical in the rehabilitation of the injured athlete and therefore should be a concern of those who are directly involved in the care and treatment of injured athletes. According to Gottlieb (1988), however, the mobilization of social support reflects the "impulses and natural activities of ordinary citizens striving to secure the resources they need to grapple with changing life circumstances" (p. 519), rather than the efforts of professional practitioners. What is needed is a framework for professionals interested in translating the research on social support into practical strategies for developing and nurturing support as well as ways of assisting individuals in the use and delivery of social support (Gottlieb, 1988; Sarason, Sarason, & Pierce, 1990a). This is particularly relevant for the injured athlete, since numerous authors have suggested that social support is an effective *psychological technique* that can be used to motivate injured athletes during rehabilitation (cf. Hardy & Crace, 1990; Wiese & Weiss, 1987). This chapter will provide (a) an introduction to the construct of social support and (b) a framework for social support-based interventions, including practical strategies for maximizing the therapeutic properties of social support when dealing with the injured athlete.

What is Social Support?

Durkheim (1952) argued that the loss of social ties or *anomie* was antithetical to psychological well-being. In his seminal study of suicide, Durkheim found that suicides were more prevalent among those with few close social ties. Although the importance of interpersonal relationships for promoting health holds intuitive appeal, "the concept of social support has been operationalized in a somewhat bewildering assortment of ways" (Wilcox, 1981, p. 98).

In its broadest sense, social support is the essence of being *"social."* Simplistic definitions view social support as the number of friendships, relatives nearby, and organizational involvements (Eckenrode & Gore, 1981). Wilcox (1981) defined social support as having a "confidant" or spouse. Kaplan, Cassel, and Gore (1977) viewed social support as the "metness" or gratification of basic social needs, approval, esteem, succor, and belonging. Moss (1973) defined social support as "the subjective feeling of belonging, of being accepted or being loved, of being needed all for oneself and for what one can do" (p. 237).

Although theorists differ on specifics, there is now wide agreement that social support is a multidemensional construct. For example, Caplan (1974) defined social support as assistance from significant others in completing tasks, in providing instrumental aid (money, tools, advice) to deal with particular situations, and in mobilizing psychological resources to deal with emotional problems. Cobb (1976) viewed social support as informational aid belonging to one or more of three categories: (a) information leading individuals to believe that they are cared for or loved; (b) information leading individuals to believe that they are esteemed and valued; and (c) information leading individuals to believe that they belong to a network of communication and mutual obligation in which others can be counted on in time of need. Thus, it is appropriate to conceptualize social support as a form of social commerce (Gottlieb, 1988). This commerce represents an exchange of resources between at least two people, with the outcome being the enhancement of the recipient's well-being (Richman, Rosenfeld, & Hardy, 1992; Shumaker & Brownell, 1984). These resources include providing emotional, informational and tangible support (Albrecht & Adelman, 1984; Cohen & Hoberman, 1983; Cohen & Wills, 1985; Conrad, 1985; House, 1981; Kahn & Antonucci, 1980; Pines, Aronson & Kafry, 1981; Sarason & Sarason, 1985; Weiss, 1974).

The Dimensions of Social Support

Richman et al. (1992) have argued that the social support process involves four elements: (a) a support provider, (b) a support recipient (c) the transaction between the provider and the recipient, and (d) the outcomes of the transaction. Members of one's social network offer emotional, informational, and tangible support by enacting various behaviors. Some support behaviors require expertise on the part of the provider, whereas others do not (Rosenfeld, Richman, & Hardy, 1989).

Recipients are perceived to be proactive elements of the support process. Recipients have personal characteristics that affect how they interact with others and how they access the needed support. The transaction between the provider and the recipient allows for an exchange of resources to take place. The recipient transmits a need for a specific type of support to potential providers who have to recognize the request for help and then be willing and capable of offering the type of support requested (Albrecht & Adelman, 1984). The recipient must perceive the behaviors of providers to be helpful in meeting expressed needs (Sarason et al., 1990a). Finally, the outcome is the enhancement of the recipient's physical and psychological well-being.

Behaviors that fulfill support functions include expressing emotional support (e.g., affection), or appraisal support (e.g., performance feedback), giving information (e.g., advice and role clarification), offering emotionally sustaining behaviors (e.g., empathy), and listening to the concerns and feeling of others (Albrecht & Adelman, 1984). These behaviors represent three general dimensions of social support: (a) emotional, (b) informational, and (c) tangible social support. Based upon the work of Pines et al. (1981), Richman et al. (1992) and Hardy and Crace (1991) have proposed that such behaviors can be grouped into eight distinguishable types of social support:

Listening Support. Behaviors that indicate people listen to you without giving advice or being judgmental.

Emotional Support. Behaviors that comfort you and indicate that people are on your side and care for you.

Emotional Challenge. Behaviors that challenge you to evaluate your attitudes, values, and feelings.

Task Appreciation. Behaviors that acknowledge your efforts and express appreciation for the work you do.

Task Challenge. Behaviors that challenge your way of thinking about your work in order to stretch you, motivate you, and lead you to greater creativity, excitement, and involvement in your work.

Reality Confirmation. Behaviors that indicate that people are similar to you–see things the way you do–help you confirm your perceptions and perspectives of the world and help you keep things in focus.

Material Assistance. Behaviors that provide you with financial assistance, products, or gifts.

Personal Assistance. Behaviors that indicate a giving of time, skills, knowledge, and/or expertise to help you accomplish your tasks.

The Measurement of Social Support

Sarason, Sarason, and Pierce (1990b) have reported that social support can be assessed by examination of *social networks, received support*, or the *perceived support*. Social networks analyses provide information on the individual's social integration into and interconnectedness within a group. Network support type measures include the network size, relationship, density, quality of relationship intensity, frequency and desirability of contact. Received support examines what individuals get from others. Received support type measures include enacted support–actions of others to assist a particular individual–and received support–the recipients' account of the support given to them by others. Perceived support focuses on the perceptions of both the need for and availability of social support. Perceived support type measures include availability, satisfaction, general status, specific status, general factor, and structural/multidimensional questionnaires.

Heitzmann and Kaplan (1988) maintained that the measurement of social support has been problematic. Although numerous scales, questionnaires, and other assessment tools purport to measure this construct, the psychometric properties of the majority of these measures have not been convincingly documented. Additionally, the measures differ substantially in length, focus, approach, and the nature of the support that is evaluated (see Bruhn & Phillips, 1984; Heitzmann & Kaplan, 1988; House & Kahn, 1985; Tardy, 1988, for a review of the measures). According to Sarason et al. (1990b) "the main problem with the measurement of social support has been that although the measures have multiplied like rabbits, relatively little work has been done to establish their comparability or lack of it" (p. 20). Moreover, relatively few measures of social support have published validity and reliability data (Heitzmann & Kaplan, 1988).

However, Heitzmann and Kaplan (1988) suggest that the state of social support measurement is not necessarily bleak, despite the lack of comparability and psychometric data. Because meaningful conclusions from research studies depend on the valid and reliable measurement of social support, research on social support must be viewed critically, with careful attention to the measurement instrument employed. In spite of the methodological concerns, the available evidence suggests that social support is an important variable in sustaining health and in the mitigation of life stress (Shumaker & Brownell, 1984).

The Functions and Mechanisms of Social Support

The overall function of social support is to enhance the recipient's well-being. The assumption underlying all models and empirical investigations is that supported individuals are more mentally and physically healthy than are nonsupported individuals. This is thought to be due to the health-sustaining and stress-reducing functions of social support (Shumaker & Brownell, 1984). The more effective the social support an individual receives, the better his or her mental and physical health. Conversely, ineffective or low quantities of social support reduce mental and physical well-being.

Social support can also moderate or buffer the impact of stress on the individual and, thus, indirectly affect well-being. At low levels of social support the relationship between stress and psychological and physiological well-being should be strong and direct, and as social support increases, the relationship should weaken. Under conditions of maximal support, the relationship between stress and well-being should be nonexistent.

Explanations for these two functions have yet to be established; however, it has been suggested that effective social support networks alter the organism's cognitions, affect, immune system function, and/or behavior. Gottlieb (1988) concluded that "by examining changes in the parties' causal and control attributions, their self-esteem and self-conceptions, feelings of deviance, and their sense of hopefulness and meaning attached to their predicaments, significant advances can be made in our understanding of the pathways whereby social support promotes adaptation and impacts health" (p. 539).

Sarason et al. (1990a) have argued that although support may be communicated through specific behaviors, the active ingredient of social support is an individual's belief that others value and care about him or her and that others are willing to assist if the individual needs support. The primary effect of these beliefs is that they "foster the feeling that we are

worthwhile, capable, and valued members of a group of individuals"
(Sarason et al., 1990a, p. 121). When individuals perceive the world as
supportive, they feel that the resources necessary for the attainment of
their goals are available to them, either from within themselves or from
their support network. That is, a sense of personal agency is enhanced by
the feeling that one's well-being is the concern of others. Thus, while
social support may have unique dimensions, the dimensions share some
common variance.

Hardy, Richman, and Rosenfeld (1991) have argued that it is possible
that the perception of the availability of social support undergirds the
buffering function, whereas one's linkages and social integration supports
the direct function (for a review see Cohen, 1988; Cutrona & Russell,
1990; Sarason, Sarason, & Pierce, 1990a, 1990b).

It should be noted, however, that social support can have negative
effects on both the recipient and the provider. For the recipient, social
support may lead to increased pressure to conform. Such pressure might
cause people to behave in unhealthy ways. Moreover, recipients may feel
smothered and controlled by, and indebted to support providers (Shumaker
& Brownell, 1984). Providing support can drain one's resource pool (i.e.,
emotions, time, finances), alter one's attitude toward the recipient, and
increase the provider's sense of personal vulnerability (Hobfoll & Stephens,
1990; Shumaker & Brownell, 1984).

A Framework for Social Support-Based
Interventions with Injured Athletes
Are we able to apply our understanding of social networks to
ourselves? In so doing we may be able to escape our own isolation
as professionals.... If we cannot model the benefits of work among
supportive networks, then we are not likely to influence others with
our findings. What is worse, without such support in our lives, our
own health and well being may suffer before we can influence
anyone. In no other activity... would the means by which we proceed
appear to be so important as in the activity of nurturance of life-
sustaining networks of social support. (Pilisuk, 1982, p. 29).

Hobfoll and Stephens (1990) have indicated that the following factors
should be considered when designing social support-based interventions:
(a) evaluation of loss, (b) intensity of support-based interventions, (c)
evaluation of other resources, (d) timing, (e) emotions and cognitions
versus action, (f) drain of resources, and (g) environmental versus

individual intervention.

The first step is to determine the nature of the stress. Injury can be categorized as a negative, uncontrollable event that involves the loss of or a threat to physical assets, relationships, achievement, and social roles (Cutrona & Russell, 1990). The next step is to determine the most effective type of social support to counter the stress of injury. Because specific types of social support facilitate coping with particular types of life stress (Cutrona & Russell, 1990; Weiss, 1974), social support will have a beneficial effect to the extent that the support actually received is appropriately matched to the specific needs activated by the stressor (Sarason et al., 1990a, p. 118). Since perception of one's needs is a subjective process, this matching process can be rather difficult. *Who* provides *what* is a crucial element for determining the utility of social support as well as in designing effective social support based interventions.

Emotional support is essential because emotion-focused coping is important in reducing the intensity of emotions as a result of the injury (Cutrona & Russell, 1990; Hobfoll & Stephens, 1990). The longer the effects of the injury last, the more emotional support will be required. For some injuries, physical limitations may necessitate tangible support to compensate for the assets lost as a result of the injury. Thus, although emotional support appears to play a key role in coping with injury, the degree to which the injury affects the athlete's capacity to function in a variety of life roles will create a broad range of support needs. Because injury can adversely affect numerous life roles, a broad range of support needs will most likely need to be provided for effective healing to occur.

Another factor to consider is the intensity of the support that is available. The limited research on natural support systems indicates that effective support is intensive and provided by the closest loved ones. Thus, the *source* of support appears to be an important factor for determining intensity of support-based interventions. Sarason et al. (1990a) suggested that when the recipient perceives that the support provider is interested, empathic, and committed, the intended support provisions will be helpful and used.

It is important to realize that social support is but one resource, and its utility clearly is dependent upon its interaction with other resources that can be harnessed during the rehabilitation process. To facilitate the rehabilitation process it is important to include other resources (i.e., personal characteristics and injury characteristics) that might interact with social support.

An additional important consideration is the timing of support behaviors. The stress of injury and the effectiveness of social support are dynamic processes. Whereas initial support efforts will need to focus primarily on emotional support, the type of support needed will change as a function of the stress sequence experienced. Emotional, tangible, and informational support are all important types of support for the injured athlete. However, the type of support that is emphasized will vary with the type of stress experienced throughout the rehabilitation process.

It is also important to remember that the use of resources is not without costs. Over time, support recipients may find it increasingly more difficult to ask for the type of support needed, and providers may feel increasingly more strained when summoned for assistance. It is important to provide ways to control for the drain in resources so that the support system will not become overtaxed, for example, by having a professional supervise the support process, making psychological and medical expertise easily accessible to the providers, and developing a multiplex network of support providers (Hobfoll & Stephens, 1990).

Finally, consideration should be given to altering the environment in ways that facilitate providing effective social support. The context of social support can be a critical factor because the stress of injury involves the loss of many tangible resources (Hobfoll & Stephens, 1990).

Utilizing this framework, and the work of Hardy and Crace (1991), and the research of Richman, Hardy, Rosenfeld, & Callanan (1989), the following strategies are offered to assist in the provision, creation, and maintenance of effective social support for injured athletes. It is important to remember, however, that "no one intervention effort is suitable for all situations, even if they concern similar stressors, because the interaction of persons, resources, and environments is too varied" (Hobfoll & Stephens, 1990, p. 474).

The Provision of Support Needs for Injured Athletes
Providing Emotional Support

Providing support that is primarily emotional in nature includes, (a) emotional support, (b) emotional challenge, and (c) listening.

Listen carefully. Active listening involves focusing on the *what* as well as the *how* of the communication (Rosenfeld, Wilder, Crace, & Hardy, 1990). One way to improve emotional support is to employ both supportive and confirming behaviors while listening. Supportive and confirming behaviors communicate the message that the injured athlete is acknowledged, understood, and accepted.

Another important aspect of effective listening is patience. Often, people are somewhat reluctant to jump right into a conversation about personal and/or emotional topics. They wish to be assured that their confidence will be protected before self-disclosure takes place. The listener may be obliged to demonstrate trustworthiness and an understanding of the particular demands placed upon the athlete in his or her sport. Active listening without giving advice or being judgmental is an excellent way to earn this type of trust.

In addition, adding emotionality to your messages may provide them the support the injured athlete needs. This does not mean throwing out your own emotions. Empathic listeners focus on the feeling as well as on the content of what the others say. By reflecting the feeling you are observing, you indicate a truer level of understanding. This tends to create a relationship that will also allow for emotional challenges where attitudes, values and feelings are explored and evaluated.

Know thyself. When strategizing the provision of emotional support for injured athletes, be aware of your emotional needs as well as your reactions to those who are distressed. The frequency with which people seek emotional support from you is often a good indication of your ability to manage your own anxiety associated with interacting with the "victim" of injury. Gottlieb (1988) maintained that providers could benefit from becoming more aware of the impact that their coping strategies had on the support process as well as from adopting more palatable strategies.

Switch hats occasionally. Too often one type of social support is used exclusively because it appears uniquely suited to the support providers, their personalities or professional role. This can result in neglect of or hesitancy to other support approaches. Unfortunately, the most underdeveloped, yet most needed, form of support is emotional support. Allow yourself to be open to providing emotional support. Gradually, you will find others turning to you for this type of support and may find this becoming a more natural part of your personality or role.

Involve the "natural helping network." Regular, informal contact with the **"natural helping network"** within sport–coaches, teammates, athletic trainers and physical therapists, and parents–should be encouraged. Injury involves rather intense emotional reactions and heightened needs that may be ameliorated by this network.

Create an open environment. As much as possible, structure the physical environment wherein you meet the athlete so that it communicates acceptance and openness. An open-door policy indicates that the injured athlete can comfortably discuss personal thoughts and feelings. Undoubtedly, this contributes to the injured athlete's commitment to the rehabilitation process. Athletes who receive high levels of emotional support from their coaches have been observed to be more highly motivated in comparison to those who receive low levels of support (Ungerleider & Golding, 1991).

Providing Informational Support

Providing support that is primarily informational in nature includes (a) task appreciation, (b) task challenge, and (c) reality confirmation.

Develop your injury knowledge base. One of the prerequisites for providing task related support is that the provider must have context expertise. He or she must be viewed by the athlete as a credible and knowledgeable person. Expertise requires an understanding not only of the technical aspects of the injury but also of the mental and emotional challenges of the rehabilitation process.

Deliver effective instructional feedback. Feedback that affirms effort and task mastery should be delivered in a sincere and personalized manner using the *sandwich principle* (Kirkpatrick, 1982; Quick, 1977, 1980; Smoll & Smith, 1979). In this approach, the technical instruction is sandwiched between affirming and encouraging statements. For example, "you're putting a lot of effort into that exercise. You may want to concentrate on getting a full range of motion so that the strength and flexibility of that muscle group will be more extensive."

In addition, the feedback should be focused on daily rehabilitation process goals rather than upon desired rehabilitation outcomes. The preferred time, place, and manner in which the recipient wants the task-related support delivered should be determined. Often, athletes desire to have this type of support delivered immediately–as soon as possible so that appropriate adjustments can be made.

Utilize technical modalities. An increasingly popular medium to deliver task support is through the use of physiological, biomechanical, and psychological tools. For example, mood inventories, biofeedback units, and computerized isokinetic strength-testing equipment provide data that the athlete can use to track the progress of rehabilitation. This technology allows the injured athlete to receive the necessary task-related support in a unique and objective manner. It is important to remember, however, that such technology is best used as an adjunct to interpersonal interaction rather than as a replacement.

Don't be afraid to challenge and confront. Injured athletes should be challenged in an honest and straightforward manner. Personal conferences should encourage the athletes to objectively assess their rehabilitation progress. Such self-assessments by injured athletes are more likely to be received in a nondefensive manner when trust and respect have been secured. When confronting the injured athlete, the support provider should be (a) accurate, (b) sensitive, (c) concrete, and (d) respectful. Modeling confrontation with these elements will likely increase athletes' receptivity to task challenge support. Perhaps the most important thing to remember is that confrontation must be delivered in a supportive manner. According to Egan (1973) "confrontation without support is disastrous; support without confrontation is anemic" (p. 132).

Provide reality touchstones. This can be accomplished in several effective ways: (a) create sharing opportunities between injured athletes; (b) have injured athletes who have successfully rehabilitated from similar injuries share their experiences with currently injured athletes; and (c) arrange small group meetings or support groups where injured athletes can openly discuss their thoughts and feelings about issues related to being injured (Weiss & Troxel, 1986; Wiese & Weiss, 1987). Athletes with similar experiences (i.e., injured athletes) profit from small group meetings where they can connect with people who understand how they feel and empathize with what they are experiencing. In addition, this type of support can facilitate the transition from sport to other life roles.

Providing Tangible Support

Providing support that is primarily material in nature includes (a) material assistance and (b) personal assistance.

Beware of boundaries. Beware that certain governing bodies within sport such as the National Collegiate Athletic Association may prohibit you from providing this type of support to athletes. Read the rules and regulations of the governing bodies for the sport you are involved with. If you are still unclear as to what the boundaries are, contact your athletic administrators for clarification. Make sure that athletes understand the rules and regulations regarding whom they can count on to provide this type of support. We are all familiar with cases where the inappropriate provision of this type of support by coaches and alumni has resulted in punishments and expulsions.

Define your boundaries. It may be helpful to establish a personal philosophy about providing this type of support. In developing this philosophy examine your motives, your past behavior, your qualifications, the rules and expectations of your administration as well as the rules and regulations of the governing bodies of the sport. Once you have developed your philosophy, communicate it to injured athletes. Let them know exactly what you can and will do as well as what you cannot and will not do. If you choose to be a provider, you may find it helpful to establish "windows of time" to assist injured athletes. This has the advantage of insuring them that you are available and focused on meeting their specific need.

Trying to please everybody all the time leads to failure. Moreover, giving to every injured athlete who needs material support can lead to *resource bankruptcy*. Rather than alleviating the stress of injury, support interventions that bankrupt the social network actually increase stress. A simple rule of thumb is to give within your means; don't overextend yourself.

Deliver on time. Tangible support, whether it be the provision of some material product or personal assistance, is best received at the time it is requested. We do not mean to suggest that you drop everything you are doing to provide for others; however, such a request usually is time limited. Thus, a timely response on your part will increase the likelihood of the support need being met. It should be noted, however, that severely injured athletes may require long-term tangible support. Thus, the use of a multiplex network is necessary to avoid a depletion of provider resources.

Offer tangible support interest-free. When you give tangible support, refrain from putting the recipient in a state of indebtedness to you, especially psychologically. Such a relationship, although supportive, is not social support. Give freely and unconditionally. Do not attach strings to your support and do not feel pressured into giving because you feel indebted to the recipient.

Creating and Maintaining an Effective Support System

Danish and D'Augelli (1983) suggested that although the ongoing support of caring others is essential, ultimately individuals must assume the responsibility of creating and maintaining the support they need. Athletes should first be encouraged to assess the structure and efficacy of their social support systems. This involves identification of (a) the types of support they feel they need, (b) the nature of their current network and (c) the level of satisfaction they have with their network in meeting their needs.

It is also beneficial to determine the type-provider match. In other words, it is important to determine *who* provides *what* type of social support. The research by Rosenfeld et al. (1989) indicates that for athletes, support that requires sport expertise is provided primarily by coaches, whereas other forms of support are provided by friends and parents. This indicates that athletes have two type-provider match systems: (a) those that require expertise on the part of the provider and (b) those not requiring such expertise.

The next step is actually to locate and determine the availability of potential support providers. Danish and D'Augelli (1983) offer the following guidelines when looking for support providers: (a) they must be someone with whom the athlete has frequent contact–someone who is available when needed; (b) they must understand the athlete's potential as well as his or her limitations; (c) they must be someone on whom the athlete can rely; and (d) they should be someone to whom the athlete can give something in return. Athletes should be discouraged from assuming that people in supportive roles are able to provide *all* necessary support. For example, although parents may provide emotional support, they may not be able to provide the task challenge support athletes need to recover successfully from the injury. In a similar manner, a member of the sports medicine staff may be able to provide the tangible and informational support, but they may not be able to provide emotional support. Moreover, it appears that reciprocity is an important element in the development of a support network.

Athletes should also be advised to invest some energy in developing new networks and utilizing *natural helpers,* such as coaches, trainers and physical therapists, and parents. These *natural helpers* can help athletes in staying motivated during the rehabilitation process, making them feel a part of the team and directing their energies toward recovery.

Coaches. Coaches can be helpful by providing emotional and informational support during recovery from injury. Coaches can serve an important social support function by encouraging the injured athlete to stay involved in team activities and meetings. In addition, injured athletes can serve as *assistant coaches* by monitoring their position during practice and competition in order to develop more effective strategies. Another commonly employed strategy is to assign the injured athlete the task of collecting game statistics. This is typically less successful because it is viewed by the athlete as a token gesture. "If this is so important, why isn't one of the non-injured athletes doing this?" It is important for the athlete's involvement to be a necessary and valued function for the team.

Perhaps the coach can schedule a weekly meeting with the injured athletes to get their feedback on what they have observed throughout the week at practice and to discuss game strategy with them. Coaches can also be most helpful by continually reinforcing the notion that the most important team function injured athletes can perform is to commit to an effective rehabilitation training program, thus facilitating a timely return to the team.

Teammates. Teammates can be helpful by providing emotional, informational, and tangible support during recovery from injury. Every effort should be made to keep injured athletes involved with the team. This involvement should include both on- and off-the-field activities. One of the best sources for this type of support are the injured athletes' teammates. According to Silva and Hardy (1991) when injured athletes are not allowed to isolate themselves from the team, feelings of letting the team down are minimized, important "family" ties are maintained, and fears of being replaced and forgotten are decreased.

Injury may cause athletes to see themselves no longer as athletes. Moreover, injured athletes may no longer be perceived as athletes by their teammates. This may have a severe impact on the interpersonal dynamics within a team. Rotella and Heyman (1986) have argued that injury has the potential to rupture friendships between teammates. To decrease this potential, teammates should work toward expanding the relationship beyond the athletic role. To the extent that athletes derive their identity through the athletic role this can be difficult. Rather than relating to them in terms of how the injury will affect their future as an athlete, teammates should be encouraged to expand their focus to how the injury impacts other life roles.

Finally, teammates can serve an important function by giving their time and talents to assist injured athletes in meeting the demands of roles outside of sport. Moreover, they may wish to give injured athletes gifts and/or tokens of appreciation for their contribution to the team.

Athletic trainers and physical therapists. Trainers and PTs can be helpful by providing emotional, informational, and tangible support throughout the rehabilitation process. Trainers and PTs can serve an important function by networking and coordinating *peer modeling.* Peer modeling involves connecting an injured athlete with another athlete who has recovered successfully from a similar injury (Wiese & Weiss, 1987). Through the interaction, it is believed that informational, emotional, and tangible support can be provided. Although the athletes do not have to come from the same sport, it is important that someone be found with as close to the same experience as possible. Because trainers and PTs are often aware of athletes with similar injuries, they are the logical linking agent. Trainers and PTs can start creating a *peer model bank* of athletes who have agreed to talk with injured athletes about the rehabilitation experience. By remaining the go-between, trainers and PTs can facilitate selecting the most appropriate peer model as well as be able to prevent the model from being bombarded with requests from injured athletes.

In addition, trainers and PTs can assist in increasing the injured athlete's involvement with team activities by coordinating the rehabilitation training around team activities. For example, physical therapy could be scheduled concurrently with team taping to encourage communication with teammates, or scheduled around team meetings so that the athlete would have a chance to attend. It is very easy for an athlete to withdraw into physical therapy in order to avoid any uncomfortable feelings associated with being with teammates or attending team functions. The more the athlete can openly discuss such feelings and be encouraged to become gradually more involved with the team, the quicker an athlete will be able to readopt the role of a teammate.

Trainers and PTs can also be helpful in establishing support groups for injured athletes (Wiese & Weiss, 1987). Although these groups are normally led by a mental health professional, the natural helpers can be quite helpful in the coordination process. Support groups represent a forum for injured athletes to discuss thoughts and emotions with similar others. The group can provide a sense of universality, a realization that the individual members are not alone in having experienced injury or the psychological reaction to the event, as well as instruction on coping strategies for dealing with the stress of injury.

Parents. Parents can be helpful by providing emotional support during the rough times of rehabilitation. In addition, it is crucial to use this opportunity to foster other roles that form an individual's identity. If athletes view themselves primarily as athletes, the impact of injury on their identity and self-worth may be devastating. Parents can gradually emphasize other important roles to indicate how positive aspects of one's life can still occur during setbacks in other areas of life.

General Considerations

Athletes should list the potential supporters for each type of support and then describe what they would like the person to do for them. Next, have them list the steps they are going to take in requesting these behaviors from the person(s) they have identified. Finally, have them identify a time frame for requesting the support they feel they need. Instruct them to continue this process until they feel that they have received the type of support they need. As with all plans, it is suggested that the athletes prepare a back-up plan or strategy.

In order to maintain the athletes' support system it is advised that they remain in regular contact with the members of their network. Encourage them to record and evaluate the effectiveness of each provider as well as the type-provider match. In addition, have them discuss with their providers any adjustments that need to be made as well as ways to nurture their involvement in the athlete's network and vice versa.

In addition, encourage the athlete to find ways that will allow the provider to feel appreciated and valued. Material and verbal rewards can be offered in a reciprocal manner, thereby building a sense of mutual caretaking. Caution should be employed, however, against developing co-dependent relationships that harm rather than help as well as those that decrease the personal agency of the people within the network.

It is important for athletes to realize that they can use their own resources as a support system for themselves and others. Although it is important to utilize the resources of others, to become totally dependent upon external support could immobilize the athlete. According to Hanson and Lubin (1986) the goal of support interventions is to "overcome the need to depend too much on environmental support by developing ourselves as a support system" (p. 63). Developing self-support involves increasing awareness of yourself, keeping agreements with yourself and others, and exercising more effective problem solving (Hanson & Lubin, 1986). To become self-supportive, therefore, the injured athlete must set clear goals about the recovery process, establish clear and specific behavioral agreements/contracts with him- or herself, and bring to closure all unfinished business surrounding the injury. These actions can lead to enhanced feelings of personal agency, the foundation of continuing self-support. The point is that the injured athlete cannot be totally dependent upon others for support, but should attempt to use the support provided by others as a base for developing a self-support system.

CONCLUSION

Research indicates that our social ties are the foundation of our interpersonal interactions and that the formation, maintenance, and severance of effective social support systems is fundamental to our well-being (Hammer, Makiesky-Barrow, & Gutwirth, 1978). More specifically, research in a variety of fields supports the conclusion that the sense of being supported may facilitate athletes' coping with the stress of injury. However, because research has demonstrated that social support can have negative health effects (Hardy et al., 1991; Hobfoll, 1985; Hobfoll & London, 1986), it is important to remember that social support is not a panacea for dealing with either injury or the demands stemming from the stress of modern life. Moreover, it is important to remember that not all social ties are supportive (Hobfoll & Stokes, 1988).

While it is unlikely that one can exist without any social support, the degree as well as the type of support needed varies as a function of both personal as well as environmental factors. Moreover, recent research indicates that the need for social support is an individual disposition (Sarason et al., 1990a) and that we can engage in behaviors that may facilitate, debilitate, and/or functionally substitute for social support (Golding & Ungerleider, 1991).

Even though the evidence to date is collectively more promising than definitive, there appears to be ample warrant for intense interest in the concept of social support, both theoretically and clinically. Indeed, it is fundamentally obvious that social support is an integral part of the quality of human life (Albrecht & Adelman, 1984). It is much more than a coping skill for the victims of extreme stress, like injured athletes; it is a life skill. As stated by Gottlieb (1988) "the enterprise of building supportive ties and networks of mutual aid is inextricably tied to the larger challenge of learning to nurture and be nurtured by our human attachments" (p. 541).

REFERENCES

Albrecht, T.L., & Adelman, M.B. (1984). Social support and life stress: New directions for communications research. *Human Communication Research, 11*, 3-22.

Billings, A.G., & Moos, R.H. (1981). The role of coping responses and social resources in attenuating the stress of life events. *Journal of Behavioral Medicine, 4*, 139-157.

Broadhead, W.E., Kaplan, B.H., James, S.A., Wagner, E.H., Schoenbach, V.J., Grimson, R., Heyden, S., Tibblin, G., & Gehlbach, S.H. (1983).

The epidemiologic evidence for a relationship between social support and health. *American Journal of Epidemiology, 117*, 521-537.

Bruhn, J.G., & Phillips, B.U. (1984). Measuring social support: A synthesis of current approaches. *Journal of Behavioral Medicine, 7,* 151-169.

Caplan, G. (1974). *Support systems and community mental health.* New York: Behavioral Publications.

Caplan, G. (1976). The family as a support system. In G. Caplan & M. Killilea (Eds.), *Support systems and mutual help* (pp. 19-36). New York: Grune & Stratton.

Cobb, S. (1976). Social support as a moderator of life stress. *Psychosomatic Medicine, 38*, 300-314.

Cohen, S. (1988). Psychosocial models of the role of social support in the etiology of physical disease. *Health Psychology, 7*(3), 269-297.

Cohen, S., & Hoberman, H.M. (1983). Positive events and social supports as buffers of life change stress. *Journal of Applied Social Psychology, 13*, 99-125.

Cohen, S., & Syme, L. (Eds.). (1985). *Social support and health.* New York: Academic Press.

Cohen, S., & Wills, T.A. (1985). Stress, social support, and the buffering hypothesis. *Psychological Bulletin, 98*, 310-357.

Conrad, C. (1985). *Strategic organizational communication: Cultures, situations, and adaptations.* New York: Holt, Rinehart, & Winston.

Cutrona, C.E., & Russell, D.W. (1990). Type of social support and specific stress: Toward a theory of optimal matching. In B.R. Sarason, I.G Sarason, & G.R. Pierce (Eds.), *Social support: An interactional view* (pp. 319-366). New York: John Wiley & Sons.

Danish, S. (1986). Psychological aspects in the care and treatment of athletic injuries. In P.F. Vinger & E.F. Hoerner (Eds.), *Sports injuries: The unthwarted epidemic* (2nd ed., pp. 345-353). Boston, MA: PSG.

Danish, S., & D'Augelli, A. (1983). *Helping skills II: Life development intervention.* New York: Human Sciences.

Durkheim, E. (1952). *Suicide.* New York: Free Press.

Eckenrode, J., & Gore, S. (1981). Stessful events and social supports: The significance of context. In B.H. Gottlieb (Ed.), *Social networks and social support* (pp. 43-68). Beverly Hills, CA: Sage.

Egan, G. (1973). *Face to face: The small group experience and interpersonal growth.* Pacific Grove, CA: Brooks/Cole.

Ganster, D.C., & Victor, B. (1988). The impact of social support on mental physical health. *British Journal of Medical Psychology, 61,* 17-36.

Golding, J.M., & Ugerleider, S. (1991). Social resources and mood among masters track and field athletes. *Journal of Applied Sport Psychology, 3,* 142-159.

Gordon, S. (1991, Summer). Sport psychology and the professional training of health care professionals. *AAASP Newsletter,* p. 15.

Gordon, S., & Lindgren, S. (1990). Psycho-physical rehabilitation from a serious sport injury: Case study of an elite fast bowler. *The Australian Journal of Science and Medicine in Sport, 22,* 71-76.

Gore, S. (1978). The effect of social support in moderating the health consequence of unemployment. *Journal of Health and Social Behavior, 19,* 157-165.

Gottlieb, B.H. (1988). Support interventions: A typology and agenda for research. In S.W. Duck (Ed.), *Handbook of personal relationships: Theory, research and interventions* (pp. 510-541). New York: John Wiley & Sons.

Hammer, M. (1981). Social supports, social networks, and schizophrenia. *Schizophrenia Bulletin, 7,* 45-57.

Hammer, M., Makiesky-Barrow, S., & Gutwirth, L. (1978). Social networks and schizophrenia. *Schizophrenia Bulletin, 4,* 522-545.

Hanson, P.G., & Lubin, B. (1986, Winter). Support systems: Understanding and using them effectively. *Organization Development Journal,* 59-66.

Hardy, C.J., & Crace, R.K. (1990). Dealing with injury. *Sport Psychology Training Bulletin, 1,*(6), 1-8.

Hardy, C.J., Richman, J.M., & Rosenfeld, L.B. (1991). The role of social support in the life stress/injury relationship. *The Sport Psychologist, 5,* 128-139.

Heitzmann, C.A., & Kaplan, R.M. (1988). Assessment of methods for measuring social support. *Health Psychology, 7*(1), 75-109.

Hobfoll, S.E. (1985). The limitations of social support in the stress process. In I.G. Sarason & B.R. Sarason (Eds.), *Social support: Theory, research, and application* (pp. 391-414). The Hague: Martinus Nijhoff.

Hobfoll, S.E. (1988). *The ecology of stress.* Washington, DC: Hemisphere.

Hobfoll, S.E. (1989). Conservation of resources: A new attempt at conceptualizing stress. *American Psychologist, 44,* 513-524.

Hobfoll, S.E., & London, P. (1986). The relationship of self-concept and social support to emotional distress among women during war. *Journal of Social and Clinical Psychology, 12*, 87-100.

Hobfoll, S.E., & Stephens, M.A.P. (1990). Social support during extreme stress: Consequences and intervention. In B.R. Sarason, I.G. Sarason, & G.R. Pierce (Eds.), *Social support: An interactional view* (pp. 454-481). New York: John Wiley & Sons.

Hobfoll, S.E., & Stokes, J.P. (1988). The process and mechanics of social support. In S.W. Duck (Ed.), *Handbook of personal relationships: Theory, research and interventions* (pp. 497-517). New York: John Wiley & Sons.

House, J. (1981). *Work stress and social support.* Reading, MA: Addison-Wesley.

House, J.S., & Kahn, R.L. (1985). Measures and concepts of social support. In S. Cohen & S.L. Syme (Eds.), *Social support and health* (pp. 83-108). New York: Academic Press.

Ievleva, L., & Orlick, T. (1991). Mental links to enhanced healing: An exploratory study. *The Sport Psychologist, 5*, 25-40.

Kahn, R.L., & Antonucci, T.C. (1980). Convoys over the life course: Attachment, roles and social support. In P.B. Baltes & O. Brim (Eds.), *Life span development and behavior* (Vol. 3, pp. 253-286). Boston: Lexington Press.

Kaplan, B.H., Cassel, J.C., & Gore, S. (1977). Social support and health. *Medical Care, 15*(5), 47-58.

Kirkpatrick, D.L. (1982). *How to improve performance through appraisal and coaching.* New York: AMACOM.

Leavy, R.L. (1983). Social support and psychological disorder: A review. *Journal of Community Psychology, 11*, 3-21.

McDonald, S.A., & Hardy, C.J. (1990). Affective response patterns of the injured athlete: An exploratory analysis. *The Sport Psychologist, 4*, 261-274.

Moss, G. (1973). *Illness, immunity and social interaction,* New York: John Wiley & Sons.

Pilisuk, M. (1982). Delivery of social support: The social inoculation. *American Journal of Orthopsychiatry, 52*, 20-31.

Pines, A.M., Aronson, E., & Kafry, D. (1981). *Burnout.* New York: Free Press.

Quick, T.L. (1977). *Person to person managing: An executive's guide to working effectively with people.* New York: St. Martin's Press.

Quick, T.L. (1980). *The quick motivation method: How to make your employees happier, harder working, and more productive.* New York: St Martin's Press.

Richman, J.M., Hardy, C.J., Rosenfeld, L.B., & Callanan, R.A.E. (1989). Strategies for enhancing social support networks in sport: A brainstorming experience. *Journal of Applied Sport Psychology, 1,* 150-159.

Richman, J.M., Rosenfeld, L.B., & Hardy, C.J. (1992). A practice model and clinical measure of the social support process. Manuscript submitted for publication in *Research on Social Work Practice.*

Rosenfeld, L.B., Richman, J.M., & Hardy, C.J. (1989). Examining social support networks among athletes: Description and relationship to stress. *The Sport Psychologist, 3,* 23-33.

Rosenfeld, L.B., Wilder, L., Crace, R.K., & Hardy, C.J. (1990). Communication fundamentals: Active listening. *Sport Psychology Training Bulletin, 1*(5), 1-8.

Rotella, R.J., & Heyman, S.R. (1986). Stress, injury, and the psychological rehabilitation of athletes. In J.M. Williams (Ed.), *Applied sport psychology: Personal growth to peak performance* (pp. 343-364). Palo Alto, CA: Mayfield.

Sarason, B.R., Sarason, I.G., & Pierce, G.R. (1990b). Traditional views of social support and their impact on assessment. In B.R. Sarason, I.G. Sarason, & G.R. Pierce (Eds.), *Social support: An interactional view* (pp. 9-25). New York: John Wiley & Sons.

Sarason, I.G., & Sarason, B.R. (1985). *Social support: Theory, research, and applications.* Boston: Martinus Nijhoff International.

Sarason, I.G., Sarason, B.R., & Pierce, G.R. (1990a). Social support, personality and performance. *Journal of Applied Sport Psychology, 2,* 117-127.

Schaefer, C., Coyne, J.C., & Lazarus, R.S. (1981). The health-related functions of social support. *Journal of Behavioral Medicine, 4*(4), 381-406.

Shumaker, S.A., & Brownell, A. (1984). Toward a theory of social support: Closing conceptual gaps. *Journal of Social Issues, 40,* 11-36.

Silva, J.M., & Hardy, C.J. (1991). The sport psychologist: Psychological aspects of injury in sport. In F.O. Mueller & A. Ryan (Eds.), *The sports medicine team and athlete injury prevention* (pp. 114-132). Philadelphia: F.A. Davis.

Smoll, F.L., & Smith, R.E. (1979). *Improving relationship skills in youth sport coaches*. East Lansing: Michigan Institute for the Study of Youth Sports.

Tardy, C. (1988). Social support: Conceptual clarification and measurement options. In C.H. Tardy (Ed.), *A handbook for the study of human communication: Methods and instruments for observing, measuring, and assessing communication processes* (pp. 347-364). Norwood, NJ: Albex.

Ungerleider, S., & Golding, J. (1991, Summer). Beyond strength: Psychological profiles of Olympic athletes. *Track Techniques, 116,* 3704-3709.

Wallston, B.S., Alagna, S.W., DeVellis, B.M., & DeVellis, R.F. (1983). Social support and health. *Health Psychology, 2,* 367-391.

Weiss, M.R., & Troxel, R.K. (1986). Psychology of the injured athlete. *Athletic Training, 21*(2), 104-109, 154.

Weiss, R. (1974). The provision of social relationships. In Z. Rubin (Ed.), *Doing unto others* (pp. 17-26). Englewood Cliffs, NJ: Prentice-Hall.

Wiese, D.M., & Weiss, M.R. (1987). Psychological rehabilitation and physical injury: Implication for the sports medicine team. *The Sport Psychologist, 1,* 318-330.

Wilcox, B.L. (1981). Social support in adjusting to marital disruption: A network analysis. In B. Gottlieb (Ed.), *Social networks and social support* (pp. 97-115). Beverly Hills, CA: Sage Publications.

SECTION 3
Counseling Athletes Who are Injured

Section 3:

Counseling Athletes Who Are Injured

Diane M. Wiese-Bjornstal and **Aynsley M. Smith** bring attention to the appropriateness of a team effort in rehabilitating injured athletes. In this first chapter of Section 3, they describe the efforts of peer athletes, physicians, athletic trainers, and sport psychology consultants in assisting the rehabilitating injured athlete. Examples of how the influence of these persons contributes to the rehabilitation effort are provided.

In two of the most unique contributions in this book, **Frances Flint**'s chapter and that of **Lance Green** (chapters 10 and 11 respectively of this section) provide creative approaches for the rehabilitation of injured athletes. Modeling is described as an effective method by **Flint** and mental imagery by **Green**.

The final chapter in this section by **Lydia Ievleva** and **Terry Orlick** reviews a number of mental factors and mental training techniques that deserve attention when designing programs for athletic injury rehabilitation. Examples are provided of athletes who were led to important insights and acceptance of their injuries, which contributed meaningfully to successful rehabilitation as well as future participation in their sport.

Chapter 9

Counseling Strategies For Enhanced Recovery of Injured Athletes within a Team Approach

Diane M. Wiese-Bjornstal
University of Minnesota
Aynsley M. Smith
Mayo Clinic Sports Medicine Center

ｌAthletes experience a variety of cognitive, emotional, and behavioral responses following athletic injury occurrence, ranging on a continuum from no change in the athlete's psychological state to extreme distress, such as attempted suicide. During the time span from immediate post-injury to full recovery, there are a variety of sports medicine team members with whom the athlete comes in contact, all of whom have important psychological roles to play in the recovery process.ｌ It is the purpose of this chapter to identify counseling and other psychological and social strategies to be employed by these various members of the sports medicine team, with the ultimate goal being the enhancement of the physical and psychological recovery of the athlete.

INTRODUCTION

Both sport-related and health care professionals have expressed concerns about the psychosocial impact of incurring athletic injury. Eldridge (1983) stated that health care professionals must understand the psychosocial dynamics accompanying sports injuries to appreciate the significance of the injury to the athlete. For example, among other possible psychological consequences, it has been noted by Scott (1984) that clinical depression, often present in injured athletes, must be identified early if optimal rehabilitation is to occur.

Limited empirical evidence exists, however, to systematically document the emotional responses of athletes to injury. In general, the preliminary research suggests that some, but not all, injured athletes manifest a variety of negative emotional reactions. For example, recent studies have provided preliminary data on post-injury emotional responses. Significant mood disturbances, such as elevations in depression, tension, and anger, have been found in more seriously injured athletes (Grove, Stewart, & Gordon, 1990; Smith, Scott, O'Fallon, & Young, 1990), in injured collegiate athletes, and in injured runners who were forced to remain out of running for two weeks (Chan & Grossman, 1988). In the Smith et al. (1990) study, it was found that mood disturbance paralleled the rating of perceived recovery, that severity of injury was the major determinant of the emotional response, and that athletes with minor injuries actually had less mood disturbance than college norms. Connelly (1991) found that physical self-efficacy was affected by injury, but that self-esteem and physical acceptance were not. These initial findings illustrate the importance of avoiding the assumption that all injured athletes will experience psychological trauma, and that they will experience the same cognitive and emotional responses. Many, it appears, may handle the injury experience quite well.

Among those athletes who do experience psychological disturbance, it is clear that negative mood states, such as depression, tension, and anger may occur almost immediately post-injury. These negative mood states may continue in the absence of intervention until the athlete returns to sport or adapts to alternative interests. In our clinical experience, athletic injury has combined with serious pre-injury stress to prompt at least five suicide attempts (Smith & Milliner, 1991). The work of Gordon, Milios, and Grove (1991) suggested that physiotherapists working with injured athletes noted many post-injury behavioral reactions resembling stages of the grief response previously identified by Kübler-Ross (1969) in her work with terminal patients. Clearly, counseling interventions are often appropriate as soon as the injury is diagnosed, the prognosis established, appropriate medical interventions arranged, and cognitive and emotional responses assessed.

However, the clinical utility of using "loss-of-health" models (e.g., Cassem & Hackett, 1971; Kübler-Ross, 1969) for understanding athletes' reactions to injury has yet to be established. Existing loss-of-health models were developed from responses of patient populations very different from injured athletes. For example, Kübler-Ross based her model on the consolidation of numerous interviews with elderly terminally ill patients, and with children having leukemia coping with impending death, during an era where treatment was ineffective for this form of cancer. Her stages of anger, denial, bargaining, depression, and acceptance represented the nonsequential coping stages of the terminally ill, and may not be the same as those experienced by injured athletes. The Cassem and Hackett model, on the other hand, describes the emotional experiences of patients who sustained heart attacks and were admitted as "critical" to an intensive care unit. Referrals of these patients to psychiatric services were primarily for anxiety, denial, and depression; responses that differ somewhat from the Kübler-Ross model.

In addition to the possibility of emotional response differences between athletes and nonathletes, there is evidence to suggest the existence of behavioral differences. Carmen, Zerman, and Blaine (1968), for example, found that athletes used a psychiatric counseling service at Harvard less than nonathletes did. Furthermore, when they finally were seen, the athletes had more problems than did the nonathletes. The reluctance of athletes to seek help was attributed to a determination not to "give in" to weakness. Pierce (1969), found that athletes held more negative attitudes toward emotional illness and were less intellectual in their interests. Furthermore, Linder, Pillow, and Reno (1989) reported that athletes who seek help or counseling from a sports psychologist may well experience discrimination. This study found that in a "mock up" of the draft selection process, athletes were rated lower if they sought assistance from a sports psychologist than if they had obtained assistance for stress management from a coach.

Although the previously cited studies suggest that athletes may be reluctant to seek assistance or counseling for their problems, the work of Little (1969) underscores the importance of having counseling services available to injured athletes. In a study of males who were experiencing depression and anxiety, approximately 75% of the middle-aged athletic group had sustained injury or illness which precipitated their symptoms compared to 11% of the nonathletes. Furthermore, the athletic group took longer in treatment and had a less favorable prognosis than did the nonathletes. Little believed that the athletic persons experienced a deprivation crisis secondary to the injury or illness that required cessation of physical activity.

In summary, differences have been noted among the following: (a) individual differences in the emotional responses of athletes to injury, (b) the ages and situation severity of psychological response models designed around terminally ill and heart attack populations, and the psychological responses of injured athletes, and (c) the reported differences between athlete and nonathlete help-seeking behaviors.

Theoretical Model of Post-Injury Response

Taken together, the results just cited suggest a need to consider athletic injury as a unique phenomenon. To better appreciate the specific psychosocial impact of athletic injury, a preliminary model of response is proposed in Figure 1. The pre-injury psychosocial model outlined by Anderson and Williams (1988) has been extended in this illustration to include the post-injury phase, incorporating the stress model of injury response proposed by Wiese and Weiss (1987). Some of the predicted precursors to athletic injury such as coping resources, social support availability, history of stressors, and personality certainly impact on the post-injury responses as well. For example, injured athletes who experience high life stress and who lack coping skills (Smith, Smoll, & Ptacek, 1990) will likely not have these pre-injury issues resolved by the time they are seen for post-injury counseling. In fact the presence of pre-injury stress and impaired coping will likely amplify the post-injury mood disturbance. An attempt is made in this model to identify some of the psychosocial factors influencing the post-injury cognitive and emotional responses, and subsequently psychological and physical recovery from injury. The key aspects of this extended model relate to the mediating role of severity of injury; sport-specific situational factors; interactions with the sports medicine team; individual differences; and the resultant emotional, cognitive, and behavioral responses of the athlete. In addition to providing a preliminary theoretical model for much needed research in this area, this model may prove to have clinical utility in assessing the post-injury cognitive and emotional responses for planning appropriate interventions. The

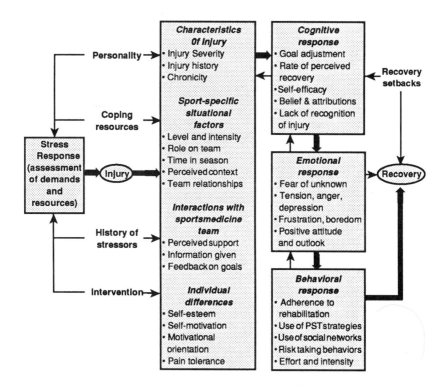

Figure 1. Predictors of cognitive, emotional and behavioral responses of athletes to injury and rehabilitation. (extended from Anderson & Williams, 1988)

specific predictions of this model will be discussed in a future article.

Implicit within this model are the various persons with whom the athlete comes into contact during rehabilitation. Each person in the sports medicine network encountered by the athlete plays an important role in his or her recovery, both physically and psychologically. Thus, the adoption of a comprehensive sports medicine team approach to assist the athlete in dealing psychologically with the injury is strongly advocated. Figure 2 identified some of the sports medicine team members with whom injured athletes at different levels of sport participation may interact. Each member of the sports medicine team can contribute unique and complementary psychosocial support services to the rehabilitation program to

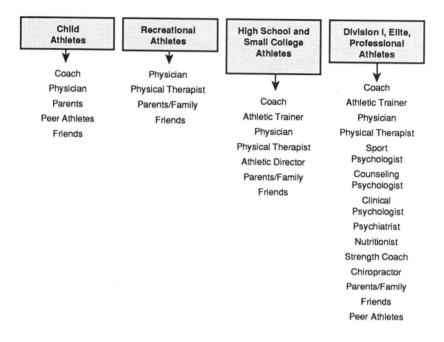

Figure 2. Members of the sports medicine team by competitive level.

enhance full recovery. However, the key is that the athlete is the captain of the team, and it is ultimately those factors which the athlete takes ownership of and has commitment to that best determine rehabilitation and recovery.

Purpose of Chapter

The primary goal of this chapter is to identify strategies for enhancing the coping resources and social support networks of athletes, as well as to suggest psychological counseling and intervention strategies. To accomplish our purpose, this chapter is organized around the framework of the various roles and responsibilities of sports medicine team members, viewed from an educational and counseling approach. It is of primary importance to involve both the sport personnel and the medical and clinical personnel in the rehabilitation process. Clear communication among the various members of the team is integral to the effectiveness of this approach.

The contents of the chapter reflect the authors' perspectives derived from their professional experiences as a sport psychology educator and researcher in a university setting and a nurse counselor in sport psychology at a sports medicine center. A number of case studies are presented with the intent of illustrating the authors' recommendations. These use the first person in an effort to stress that reported interactions and practices on behalf of one or both of the authors actually occurred. Although these case studies are based on actual experiences with injured athletes, some aspects have been altered to protect the identity of those involved.

SOCIAL SUPPORT AND EDUCATIONAL STRATEGIES FOR SPORT-RELATED PRACTITIONERS

The involvement of sport-related practitioners in the rehabilitation of the athlete will depend to some extent on the competitive level and sponsor (e.g., school-based, national team, youth sport) as identified in Figure 2. The work of Duda, Smart, and Tappe (1989) suggested that adherence to rehabilitation programs is related to athlete perceptions about the effectiveness of the rehabilitation protocol, social support for injury rehabilitation, the degree of self-motivation, and involvement in sport for primarily task-related motives. Clearly the first two factors can be influenced by various sport-related members of the sports medicine team. Some suggested strategies follow.

Athletic Trainers

The recent establishment of the Nuprin[R] Comeback Award at the U.S. Olympic Festival 1990 in Minneapolis/St. Paul pays tribute to the important role athletic trainers play in the rehabilitation of athletes from injury. The award, presented again at the 1991 festival in Los Angeles, recognizes not only athletes who make an exceptional recovery from sports-related injuries to distinguish themselves in elite level competition, but also their athletic trainers who enhance their rehabilitation.

In understanding the role of trainers, it is important to examine their psychosocial, as well as their more familiar physical responsibilities in the rehabilitation process. Clear, controlled communication is a primary responsibility of athletic trainers during the initial management of injury (Wiese & Weiss, 1987). Often athletic trainers are the first responders when athletic injury occurs. What they say, and perhaps even more importantly, how they say it immediately following injury is extremely critical. All interactions should be calm and professional when injury occurs, as many athletes will turn to the trainer for reassurance and information about the nature of the injury. Trainers should be empathic and reassuring. It is sometimes helpful to encourage athletes to talk, thereby distracting them from overreaction to injury. Diagnoses and hasty impressions must be avoided, as they might precipitate unnecessary emotional reactions.

Later in the chronological progression, at least in high school and university team settings, the athletic trainers are the ones to plan, monitor, and evaluate rehabilitation programs. Thus the training staff has the most frequent contact with injured athletes, usually even more than coaches and teammates have. Rehabilitation must be viewed as an educational process, and the psychosocial role that the trainer plays at this time is crucial to the recovery process. Athletes experience many different emotional and cognitive states during the course of an extended rehabilitation. Usually, depending on the nature and severity of the injury and the rehabilitation protocol, performance plateaus occur when the athlete does not seem to make further progress. Support, encouragement, and reassurance that this is a normal part of the rehabilitation are helpful from the trainer dur-ing these times. Positive rather than negative communication skills are essential, including good listening skills on the part of the trainer. The focus should be on aspects of the rehabilitation program that have been performed correctly, and emphasis placed on the use of praise and rewards as a means of further encouraging desired recovery behaviors. Trainers may insert corrective feedback between positively reinforcing comments.

Trainers should also ensure that athletes have realistic goals and expectations for their recovery. Some athletes apply their same high levels of self-motivation enjoyed in sport to their rehabilitation programs; for these athletes the biggest challenge will be helping them to be realistic and not overdo, consequently risking reinjury. Other athletes may have a tendency to give up in the face of a difficult rehabilitation. In this case the challenge to the trainer is to find appropriate motivational strategies. In both of these situations, realistic, short term goals (i.e., daily goals) should be employed to allow plenty of room for goal adjustment based on the current progress. The provision of specific performance-based feedback regarding attainment of goals should be central to trainer's job.

The athletic training staff can provide social support to the athlete in the form of encouragement, as just described. However, the athlete must not rely solely on the trainer for social support. The trainer may have to

Injured Athlete Survey

1. Name _____ Date: _____

2. Injury: _____ Sport: _____

3: What would you like from your coaches during your rehabilitation?
   (e.g., encouragement, keeping you involved with the team, leaving you alone,
   monitoring your progress, etc.)

_____
_____
_____

4. What would you like from your athletic trainer or physical therapist?
   (e.g., explaining more about the injury to you, taking an interest in you outside
   your sport background, helping you set goals, etc.)

5. What would you like from your teammates? (e.g., telling you about practice,
   checking up on how you are doing, asking you to help them with their
   technique, not talking about the team in front of you, etc.)

_____
_____
_____

6. What would you like from your family? (e.g., taking time to talk to you, not
   fussing over you, still attending games, etc.)

_____
_____
_____

7. What would you like from your friends? (e.g., spending more time with you,
   encouragement, an ear to bend, etc.)

_____
_____
_____

Figure 3. Injured athlete survey.

remind the athletes to also rely on others, such as their coaches, teammates, parents, and significant others. One tool that might be helpful in
assessing both the available social support networks and the desires of the
athlete with respect to involvement by these persons is provided in Figure
3. This simple questionnaire allows the athlete to express his or her
preferences. However, it may not be best administered by the athletic
trainer if other options are available. The effect of social desirability is

high, and it may be more beneficial to have a sport psychology consultant, when available, administer and read the questionnaires and convey the information to the appropriate persons. Or, better yet, the injured athletes should be encouraged to express their own thoughts honestly and directly to the persons involved if they are assertive enough to do so. In either case, the survey encourages injured athletes to think through what behaviors they desire from various individuals.

Other specific psychosocial strategies that can be employed by athletic trainers are highly dependent upon their personal training and education. Results of studies which have tapped an important source of psychological data based on the interactions of athletic trainers and physiotherapists with injured athletes (e.g., Gordon et al., 1991; Wiese, Weiss, & Yukelson, 1991) have demonstrated that these practitioners have experiential knowledge about responses to injury, but often lack systematic and specific educational preparation which might provide a context or framework for understanding and interpreting these emotional, cognitive, and behavioral responses. It is of the utmost importance that future preparation programs for athletic trainers mandate formal educational consideration of involved psychosocial factors (Wiese et al., 1991). If the trainer had had such educational preparation, they might well be able to assist the athlete with such strategies as more systematic goal setting, relaxation training, and imagery as methods of enhancing recovery. We are attempting to work toward this end at the University of Minnesota, where students preparing to become athletic trainers are strongly encouraged to take at least one course in applied sport psychology. In this course they receive at least basic education regarding psychosocial factors related to athletics and experience in employing Psychological Skills Training (PST) (Martens, 1987) techniques. These may prove to be beneficial to athletes in enhancing their recovery, and it is hoped that in the future such education will be central to the preparation of all athletic trainers.

Coaches

In some cases, unfortunately, coaches pay little attention to injured athletes because they are no longer useful to the team, or perhaps because they feel awkward around injured athletes and do not know what to say or do. When this occurs it may be because the coach knows little about the athlete's life outside of the sport context, his or her responses to stress, the injury and rehabilitation protocol, or even whether or when the athlete can return to sport. Unfortunately many coaches expect athletes to "tough it out" and feel that they should not need support from the coach or others during rehabilitation.

Case 1: A collegiate athlete playing for a national caliber hockey program sustained two serious knee injuries during his career. After his collegiate career ended, he retrospectively expressed to me several concerns about the rehabilitation process that he experienced. One concern was that injured athletes were virtually ignored by the coaching staff, indicative in his opinion of the coaches' general attitude toward "treating athletes as pieces of meat." His feeling lends support to the suggestion stated earlier that some coaches lose interest in athletes when they are no longer of immediate usefulness to the team and, more importantly, in winning games. On the other hand, this athlete expressed a preference, perhaps learned during the course of several rehabilitation experiences, to not be too extensively involved with the team during his recovery. He felt that he wanted to prove to the coaches and his teammates that he could come back from the injury on his own and return to play. This may possibly be reflective of high self-motivation and determination. More likely, however, his behavior was in response to his perception that if the coaches did not care about him, he would not care about the team. This athlete took great pride in recovering faster than the timeline initially determined for him, perhaps in part due to the use of short- and long-term goal setting. It was almost as though this pride in recovery was based primarily on his recovery in spite of being ignored by the coaches, sort of an "in your face" response. In either case, this athlete recovered successfully and went on to become a high school coach.

Coaches should strive to provide evidence that they care about their injured athletes. This may be done by recognizing and supporting their rehabilitative progress, whether or not their return to team activities is anticipated during the current season or in the future. Coaches are educators, and it therefore behooves them to be concerned with the psychosocial and physical aspects of their athletes' growth and development.

Moreover, it is important to keep injured athletes integrated with the team in order that they retain a sense of self-worth and of importance to the team. For example, injured athletes may continue to attend practice and participate as drill leaders or peer coaches. They may be able to help referee or officiate a scrimmage, thereby freeing the coach to evaluate the performance of others. They can keep scores, times, or statistics during contests. Some young athletes might wish to serve as an extra team manager as a means of retaining involvement with the team. Injured athletes can provide support and encouragement to teammates during practice and competition, although this may be difficult for those who are used to receiving high and frequent praise for their past competitive performance. In fact, this may be a good lesson for some elite injured athletes to learn.

In addition, the coach may also suggest activities to injured athletes in order to keep their sport knowledge and insights current. Mental rehearsal of individual skills or team strategies might prove helpful to athletes. Athletes may also be referred to books about their sport, be encouraged to take coaching or officiating classes, or to attend a clinic to learn more about various aspects of their sport. Injured athletes could even obtain officiating certification. The coach might also make the injured athlete feel involved in the team effort by asking her or him to view game films and provide notes, comments, or feedback. The goal of these strategies is to further the injured athlete's skills, knowledge, and understanding about competitive sport during a time of reduced physical involvement, given that the athlete expresses an interest in learning about other aspects of the sport. However, the coach must be sensitive to maintaining realistic time demands for injured athletes, as they will have the added time commitment of their rehabilitation regimens. Certainly athletes should not be expected to accomplish all of the above, but rather should be allowed some choice from among involvement alternatives.

Peer Athletes

Peer athletes play an important role in the rehabilitation process. Both healthy and injured peers can offer social support to the injured athlete. For example, healthy teammates and other peer athletes can simply serve as friends who take an interest in both the recovery of the athlete and in the life of the athlete outside sport, as appropriate. These peers may also keep the athlete informed and involved in the activities of the team, so that the injured athlete still feels an integral part of the group. Teammates should make sure to include the injured athlete in social gatherings and other functions.

Another more structured way in which peer athletes might become involved is via establishment of injury support groups (Weiss & Troxel,

1986). This involves meeting a facilitator and other injured athletes to discuss thoughts, emotions, and challenges associated with injury and rehabilitation. Injured athletes may share common concerns; this provides an opportunity to find out that they are not alone in their recovery triumphs and struggles.

This strategy has been tried in a limited fashion at the University of Minnesota, with injured athletes attending group meetings led by a licensed clinical psychologist who is also knowledgeable about sport. Many of the recommendations for future efforts that arose from this initial attempt related to the frequency of meeting and attendance requirements. For example, some athletes recommended meeting with limited frequency, such as once every month, due to the other time constraints that they faced in rehabilitation and practice. Others suggested that attendance not be made mandatory by coaches or athletic trainers, but that each injured athlete make a personal decision about attending. Some athletes indicated that they found the groups very useful and that it gave them a chance to primarily share the emotions associated with injury, whereas others did not feel that they needed to attend and were coping with the injury quite well on their own.

An example of the important role played by peer athletes, particularly those who have sustained the same injury, was provided following the recent permanent paralysis sustained by football guard Mike Utley of the Detroit Lions. Former New England Patriots wide receiver Darryl Stingley who incurred a football injury that resulted in permanent paralysis of his lower body, was quoted as saying, "It doesn't mean that life is over. It means you have to make a few more adjustments. My advice is to be strong. If he survives, the sky is the limit as to what he can do, depending on his competitive nature and spirit. Just never get down" (*NFL Notebook*, 1991, p. 3c). His public support and encouragement to Utley was likely gratefully received.

Other Sport Professionals and Nonsport Individuals

Examples of other professionals who are often involved with the injured athlete are the athletic director, strength coach, and sport nutritionist, whereas nonsport related persons involved in the process might be teachers, friends, peers, and family members. It is important for these individuals to share in the rehabilitative process and show concern for athletes' recovery efforts. Because injured athletes frequently maintain keen interests in their sport, efforts should be made by nonsport–as well as by sport-related peers, friends, and acquaintances to discuss sport issues, results of current competitions, and other pertinent events. It is also important to discuss other aspects of the athlete's life, such as school, work, or church activities. Parents, family, and friends are perhaps the most important source of social support for injured athletes, depending on the level of competitive involvement and age of the athlete. For example, in the youth sport setting, parents and family members provide the primary social network for young athletes and thus must be extremely sensitive to their cognitive and emotional responses during recovery. Just "being there" for the injured athlete to talk to is very important during the recovery process. However, injured athletes will need to feel a sense of trust in the relationship before they will reveal their innermost fears and concerns. It is also important to be sensitive to the motives, desires, and values of the athlete, rather than impose those of the parents or friends. In many cases, what the athlete wants and is willing to risk in order to return to sport may be quite different from that which the parent desires. Sometimes injured athletes feel the stakes and demands are too high, and they are not prepared to take further risk. In other situations, the athletes are insistent on a return to sport even though it means persevering in spite of recommendations.

In summary, the sport-related professionals and personal relatives and friends are very important in helping athletes recover from injury and return to sport. Should the return to sport not be possible or desired, the same persons play an important role in helping injured athletes recover and adapt to normal life without their sports.

COUNSELING STRATEGIES FOR PSYCHOLOGICAL AND MEDICAL PRACTITIONERS

The extent to which psychological and medical practitioners will be involved in an athlete's rehabilitation will depend on such factors as the severity of the injury, the athlete's competitive level, and sport sponsor (e.g., school, national team, youth sport league) as previously identified in Figure 2. Figure 4 illustrates a specific example of a sports medicine team approach flow chart. Injured athletes who seek treatment at the Mayo Clinic Sports Medicine Center may interact with these and other sports medicine team members, depending on the nature of the presenting problem.

Coping and the Counseling Approach
Coping has been defined by Folkman and Lazarus (1986) as transient

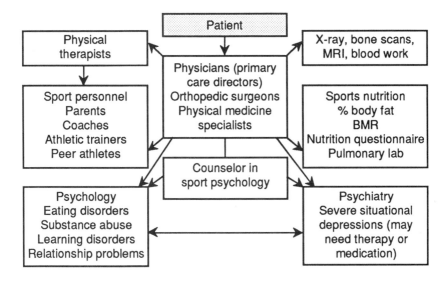

Figure 4. Sports medicine team approach flow chart.

behavioral efforts to change specific external and internal demands that are appraised as taxing or exceeding a person's resources. As described by Tunks and Bellissimo (1988), some individuals seem able to transform calamities into opportunities for growth whereas others transform everyday hassles into overwhelming adversities. Coping skills vary in appropriateness, may be adaptive or maladaptive, and can be taught and used as a situation requires. Coping skills are organized primarily into three domains: (1) the appraisal aspect of coping attempts to understand and find meaning in a crisis, evaluating what the demands are of a situation (primary appraisal) and the coping resources available (secondary appraisal): (2) problem-focused coping confronts the reality of the crisis and deals with tangible consequences by constructing a more satisfying situation; and (3) emotion-focused coping aims to manage the feelings provoked by the situation (stressor) and to obtain effective equilibrium. It is believed that most stressful situations are responded to with both problem-focused and emotion-focused coping.

Extensive research on the effectiveness of counseling interventions with injured athletes is not yet available, but based on what is known of athlete and nonathlete differences, it seems likely that athletes in general would prefer a rehabilitation program that "stresses concrete, behavioral goal setting and accurate data feedback on their progress in preference to a program of abstract planning and detailed scientific explanation" (Rohe & Athelstan, 1982). These recommendations are consistent with suggestions by other health care researchers who suggest problem-focused coping strategies for their heart attack (Christman, 1988), adolescent (Yarcheski & Mahon, 1986), and spinal-cord-injured patients (Rohe & Athelstan, 1982). This approach seems ideal for injured athletes, as it is congruent with goal-setting and performance-enhancement programs common to exercise and sport training.

Sport Psychology Counselor
Medical History and Intervention Plan

Sport psychology counselors, particularly those in hospital or medical clinic settings, are often asked to see injured athletes within a few days of their injury. Prior to meeting the athlete, the first task is to conduct a thorough assessment of the athlete's situation, which begins with a review of the patient's medical history, relevant physician and physical therapy notes, as well as X-ray, bone scan and MRI reports. Associated illnesses or conditions such as insulin-dependent diabetes, exercise-induced asthma, scores on standardized psychological tests, and the presence of a psychiatric history should be noted. The medical plan for the patient (e.g., surgical or nonsurgical rehabilitation) should be identified and the patient and physician expectations recorded. Review of these records and any additional necessary communication with the physician or physical therapist should take place before the patient is directed to the counselor.

Assessment Meeting with Injured Athlete
Ideal Counseling Atmosphere

Counseling offices in a sports medicine center can be designed specifically to decrease athlete discomfort and increase a sense of trust and intimacy. Ideally, the injured athlete and counselor are seated in chairs of the same size so that both parties occupy the same space. A round table allows for a sense of togetherness and mutuality as the guided interview progresses and necessary forms are completed. Colors in the office should be attractive and coordinated, with the decor reflecting an interest in sport (e.g., sport photos or pictures on the wall). These physical details reflect a desire on the part of the interviewer for mutual respect and understanding, a necessary prerequisite to a meaningful interaction.

Interviewing Alone

By being interviewed alone, in the absence of coaches, parents, athletic trainers, teammates, or other members of the sports medicine team, the athlete has the opportunity to convey honest concerns and not simply say what others want to hear. When interviewed alone, athletes are often inclined to acknowledge the pressures they experience, their readiness to quit a sport, the degree of physical and emotional pain they experience, or on the other hand, their sincere desire and intent to continue, despite injury and the need to persevere with their extensive rehabilitation therapy. For example:

Case 2: A few years ago, an injured college athlete, captain of his varsity football team, was seen in the sports medicine center. The athlete was on a scholarship and had experienced two years of severe, chronic back pain. The athletic trainer had accompanied the athlete to all of his previous appointments. I gently stopped the athletic trainer from entering the counseling room, and later, the athlete expressed appreciation. "This is the first time I've seen a member of the sports medicine team alone. Frankly, I've had two years of pain. I've worked hard for my scholarship, and I've produced well. I don't plan to continue my sport beyond college, and I'd rather stop now, rehabilitate, and know I won't be risking permanent disability. I'm O.K. with not playing any more, focusing on my academic career and on life beyond sport." As a nurse counselor, my role is to serve as the patient's advocate. With the athlete's permission, I shared his concerns and other pertinent findings from our interview with the sports medicine physician who was directing the evaluation and treatment. The physician had the difficult task of considering and coordinating all professional input and then together with the injured athlete determining the best course of action.

Interview Format

When the counselor meets initially with the injured athlete, it is important that a thorough explanation of the counselor's role and qualifications be provided. The guided interview then follows the Emotional Responses of Athletes to Injury Questionnaire (ERAIQ), adapted slightly from the version previously published (Smith, Scott, & Wiese, 1990). The clinical version of this questionnaire was developed over a period of several years and is based on interviews with hundreds of injured athletes (see Figure 5).

The instrument's first question offers an opportunity for the interviewer to gain insight into the athlete's values and priorities. The athlete can share dreams of music, academics and nonsport career goals. The athlete who is tired, burned out, or conversely burning with desire, can often be identified through question number one. The second question helps the interviewer determine whether the injury has occurred at a more or less critical time in the year or season. This information allows a better understanding of the psychosocial impact of injury. The third question permits the interviewer a glimpse into the athlete's motivation for sport or exercise and heightens the interviewer's appreciation of what is lost to the athlete when injury occurs. Post-injury intervention strategies often incorporate information from this question. The questions on perceived athleticism, goals, nature of the injury (patient's perception), pressures to be in sport and perform up to the expectations of others, stress, and social support are self-explanatory. The last two factors are integrated into the view taken of the injured athlete, illustrated in our earlier model of post-injury response.

The question that asks the athlete to rank emotional responses is central to the ERAIQ. This question is deliberately placed well into the interview, so that ideally a trusting relationship has already been established. More seriously injured athletes have rated frustration, depression, and anger highest on the ERAIQ, which correspond with the depression, tension, and anger scales of the Profile of Mood Scales (POMS) (McNair, Lorr, & Doppelman, 1971), a popularly used standardized instrument used to assess mood. This information tells the interviewer which emotions are the most bothersome to the injured athlete, and thus need to be addressed with appropriate intervention so they do not adversely impede rehabilitation. When athletes who have a chronic injury or who are being seen preoperatively are interviewed, pain may be ranked near the top of the athletes' concerns. The interviewer has an obligation to ensure that the injured athlete is physically comfortable during the interview.

The injured athlete's understanding of the injury and the planned surgical procedure or the goals of the nonoperative rehabilitation program should also be assessed. If the athlete does not understand the problem or procedure, the counselor can provide the correct information. If this is not within the counselor's expertise, assistance should be sought. Usually the physicians and therapists have instructed the patient carefully, and the

Name: _____   Date: _____
Address: _____   Age: ___ ___Date of Birth ___/___/___
City:_____State:____ Zip: _____   Clinic #: _____
Tel: home: _____ work: _____   Ht::_____ Wt:._____
Interviewer_____   Level of Participation: _____
****

1. If you could be anything you wanted to in life, what would that be?_____
   _____

2. List in order of preference the sports and activities that you participate in:
   1._____   2._____   3. _____   4. _____

3. What are your reasons for participating in sport? Rank 10=high, 0=low
   (in declining order of importance):

   Stress management _____   Competition _____   Socialization _____
   Pursuit of excellence _____   Fitness _____   Self-discipline _____
   Personal improvement _____   Fun _____   Outlet for aggression _____
   Weight Management _____   Other _____   (e.g., well-being)

4. Would you describe yourself as an athlete?
   1. _____   2. _____   3. _____   4. _____   5. _____
   (absolutely not)   (absolutely yes)

5. What specific goals do you have in sport?_____
   _____

6. Have they changed since the injury? __Yes __No   If yes, how?_____
   _____

7. What is the nature of your injury?_____
   _____

8. What sport were you injured in?_____ How did it happen?_____
   _____

9. When did the injury occur? __/__/__ (before season?, mid-season?, end-season?)

10. Are you encouraged in sport by significant others? _____Yes _____No

11. Do you interpret this support as: ____pressure ___reluctant support ___ just right

12. Who exerts most of the pressure? __self __father __ mother __ coach __other

**Figure 5. Emotional responses of athletes to injury questionnaire
(ERAIQ) (adapted from Smith, Scott, & Wiese, 1990)**

13. How many hours per week were you in practices or competition before the injury?
0-2   3-5   6-10   11-15   16-20   21-25   26-30   31 & over

14. Were you under any recent stress (life changes) before the injury? ___Yes ___ No
If yes, could you please describe? _____
_____

15. Do you have a strong family support system or close friends who know about your injury?
_____ Yes _____No If yes, who are they? (i.e., coach, friend, parents, teammates, others)
_____

16. How have you been feeling emotionally since the injury?
        1. _____   2. _____   3. _____   4. _____

17. How would you rank these emotions in significance as to how you are feeling because of
    the injury? (Rank 12=high 0=low)

Helpless	_____	Angry	_____	Frightened	_____
Tense	_____	Frustrated	_____	Optimistic	_____
Bored	_____	Shocked	_____	In pain	_____
Depressed	_____	Discouraged	_____	Relieved	_____
Other_____			_____		

18. If 0% is no recovery, what percentage of recovery have you made to your preinjury status:
0%   10%:   20%   30%   40%   50%   60%   70%   80%   90%   100%

19. When is your estimated date of return to sport? ___/___/___

20. Do you have fears about returning to sport? ___Yes _____No
        If so, what are they?_____

21 Are you a motivated person for exercise?
1   2   3   4   5   6   7   8   9   10
(not at all)   (extremely)

22. What is your current rehabilitation program?:
        exercise _____ number of times per week _____

23. Are you able to work out on exercise equipment or modalities? ___Yes ___No
If yes, please describe _____
_____

**Figure 5 (Cont'd). Emotional responses of athletes to injury
questionnaire (ERAIQ) (adapted from Smith, Scott, & Wiese, 1990)**

athlete's understandings are accurate.

Information of a subjective nature obtained during the interview (e.g., tendency towards making eye contact with the counselor, energy level, and posture) are considered in addition to the athletes' answers to the interview questions. Sometimes information omitted from the athlete's responses is very important. For example, an athlete suffering from an exercise addiction or an eating disorder will frequently rank weight management and stress management lowest on the list of motivators, perhaps in a conscious or unconscious effort to draw the interviewer's attention away from some major concerns and areas of discomfort.

The POMS or other psychological tests may be used when appropriate, if the counselor is trained in their use. The POMS instrument measures several aspects of mood state, and has been used in other sport and medical research and practice. The results from this test provide objective quantitative data to support the emotional response findings on the ERAIQ. On occasion, high depression, tension, and anger scores have been seen in injured athletes, prompting a referral—with the patient's permission—to a psychologist or psychiatrist for therapeutic intervention. Most often mood disturbance, measured objectively on the POMS, is moderate and simply supports the mood state identified on the ERAIQ. However, more elevated depression, tension, and anger scores, reinforced by the ranking of emotional responses on the ERAIQ, provide a blueprint for counseling intervention.

Again, assessment of the injured athlete is based on a review of the medical findings, the treatment plan (contingent upon severity of injury), the interview (ERAIQ), subjective findings, and any appropriate psychometric testing. Emphasis is also placed on how the athlete's personality, history of stressors, and coping resources might influence the post-injury emotional response. Personality vulnerabilities, frequent and intense life stressors, and poor coping skills do not disappear when injury occurs; rather, they may become exacerbated, and injury may be the last link in a culmination of events.

The most significant factor that determines the magnitude of emotional response related to sport injury appears to be the athlete's perception about the severity of the injury and its consequences (Smith, Scott, O'Fallon, & Young, 1990). Typically, the most seriously injured athletes will demonstrate the most significant emotional response. An example of this is seen in the following case, which also serves to illustrate how the assessment criteria discussed above may be incorporated by the counselor.

Case 3: This athlete was a high school senior from the southwestern United States. He excelled in baseball, football, and basketball. His older brother had received numerous college scholarship offers in several sports, but was seriously injured during his senior year and regretted being unable to accept one. During the athlete's sophomore year he sustained a foot injury that was diagnosed as a ligament sprain. He played on the foot all season, despite the pain. Later it was discovered that the foot had been fractured, and continued use over the season made surgery necessary. Despite surgery, pain and swelling lingered. Some months later, he was injured again, this time by a jealous teammate, and seriously damaged his shoulder. In spite of his doctor's and therapist's rigorous efforts, he failed to respond to therapy and was referred to our sports medicine center. On clinical examination, the physicians found the shoulder sore and the range of motion impaired. Consultation was made with the sports counselor to assess the psychosocial impact of injury. It was apparent from the onset of consultation that the injury had tremendous psychosocial impact on this young athlete. He was the second son and according to his coaches was a "gifted athlete". He often scored nearly 75% of his team's total points per game in basketball and gained at least half of the total team yardage in football. In baseball, his defensive play at third base and his offensive production kept the team together. His dream had been to be a professional athlete, and he wanted a college scholarship. The shoulder injury "robbed" him of his junior season, which was very crucial as he felt this was "when scouts notice ball players." He was very depressed and angry. He described himself as "straight" (i.e., someone who did not attend parties involving alcohol or drugs), and he felt totally left out of any peer group when he could not play and help the team. During our interview, his affect was flat, and he sat slouched in the chair, unable to make eye contact. It became increasingly apparent that he was very depressed and was unable to assure me that he would not harm himself before our next visit. I suggested he see our sports psychiatrist. He resisted, stating he was tired of doctors. I asked him to complete the POMS to obtain objective data to support our interview findings (which followed the ERAIQ) and my subjective observations. His resulting mood scores were depression = 49; tension = 37; and anger = 35. These negative mood state scores were significantly higher than college norms and than those observed in our study (Smith, Scott, O'Fallon, & Young, 1990) for seriously injured athletes (in which the mean scores were depression = 23.1; tension = 19.1; and anger = 19.1). When these findings were integrated with his highly self-motivated personality, the stress of physical and emotional violation, pressure from parents and coaches, a lost season in his preferred sport, pain and reduced range of motion, and the lack of a supportive peer group, it was apparent that profound mood disturbance existed. Somewhat reluctantly, he granted me permission to discuss the situation with his parents. They agreed that a consultation with our sports psychiatrist was appropriate. I wondered if the physicians might feel that he was a candidate for short-term intensive psychotherapy and possibly a course of antidepressant drugs. However, he failed to keep his appointment with the psychiatrist. His reluctance may have been related to his determination not to give in to weakness (Carmen et al., 1968), a negative view of emotional illness (Pierce, 1969), or a fear of discrimination (Linder et al., 1989). It may also be that he had simply lost hope. Fortunately, he returned one week later to see me, and we worked through several other major issues. He was provided with support, coping skill interventions, homework, some inspirational reading, and hope. When he returned for his final visit one month later, his affect, shoulder, and POMS scores all showed marked improvement. Although professional licensed psychotherapy was offered, the patient declined and fortunately seemed to work through this situational depression with the support of both family and the nurse counselor.

Counseling Interventions

Referrals to the sports counselor may involve preoperative, postoperative or nonoperative counseling; each requiring different emphases. Overall, the pre- and postoperative counseling sessions are ordered by the physician, and counseling interventions are based on the athlete's injury and concerns that are identified from the medical history and guided interview (ERAIQ). Most sports medicine surgical and nonsurgical rehabilitation programs require a great willingness on the part of the patient to commit a large amount of time and energy to regaining pre-injury status. The flexibility and strengthening exercises are often demanding and force athletes to push through pain and swelling, while adhering to rigorous appointment schedules or, equally as difficult, maintaining the motivation to exercise on their own. The goals of each individual athlete are integrated with the reality of the injury, the potential for rehabilitation and any short or long-term limitations. The counselor must decide which strategies will help athletes cope psychologically with present and future events.

Preoperative Consultation

In preoperative counseling the primary focus should be on helping the athlete to understand the goals of the forthcoming surgical procedure and on the developing or strengthening the commitment to rehabilitation. Athletes are asked to make decisions about anaesthetic choices, pain management, and certain aspects of the rehabilitation regimen that will follow. Aspects of attribution theory (Weiner, 1974), which explain differential tendencies to account for behavior outcomes, may be described to athletes in order to emphasize the need for intrinsic motivation for rehabilitation. Athletes should be made aware that much of the potential for successful rehabilitation is under their control. Specifically, athletes are encouraged to become involved in their own stress management, pain control, and motivation and to assist the sports medicine team in setting and revising daily rehabilitation goals.

This attributional approach appeals to the problem-focused athlete as it increases the athlete's sense of control. However, in spite of helping the athlete exercise control over some aspects of post-injury experience, it is also important to discuss prospective issues of dependency, helplessness, and potential lapses in motivation that occur during the long rehabilitation process (Dishman, 1985; Duda et al., 1989; Fisher, Domm, & Wuest, 1988). Practical issues such as dealing with six weeks on crutches or in casts, transportation to rehabilitation sessions, and boredom resulting from repetitive performance of exercise routines are also addressed.

A goal-setting model used for rehabilitation can be applied (Smith, 1991). Following an interview, it is helpful for the counselor to draw a target model and insert the individual athlete's dream goal and rehabilitation program. The "target model" (see Figure 6) has appeal to injured athletes and integrates long-, intermediate- and short-term or daily goals. In the outer ring the "dream goal" is inserted, which serves to stimulate

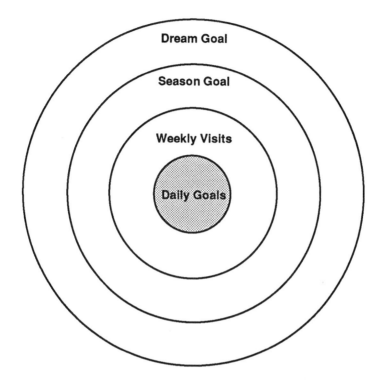

**Figure 6. Target approach for goal setting
(adapted from Smith, 1991)**

motivation. Nestled inside can be any number of rings. The center is always anchored with the bull's eye, which is darkened to attract the eye. The model is bidirectional in the sense that having a dream provides the inspiration to meet daily goals but only by doing the daily exercises will athletes return to sport and fulfill their dreams.

For example, the counselor can explain that during the postsurgical rehabilitation of an anterior cruciate ligament reconstruction, the postoperative course to recovery might resemble a "rum line in sailing". Just as a sailor tacks back and forth across the wind in order to progress to the destination, so will the injured athlete experience physical and psychosocial ups and downs during the rehabilitation period. Overall, the athlete must always mentally go back to the starting point to see how far he or she has come or how much progress has been made.

1. Find a quiet, comfortably warm room where distractions are minimal.
2. Attention must be focused on something such as your breathing.
3. It is essential to have a passive attitude and to let thoughts and images move through your mind in a passive manner. Gently bring your attention back to the object of focus when your mind wanders.
4. A comfortable position is essential, but you should not be so comfortable that you fall asleep.
5. Instructions:
    a. Sit in a comfortable position and close your eyes.
    b. Contract your muscles as hard as possible, harder yet, for count of 10.
    c. Start by pulling your toes up toward your nose (tightening calves) for a count of 10; tighten quadriceps (thighs); then abdominals; hand grip; biceps and triceps (make a muscle); and then pull your shoulders up toward your ears (muscles are contracted one group at a time starting with the toes).
    d. Feel the relaxation that follows, the warm feet, warm hands.
    e. Allow the muscles to remain deeply relaxed.
    f. Now settle in to the deep breathing phase. The breaths are slow, deep. On the way out say the word "calm".
    g. Allow all the air to escape so that you feel like a deflated balloon. Continue this practice for about 10 minutes. Keep your mind on the movement of air in and out of your lungs, gently bringing your attention back if your mind wanders.
6. Practice this at least once daily. Gradually use it as a form of emotional and arousal control for sport or stressful life situations. Learn how to use it to help you maintain an optimal flow zone for sport.

**Figure 7. Adapted relaxation method
(adapted from Smith, Scott, & Wiese, 1990)**

Relaxation and imagery are used preoperatively to reduce anxiety. The counselor suggests that relaxation and imagery may also be used prior to rehabilitation exercises when it may be appropriate to decrease muscle tension. A sample relaxation exercise that has been used with some success is provided in Figure 7. This technique combines elements of cognitive and physical relaxation, with an emphasis on clearing the mind of distracting thoughts and progressively tensing and relaxing various muscle groups of the body. In addition to the interventions discussed, sources of social support, recent stresses, and any maladaptive coping methods are identified. Issues of school and college grades, drug and alcohol use and abuse, sexuality, and other concerns should be discussed and assistance provided as appropriate. Should risk factors such as single organs, infectious disease, or drug use be identified as risk factors that might endanger the health of the patient or surgical team, they are discussed with both the patient and physician.

Postoperative Consultation
During the first postoperative meeting the counselor may use the ERAIQ and a sport preference inventory to assess the athlete's psychosocial status in relation to the injury. Sometimes this is the first time the counselor and injured athlete have met, whereas at other times it is the postoperative follow-up to the preoperative interview. The interview is therefore conducted accordingly. It is also important at this time to evaluate the athlete's compliance with the actual rehabilitation protocol. The counselor must determine whether progress or lack thereof, relates to the injured athlete's attitude (i.e., motivation, ability and effort) or to complicating factors, such as lack of insurance coverage for rehabilitation services, inadequate access to exercise or rehabilitation equipment, or medical complications such as infections, thrombosis or adhesions.

The counselor should assess stress, social support, and coping skills as well as age group, sex, team and individual sport differences. It is preferable to assess the athlete's mood states, and real and perceived progress on a monthly basis. The counselor must also discuss sleep deprivation and pain management issues. For example, pain and activity restriction due to large braces and immobilizers often interfere with sleep patterns. Other factors associated with athletic injury that have psychosocial ramifications for recovery include interactions with significant others, teammates, coaches, or parents as discussed earlier. These persons may be sources of stress or worry, or conversely towers of strength and support. Additional factors that seem to affect athletes at this stage may relate to loss of recognition (e.g., no rewards or positive feedback) and loss of financial and/or physical independence.

Strategies for intervention must be appropriate to the etiology of the problem. It may be necessary to see injured athletes every few days for a few weeks if they are very depressed. These injured athletes are also referred to a licensed clinical psychologist or a psychiatrist. The physician and physical therapist usually can best determine whether or not a lack of progress is related to factors under the athlete's control. Exercise logs or diaries are often helpful to increase compliance and permit evaluation of the effort exerted.

Nonoperative Consultation

Nonoperative referrals to the sports counselor can be from athletes, physicians, patients, physical therapists, coaches, athletic trainers, athletic directors, or parents. Consultations that are not from physicians should be cleared by the medical directors for appropriateness before the appointment is made with the counselor. These athletes are usually referred for one of the following reasons:

1. To assess the impact of the injury on the athlete for whom surgery is not an appropriate solution. These injured athletes, for example, may have back pain, rotator cuff injuries, patellar-femoral pain, Osgood-Schlatter's disease, or stress fractures.
2. To assess performance decrements or assist with performance enhancement strategies.
3. To determine the athlete's goals, motivation for rehabilitation,and existing pressures.
4. To explore concerns about eating disorders, exercise or substance abuse, fear of failure,or fear of success.
5. To interview injured athletes where pain is chronic and the injury has not resolved.

Some injured athletes have been seen at numerous institutions, have had several surgical procedures, and have pain that remains refractory to treatment; and psychological or psychiatric intervention is glaringly absent in their medical history. Such patients are often frightened of and therefore resistant to psychological intervention. Occasionally they may be less inhibited by an interview with a nurse counselor, but unfortunately, when a more in-depth evaluation by a psychologist or psychiatrist is warranted, these patients often leave the sports medicine center in search of yet another scalpel or surgical cure. Often chronic unresolved pain causes psychosocial issues that become associated with the physical pain. In such cases breaking the cycle of pain should take priority over resolving issues of a psychological nature. Resolution or adaptation to chronic post-injury pain is a very different problem that usually requires a multidisciplinary or holistic approach. Professionals in the pain clinic or pain management center are often consulted to assist in the management of these patients.

As briefly discussed earlier, when appropriate to the situation, the counselor may introduce a variety of strategies such as relaxation, guided imagery, cognitive restructuring (e.g., "channel-clicking," or cognitively switching from the negative talk channel to the positive talk channel), aerobic exercise (e.g, maintaining exercise logs with an emphasis on adherence to a training regimen for general, overall conditioning), and various performance-enhancement strategies (e.g., goal setting, mastery mental rehearsal of sport skills). Strategies to maintain reaction time, such as juggling and acu-vision, mental training programs, and biomechanical analysis of taped videos featuring the athletes in their sport, can be motivating, informational tools (Smith, Scott, & Wiese, 1990). Selected reading that is inspirational and appropriate to the athlete's sport may also be helpful (Wiese & Weiss, 1987).

Because injured athletes often respond to problem-focused coping, they may be engaged in sport-related experiences that interest them, such as participating in self-study programs to obtain coaching certification in the American Coaching Effectiveness Program (ACEP), acting as coordinators of marketing efforts for their teams, providing assistance in coaching younger athletes, reviewing available sports psychology tapes, or reading materials appropriate to their sport and level of participation. In addition, every attempt is made to maintain the athlete's strength and conditioning during the rehabilitation period to ensure readiness to return to sport. The following case study illustrates this strategy.

Case 4. A 17-year-old female high school senior was referred to the sports psychology counselor by the high school athletic director. The injured athlete, whose aspiration was to play college tennis, had developed a vascular necrosis of the hip. Our counseling strategy employed gradual attempts to change her dream from one of playing sport into one of a career in sport management. The athlete ultimately remained involved with sports by organizing a large philanthropic marketing effort for a community sports team, giving a radio interview presenting an athlete's perspective on dealing with injury, and becoming affiliated with a high school athletic director in a clerkship role. After probing her interests further, it was discovered that she also wanted to learn more about coaching. We were able to provide her with the means to become leader-level certified through ACEP. At the time of this writing, she is coaching a youth tennis team and has been accepted to a fine college. We continue to emphasize her sense of self-control over her destiny, and she has responded well to this challenge. Consequently we hope to minimize depressive tendencies that might otherwise occur. Communication of her progress, with her permission, is

ongoing between the high school athletic director and sports medicine team.

Physicians in Sports Medicine

As indicated earlier in Figure 4, physicians are often at the center of the injury treatment team. Consequently, it is of the utmost importance for them to keep abreast of both the physical *and* psychological progress of athletes during recovery. Physicians who treat sport injuries are usually trained in orthopedic surgery, physical medicine and rehabilitation, family practice, or community medicine. The practice of sports medicine, although primarily concerned with sport-related injuries, also encompasses prevention of injury, conditioning, performance enhancement, and other activity-related situations.

Most sports medicine centers try to accomodate injured athletes promptly to ensure accurate, immediate diagnosis and appropriate treatment. Many are equipped to serve as small emergency rooms with diagnostic, suturing, cast application, and cast removal capabilities. Frequently, the injured athlete meets the physician "on the field." The physician will diagnose the injury, explain the treatment options, perform whatever procedures are required, order pain and other medications as appropriate, and consult other members of the sports medicine team as indicated. If the athlete needs physical therapy, has nutritional concerns, or requires psychosocial assessment or counseling, the physician most often writes the orders. In some medical practices, physical therapists or athletic trainers are the first to evaluate the injured athlete, and they consult the physician as appropriate.

In either case, the key for these team members is to acknowledge the psychological reactions and progress of the athlete, and to refer to sport psychology consultants, clinical psychologists, and psychiatrists as needed. A recent survey of sports medicine physicians conducted by Brewer, Van Raalte, and Linder (1991) found that behavioral and psychological problems were perceived by the physicians to occur with some frequency in conjunction with athletic injuries, thus suggesting the importance of having a referral network in place. Physicians were also found to have a moderately positive attitude toward the involvement of sport psychologists in the recovery process as appropriate. As these authors indicated, it is important to continue to build on this perceived value as physicians become more aware of the potential role of sport psychology practitioners as members of the medical team.

Physical Therapists in Sports Medicine

Physical therapists conduct a thorough evaluation of the injured area, determine the exercises or modalities that will be helpful, explain the therapy regimen, and set up goals for rehabilitation. The therapist instructs the injured athlete about when evaluations will be scheduled and accordingly provides appropriate feedback emanating from such evaluation. For example, on postsurgery status the athlete must satisfy prescribed and agreed-upon rehabilitation goals relative to regaining range of motion and strength. Such anticipated progress may be delineated and clarified by the physical therapist who in concert with the physician decides upon treatment modification. Should the athlete not progress as expected, further diagnostic procedures may be indicated. Occasionally, if an aggressive nonoperative therapy program is unsuccessful, a surgical procedure may be indicated. Physical therapists use handouts, anatomical models, and actual demonstrations to instruct their patients. Physical therapists also initiate consultations with other members of the sports medicine team when additional input is in the best interests of the patient.

Psychiatrists and Psychologists

Psychiatrists and clinical psychologists may be consulted directly by physicians, although in the Mayo Clinic program many of these consultations are made on the recommendation of the sport psychology counselor. A telephone call is usually made to the sport psychiatrist regarding the appropriateness of a prospective referral. If the psychiatrist agrees that such intervention is indicated, an appointment is arranged. After the psychiatrist sees the injured athlete, we usually receive a call with a summary of the psychiatric interview and the goals of the recommended treatment regimen. A more detailed copy of the content from the interview is then placed in the confidential file. In this way, members of the sports medicine team who may continue to work with the injured athlete are informed of the basic treatment objectives, thus ensuring a consistent, integrated approach. Feedback from psychologists and dietitians seeing injured athletes occurs in a similar way.

CONCLUDING COMMENTS

Many team members from both the sport and medical communities are involved in the recovery process for injured athletes. Each has unique and, it is hoped, complementary offerings to enhance the injured athlete's physical *and* psychological rehabilitation. It must be emphasized that paramount in the process of rehabilitating the injured athlete is the delicate balance between confidentiality and the need for a holistic integrated sports medicine team approach to the client's care. Respect and empathy for injured athletes dictate the manner in which sports medicine is practiced.

It is also important to review information on academic progress, career goals, and alternative interests in the event that injury severity precludes the athlete's return to sport. Athletes will benefit from working with a sports medicine team that communicates not only among themselves but also with the coach, family, and trainer to insure a safe, productive return to sport.

REFERENCES

Anderson, M.B., & Williams, J.M. (1988). A model of stress and athletic injury: Prediction and prevention. *Journal of Sport and Exercise Psychology, 10,* 294-306.

Brewer, B.W., Van Raalte, J.L., & Linder, D.E. (1991). Role of the sport psychologist in treating injured athletes: A survey of sports medicine providers. *Journal of Applied Sport Psychology, 3,* 183-190.

Carmen, L., Zerman, J.L., & Blaine, G.B. (1968). The use of the Harvard psychiatric service by athletes and non-athletes. *Mental Hygiene, 52,* 134-137.

Cassem, M.H., & Hackett, T.P. (1971). Psychiatric consultations in a coronary care unit. *Annals of Internal Medicine, 75,* 9-14.

Chan, C.S., & Grossman, H.Y. (1988). Psychological effects of running loss on consistent runners. *Perceptual and Motor Skills, 66,* 875-883.

Christman, N.J. (1988). Uncertainty, coping and distress. *Research in Nursing and Health, 11,* 71-82.

Connelly, S.L. (1991). *Injury and self-esteem: A test of Sonstroem and Morgan's model.* Unpublished masters thesis, South Dakota State University, Vermillion.

Dishman, R.K. (1985). Medical psychology in exercise and sport. *Medical Clinics in North America, 69,* 123-142.

Duda, J.L., Smart, A.E., & Tappe, M.K. (1989). Predictors of adherence in the rehabilitation of athletic injuries: An application of personal investment theory. *Journal of Sport and Exercise Psychology, 11,* 367-381.

Eldridge, W.E. (1983). The importance of psychotherapy for athletic-related orthopedic injuries among adults. *International Journal of Sports Psychology, 14*, 203-211.

Fisher, A.C., Domm., M.A., & Wuest, D.A. (1988). Adherence to sports-injury rehabilitation programs. *The Physician and Sportsmedicine, 16*, 47-52.

Folkman, S., & Lazarus, R.S. (1986). Stress responses and depressive symptomatology. *Journal of Abnormal Psychology, 95*, 107-113.

Gordon, S., Milios, D., & Grove, J.R. (1991). Psychological aspects of the recovery process from sport injury: The perspective of sport physiotherapists. *Australian Journal of Science and Medicine in Sport, 23*, 53-60.

Grove, J.R., Stewart, R., & Gordon, S. (1990, October). *Emotional reactions of athletes to knee rehabilitation.* Paper presented at the Annual Meeting of the Australian Sports Medicine Federation, Alice Springs.

Kübler-Ross, E. (1969). *On death and dying.* New York: MacMillan.

Linder, D.E., Pillow, D.R., & Reno, R.R. (1989). Shrinking jocks: Derogation of athletes who consult a sports psychologist. *Journal of Sport and Exercise Psychology, 11*, 270-280.

Little, J.C. (1969). The athletes' neurosis: A deprivation crisis. *Acta Psychiatrica Scandinavia, 45*, 187-197.

Martens, R.M. (1987). *Coaches' guide to sport psychology.* Champaign, IL: Human Kinetics.

McDonald, S.A., & Hardy, C.J. (1990). Affective response patterns of the injured athlete. *The Sport Psychologist, 4*(3), 261-274.

McNair, D., Lorr, M., & Doppelman, L. (1971). *Profile of Mood States Manual.* San Diego: Educational and Industrial Testing Services.

NFL Notebook. (1991, November). St. Paul Pioneer Press, p. 3C.

Pierce, R.A. (1969). Athletes in psychotherapy: How many, how come? *Journal of the American College Health Association, 17*, 244-249.

Rohe, D.E., & Athelstan, G.T. (1982). Vocational interests of persons with spinal cord injury. *Journal of Counseling Psychology, 29*, 283-291.

Scott, S.G. (1984). Current concepts in the rehabilitation of the injured athlete. *Mayo Clinic Proceedings, 59*, 85-90.

Smith, A.M. (1991). *Power play: Mental toughness for hockey and beyond.* Unpublished paper, Mayo Clinic Sports Medicine Center, Rochester, MN 55905. Aynsley M. Smith, Mayo Clinic Sports Medicine Center, Rochester, MN 55905).

Smith A.M., & Milliner E.K. (1991). *Suicide risk in injured athletes.* Manuscript under review.

Smith, A.M., Scott, S.G., O'Fallon, W., & Young, M.L. (1990). The emotional responses of athletes to injury. *Mayo Clinic Proceedings, 65,* 38-50.

Smith, A.M., Scott, S.G., & Wiese, D.M. (1990). The psychological effects of sports injuries: Coping. *Sports Medicine, 9,* 352-369.

Smith, R.E., Smoll, F.L., & Ptacek, J.T. (1990). Conjunctive moderator variables in vulnerability and resiliency research: Life stress, social support and coping skills, and adolescent sport injuries. *Journal of Personality and Social Psychology, 58,* 360-370.

Tunks, T., & Bellissimo, A. (1988). Coping with the coping concept: A brief comment. *Pain, 34,* 171-174.

Weiner, B. (1974). *Achievement motivation and attribution theory.* Morristown, NJ: General Learning Press.

Weiss, M.R., & Troxel, R.K. (1986). Psychology of the injured athlete. *Athletic Training, 21,* 104-109, 154.

Wiese, D.M., & Weiss, M.R. (1987). Psychological rehabilitation and physical injury: Implications for the sports medicine team. *The Sport Psychologist, 1,* 318-330.

Wiese, D.M., Weiss, M.R., & Yukelson, D.P. (1991). Sport psychology in the training room: A survey of athletic trainers. *The Sport Psychologist, 5,* 15-24.

Yarcheski, A., & Mahon, M.E. (1986). Perceived stress and symptom patterns in early adolescents: The role of mediating variables. *Research in Nursing and Health, 9,* 289-297.

Chapter 10

Seeing Helps Believing: Modeling in Injury Rehabilitation

Frances A. Flint
York University

Modeling has been used extensively within sport as an instructional tool for the learning of motor skills and social behavior. The extension of this technique into the realm of sport injury rehabilition affords motivation, injury-rehabilitation information, and behavioral cues for recovering athletes. For athletes who have never experienced a major injury, a key component of a successful recovery involves learning how to cope with the process of rehabilitation and return to competition. Thus, athletes who have already effected a complete recovery from injury are ideal models. Seeing someone similar to you successfully overcome the obstacle of an injury can help an injured athlete believe that recovery is possible. In this sense, "seeing helps believing."

"I thought I was invincible until this happened." Such were the words of a highly recruited, first-year university basketball player as she recounted her reactions to a season-ending knee injury. Never having experienced a major injury before, she suffered through the loss of the image she held of being a physically active, elite level athlete. In addition, the daily exercise and competitive pursuits to which she was accustomed

were now replaced with dependency and physical disability. Consequently, in the hours and days immediately after the injury, despair and
depression dominated the psyche of this injured athlete.

Certainly with the current surgical techniques and rehabilitation programs available, this kind of injury scenario no longer need be considered
devastating and potentially career ending. But what of the psychological
trauma sustained by the injured athlete? How can therapists, coaches, and
teammates support the injured athlete through the difficult periods of
depression and despondency that may result from injury, and aid in the
recovery process? It has been suggested that psychological skills such as
goal setting, visualization, relaxation training, and negative thought
stoppage be used to provide psychological rehabilitation in conjunction
with physical recovery protocols (Feltz, 1984; Gordon, 1986; Weiss &
Troxel, 1986; Wiese & Weiss, 1987). One technique that has been given
minimal attention in the psychological rehabilitation of athletic injuries is
the use of modeling or observational learning.

Modeling has been described as an ideal way to communicate skills,
attitudes, and behaviors through the observation of behavioral or verbal
cues provided by a model (Bandura, 1986a). Modeling has been used
extensively in sport, and teachers and coaches have often relied on this
teaching tool for the transmission of knowledge in motor skill learning
(McCullagh, Weiss, & Ross, 1989; Weiss & Klint, 1987). Thus, athletes
are familiar with observing models either in a live or filmed format for the
purpose of motor skill learning or for the transmission of psychological
information (e.g., motivation). In order to understand the potential
beneficial effects of modeling in a therapeutic context, it is important to
understand common affective reactions to injury and the psychological
needs of recovering injured athletes.

Psychological Reactions to Athletic Injury

When a university-level basketball player was asked how she felt after
suffering a major knee injury she responded,

> That week between the time of the injury and surgery, ...if you
> excuse it—it was hell—because I didn't know what to think... That
> was the worst week I can ever comprehend in my life... my school
> suffered and I was trying to get around campus on crutches. My
> social life suffered with respect to relationships with other people,
> because I was so confused and I was angry...I had so many emotions
> running through my head (Flint, 1991, p. 142).

The athlete also remarked that she was having to contend with an overload of medical information on injury and surgery that she did not understand, while trying to deal with the reality of the sudden end to her playing season. In addition, because she was only a freshman, doubts about whether she would be able to complete a university athletic career were evident.

When a severe injury occurs, it is common that the injured athlete must cope with an excess of medically based information, the loss of physical capability, the emotions of withdrawing from a desired activity, and a dependency on others to fulfil daily needs. At the same time, anxiety about the uncertainty of the future may be exacerbated by the severity of the injury and the limitations imposed by the injury (Lynch, 1988; Purtilo, 1978). All of these experiences and emotions may flood the injured athlete and create confusion and feelings of helplessness (McDonald & Hardy, 1990; Yukelson, 1986). The athlete may minimize or exaggerate the extent of the injury and draw unwarranted conclusions as to the implications of the injury. In addition to irrational thoughts, affective reactions can become influential and may partially determine the actions and behavior of the injured athlete (Rotella, 1988; Yukelson, 1986). Anger, depression, and despair emanating from this sense of loss and confusion may become overwhelming and interfere with the recovery process (Feltz, 1984; Yukelson, 1986).

Thus, the athlete who becomes injured may experience a myriad of emotions that may be detrimental to the recovery process. Helping the athlete deal with these emotions is an important component in the psychological rehabilitation program.

Psychological Needs During Recovery

For athletes who are accustomed to seeking control over opponents and game situations, their own helplessness due to injury can be overwhelming. Specific psychological needs of injured athletes must be satisfied and strategies developed to promote a complete healing process. In the same way that the athlete requires technical information from coaches in order to develop skill, so too the injured athlete needs guidance from physicians, therapists, and others so that the recovery process can be as comprehensive as possible.

Yukelson (1986) has suggested that athletes can overcome injury by employing the same psychological qualities that helped them to excel in their athletic endeavors (e.g., pride, determination, and hard work). Bev Smith, a former Canadian National Women's Basketball team member and All-American, provides an excellent example of this transfer of athletic excellence determination to injury recovery. She had sustained several knee injuries and surgery in her illustrious career and remarked that,

> If you keep your perspective on it and look one day at a time, then that'll come, but, I mean, you have to get up every morning and you have to do your leg weights. It's the most unromantic thing in the morning... a lot of people think comebacks...they see TV documentaries on these athletes who have come back and it's all really spectacular and romantic... but it's not—it's drudgery, it's getting up every morning and doing these small little things, doing the leg weights, doing them at night before you go to bed even though you're tired—those things really pay off (Flint, 1991, p. 151).

Bev's dedication to her injury recovery consisted of the same psychological factors (i.e., goal setting, persistence) as her basketball skill development.

With this in mind, an identification of the specific psychological needs and strategies for recovery must be the first step in the rehabilitation process. Athletes who have recovered from injury consistently identify the same emotions, needs, and factors as helpful in overcoming injury. For instance, taking an active role and responsibility for the recovery process is perceived as being vital (Ievleva & Orlick, 1991; McDonald & Hardy, 1990). Also, having a social support structure either through family, peers, and coaches, other injured athletes, or therapists, provides a valuable foundation from which to tackle the hardships of recovery from injury (Flint, 1991; McDonald & Hardy, 1990; Smith, 1980; Wiese & Weiss, 1987).

Fisher (1990) concurred with the importance of psychological factors in injury rehabilitation and has identified self-confidence as a primary component in this process. According to Fisher, three aspects of self-confidence that become important in the recovery process include *competence, control,* and *commitment.* Competence relates to the feeling that a task can be accomplished successfully and in the instance of an injured athlete this means a successful return to competition. The control aspect describes the athlete's feeling that he or she has the ability to take command of a certain situation such as the rehabilitation program. The last aspect, commitment, refers to the athlete's willingness and capability to stay with a task. Fisher (1990) indicated that, "Any strategy that promotes any of these three ends will increase the likelihood of treatment adherence" (p. 154). Thus, pertinent injury and rehabilitation information and strategies for coping become critical components for increasing the athlete's confidence in a successful recovery from injury.

Much of the information needed by the injured athlete to promote the psychological aspects of recovery can be gained through the use of modeling. Listening to someone like Bev Smith talk about setting daily goals for recovery and dedication to the small details of rehabilitation, seeing another athlete struggle through reconditioning, or hearing a similar other talk about the frustration of injury and the joy related to returning to play can all be influential for the recently injured athlete. This is especially true if the athlete has never before experienced a major injury and has no experience on which to base hopes for recovery. Not knowing what to expect, how to behave under injury conditions, or how to tackle the challenges of recovery may present a quandary for the injured athlete.

Modeling–What is it?

Modeling has long been regarded as a powerful instructional tool for the learning of motor skills and social behaviors (McCullagh et al., 1989). The theoretical strength and empirical support for the effects of modeling make it a viable intervention strategy particularly in the area of sport and exercise.

A number of theories have been forwarded to explain the modeling-behavior relationship. The most consistent efforts have been made by Bandura (1969, 1977, 1986a, 1986b), with social-cognitive theories of modeling being the most popular. This theory proposes that modeling or observational learning is one of the primary modes used by individuals to gain socialization information and cognitive skills. Behaviors, attitudes, and skills can be learned through modeling via behavioral and verbal cues provided by the model (Bandura, 1986a). As the observer views a model, symbolic representation or verbal coding takes place, and these cues are placed in memory. Through this vicariously gained information, judgment criteria are established and new behavioral patterns can be learned. Judgments about capabilities are often comparative in nature and, therefore, seeing someone similar to oneself perform a novel task or particular behavior can enhance the perception about the observer's capacity to recreate the action (Bandura, 1986a).

A number of significant factors help to determine how effective the modeling experience has been and whether the observer will have incentive to copy the modeled behavior. These factors may include physical characteristics of the model (e.g., physique, age, sex); model type (e.g., mastery vs coping); and the number of models. Multiple, diversified models are presented because it is hoped that at least one of the models will demonstrate characteristics similar to the observer and will capture the attention of the observer creating a common bond.

The importance of model/observer characteristics has been stressed by Bandura (1977) and McCullagh et al. (1989). It is proposed that the observer will form a bond with the model through the identification of similarities, and thus, the observer will be more motivated to pay attention to the message the model is conveying (McCullagh et al., 1989). In sport these similarities may relate to playing position, level of competition, or style of play. Therefore, the selection of specific characteristics of the model, creating a "similar other," is critical for effecting behavioral change in observers.

Model similarity is a particularly salient aspect of the observer/model relationship because it may determine if the observer will pay attention to the model. A perfect example of the effect of model/observer similarity was provided by an injured female basketball player who had just undergone anterior cruciate ligament surgery. While watching a videotape of other female basketball players who had experienced the same surgery, she described one of the models who had caught her attention and the reason she had noticed the model. "One of the girls who talked about the pain after coming out of surgery, I had it too. Because I could relate completely to what she was talking about, I understood it" (Flint, 1991, p. 246). Obviously this model had an impact on the observer through the shared experience of pain. This common bond, which had been formed between the two, may have been influential in encouraging the observer to pay attention to the verbal and behavioral cues provided by the model.

Another important aspect of the model/observer relationship is the type of model presented. Model similarity is established through the level of expertise displayed by the model such as a mastery or expert model as compared to a coping model. Mastery or exemplary models demonstrate errorless task execution and show tasks as they are to be performed perfectly (Schunk, Hanson, & Cox, 1987). On the other hand, coping models initially demonstrate negative cognitions and affects and an imperfect performance. Gradually, the coping model demonstrates positive thoughts, high self-efficacy, and strategies needed to overcome problems and improve performance. The use of coping models is particularly pertinent to injury rehabilitation because the injured observer can relate to the stages of recovery demonstrated by the model who is overcoming an injury.

The last factor, the use of multiple, diversified models, has also been demonstrated as effective in the learning of new behaviors and motor skills (Thelen, Fry, Fehrenbach, & Frautschi, 1979). This modeling strategy entails the use of at least two, but possibly more, persons who demonstrate the target behavior. The models should be diverse, however, in terms of personal characteristics (e.g., sex, age) and physical attributes (e.g., size, physical abilities) to increase the likelihood that the observer will be able to identify with at least one of the models. The visible characteristics of the model may result in a psychological bonding effect by the observer because a similarity with the model is recognized. This aspect of bonding may have a motivational effect on the observer and may prompt the observer to expend more effort to "be like" the model. The use of multiple models also provides the observer with more than one exposure to the target behavior, which enhances the opportunity for learning.

When modeling is used as a psychological intervention in therapeutic situations, it is felt that the model/observer relationship will act as a catalyst to effecting a positive approach to the rehabilitation process. By watching the model, injured athletes gain knowledge about rehabilitation, strategies for handling setbacks, and the confidence that, if others can recover from injury, so can they. Feltz (1988) suggests that the effect of modeling resides in experience with the task or behavior: "The less experience one has had with a task or situation, the more one will rely on others to judge one's own capabilities" (p. 427). Thus, athletes injured severely for the first time would be considered extremely naive in terms of what is required to accomplish a complete recovery.

In summary, strong empirical evidence exists for the powerful effects of modeling on performance, cognitions, and emotional responses in observers. In particular, the use of specific strategies such as similar, diversified, and coping modeling has been shown to have enduring beneficial effects in anxiety-producing, clinical, and therapeutic settings. The provision of coping models via videotape presentation may be particularly salient to athletes as they pursue physical rehabilitation after injury. The psychological benefits of watching a similar other recover from injury could have far-reaching effects on effort and persistence in adherence to rehabilitation programs.

Informal and Formal Modeling in the Medical Context
Both informal and formal modeling techniques have been used within

a medical context to bolster the observer's sense that recovery from a serious health threat is possible. In many cases, these observer/model situations occur informally and naturally within a rehabilitation setting as a therapist points out another person with the same injury who is progressing with the rehabilitation process. Often, an athlete who has returned to competition after recovering from a serious injury is identified by coaches or therapists as an example for the injured athlete. This is a form of informal modeling where the main benefit to the observer is a motivational boost, and very little hard data on psychological strategies or ways of overcoming obstacles to recovery is conveyed.

An excellent example of informal modeling was provided by Kerrin Lee-Gartner at the 1992 Winter Olympics, when she won the gold medal in women's downhill skiing. The head coach of the Canadian women's ski team remarked, "It'll make us believe again. It'll make injured skiers like Kate Pace and Lucie LaRoche say, 'I can win again'" (Byers, 1992, p. E18). Kerrin became a model for injured skiers because, despite five knee surgeries and a broken ankle, she was able to recover and win Olympic gold. This is an instance of informal modeling because strategies for recovery were not provided by Kerrin, but rather, a motivational example was set for others to follow.

In order to ensure that pertinent, useful information and strategies for a complete rehabilitation process are being displayed by the model, the modeling process should be formalized. In formal modeling, a situation is created whereby one or more models present specific verbal or visual cues that expose the observer to vicarious experiences, verbal persuasions, and emotional exhortations. Depending on how the modeling experience is structured, all three of these sources of self-confidence information can be presented or one specific source can be isolated and highlighted. In formal modeling, the model/observer situation is created to gain the maximum benefit from the exposure.

For instance, in order to reduce preoperative anxiety, increase postoperative ambulation, and decrease the number of days in the hospital after surgery, newly hospitalized patients can be exposed to postsurgical roommates who demonstrate various coping behaviors (Kulik & Mahler, 1987). The exposure to postoperative sensations and events through a coping model better prepares the observer by providing accurate information on which cognitive appraisal of the situation can be made (Kulik & Mahler, 1987). According to Lazarus (1966) the observer will experience less stress in these situations because the events are now interpreted as less threatening due in a large part to the newly acquired cognitive and behavioral responses. In other words, because of the modeling experience, the preoperative patient now knows what to expect, and this may help alleviate fear.

In order to provide the observer with a maximal amount of pertinent information regarding medical procedures and outcomes, videotape or film modeling may be used to augment therapy in clinical settings (Melamed & Siegel, 1975; Thelen et al., 1979). Recently, videotape modeling was used as a psychological intervention within an athletic population (Flint, 1991). Female athletes who had just undergone a surgical repair of the anterior cruciate ligament in the knee watched a videotape of several coping models. The videotape consisted of interviews with seven basketball players who had all recovered from knee ligament surgery. Six of the players in the videotape were interviewed at various stages of recovery from anterior cruciate ligament surgery extending from 2 weeks to 7 years after surgery. The seventh player was an example of complete progress of a full recovery from a few weeks postsurgery to 16 months after surgery. These players were interviewed in a question-and-answer format describing the playing situation when they were injured, the problems and fears they experienced during their recovery from surgery, and various aspects of their rehabilitation. Heavy emphasis was placed on how they had overcome the problems they faced during recovery and on a positive outlook with respect to their return to a basketball career. At the end of each interview there were scenes of the recovered player demonstrating a total capability to participate during practice and game sessions.

The modeling videotape was seen by the injured athletes on three separate occasions: immediately after surgery, at 2 months after surgery, and at 4 months after surgery. Pertinent insights into the needs of the recovering athletes was provided, and this information provides a guideline for the designing of modeling interventions for athletic injury rehabilitation.

In general, immediately after surgery, the injured athletes tended to notice things that related to the emotions associated with the injury and the surgery. For example, one subject picked out a specific model in the videotape as similar to herself "because when she injured it she said 'F___' and I knew exactly what she was going through because the same thing was going through my mind too!" (Flint, 1991, p. 243). Another recovering athlete commented that she felt comforted knowing "that other basketball players had some of the same feelings about the injury. Even though I feel a lot of support from parents and teammates it is good to know that other injured athletes have similar feelings and that I'm not going crazy" (Flint, 1991, p. 246). Most of the comments initially noticed by the injured athletes who watched the videotape were in some way connected to affective responses to the injury and surgery that were verbalized by the models.

Later, at 2 and 4 months after surgery, the verbal statements and actions of the models that attracted more notice tended to change as the rehabilitation process continued. One injured athlete summed this up perfectly when she said, "Everybody in the tape said something that I could relate to, but it has changed as my rehab. progressed" (Flint, 1991, p. 246). Several of the injured athletes remarked about their recovery and said that some of the statements made by the models meant more to them now that they were experiencing the struggles of rehabilitation. One injured athlete commented that the model who was cycling with one leg and then with both legs caught her attention because "I remember how frustrated I was when I couldn't do a single rotation and finally being able to cycle without any pain and actually sweating!" (Flint, 1991, p. 241). In general, there was an overwhelmingly positive response to the verbalizations and actions of the models, and it appears that a bonding effect did occur between models and observers.

Injured athletes who watched the videotape also provided insight and qualitative information on their perceptions relative to their rehabilitation progress. They were asked to outline the factors that had helped them adhere to the rehabilitation program or the reasons that they had not persisted in their physical rehabilitation. They were also asked to reflect on their experience and discuss what assistance would have been helpful to them in their recovery (i.e., more social support, more advice). It was interesting to note that the injured athletes who watched the videotape appeared to be motivated to adhere to their rehabilitation programs, had knowledge about what had helped them throughout rehabilitation, and were definitive with their needs (e.g., goal setting) during the recovery period. The videotaped modeling experience appeared to have a positive effect on the perceptions of the injured athletes in terms of their ability to handle a physical rehabilitation program.

When combined with the use of the videotape medium, coping models can be effective in reducing fears and anxiety in therapeutic settings. Thelen et al. (1979) supported the efficacy of videotape or film modeling over live modeling because the opportunity to present naturalistic modeling sequences would be difficult or unrealistic in a clinical setting. The videotape format also allows for the reconstruction of the most desirable scenes and the multiple viewing of specific situations or conditions (Anderson, DeVellis, & DeVellis, 1987). This format is versatile in that it affords self-administration by the injured athlete at times when the need is greatest, such as when setbacks occur in the recovery process. In terms of costs, after an initial relatively high expenditure, the videotape becomes an inexpensive tool for augmenting the rehabilitation process. Much support exists in the literature for the use of videotape modeling in therapeutic settings (Anderson et al., 1987; Kendall & Watson, 1981; Thelen et al., 1979).

Information Provided Through Modeling–the Specifics

What information should be provided through formalized modeling experiences? Is there information that would be of prime benefit to the observer and other information that could be harmful? These questions and others related to the modeling experience have been posed in the medical psychology literature (Weinman & Johnston, 1988). Within the dimensions of sport psychology and sports medicine, however, the use of multiple coping models to demonstrate behavior and attitudes conducive to the rehabilitation of athletic injuries is a relatively new strategy. Thus, it is important that direction be sought from allied medical and health fields in order to discern valid content and composition guidelines for modeling interventions in rehabilitation.

In addition to injury and rehabilitation information, common questions asked by injured athletes, parents, and coaches relate to the procedures of surgery, its potential disfiguring effects, and the prospects for complete recovery. Often, the shock of a major injury and the fear of possible surgery create a mental obstruction, and the injured athlete is unable to be receptive to injury information. In some cases, too much information or too many medical technicalities create a cognitive overload situation, and details of the injury are forgotten or misunderstood (Flint, 1991; Samples, 1987). If a videotaped presentation by a former injured athlete, outlining some pertinent injury information, was available through either the physician's or therapist's office, then the injured athlete could refer to it as needed.

Van der Ploeg (1988) provides us with useful information on the perceptions of hospital patients relative to stressful medical situations, and this furnishes guidance on the development of modeling experiences.

He found that hospital patients described the most stressful medical situations and events to include pain, the inability discuss one's problems, and the lack of sufficient information on medical conditions. Thus, information provided to medical patients should be designed to ameliorate these stressful situations. In terms of athletes, the only concrete guidelines concerning patient information comes from Heil (cited in Samples, 1987, p. 174). He stated that the information should include the exact nature of the injury, the procedures and rationale for rehabilitation, the potential obstacles ahead and the means of overcoming them, and the feelings that the athlete may experience through the recovery period. Thus, Heil's recommendations concerning injured athletes are in concert with Van der Ploeg's (1988) research.

Kulik and Mahler (1987) suggest that, in general, the more information a patient has preoperatively about what to expect, the better are the chances of recovery being facilitated. Concerns with this approach of full injury and surgery disclosure are the aspects of fear and the impression of control. If the information provided to the injured athlete is too detailed and graphic, then the fear experienced may be overwhelming, and the athlete will suffer from a feeling of loss of control over the situation. In this case, the stress and fear created by explicit details of the injury and surgery may be greater than the perception that the athlete has of his or her ability to overcome the injury. It is vital that any information provided or psychological interventions applied help injured athletes gain more confidence that they are capable of performing activities that may benefit overall recovery. Gaining insight from a similar other who has successfully rehabilitated an athletic injury could help reduce fear and increase confidence for a complete recovery.

The concept of fear reduction and perceptions of control are two important aspects of information provided to the injured athlete. Few guidelines exist for the composition or content of information designed to reduce stress in medical settings (Johnson, 1984; Wilson, 1981). According to Anderson and Masur (1983), the best kind of information is a combination of sensory and procedural details that can help foster accurate expectations and allow for correct cognitive interpretations of sensations to be experienced. Through this information, both procedural stress (immediate aspects) and outcome stress (long-term factors) can be alleviated (Weinman & Johnston, 1988). The procedural stress relates to details of the surgery (pain, disfigurement), and the outcome stress is associated with the prognosis for a complete recovery. Perhaps in this situation, a previously injured athlete who has recovered from a similar injury can provide valuable information on the immediate effects of injury and surgery, obstacles to be expected, strategies to encourage adherence to rehabilitation, and realistic expectations for future recovery.

Athletes sustaining injury for the first time have no experience on which to base their expectations for a full recovery. Fear of the unknown may result in dysfunctional attitudes on the part of the injured athlete and may delay the recovery process (Rotella & Heyman, 1986). This situation creates the perfect opportunity for vicarious learning from a similar other who can provide an accurate account of the road ahead (Kulik & Mahler, 1987; Weiss & Troxel, 1986; Wiese & Weiss, 1987). Models who provide cues to coping behavior and effective strategies for dealing with challenging or threatening situations are an untapped resource in the rehabilitation of athletic injuries.

SUMMARY

The old adage "Treat the person, not the injury" has specific implications in the rehabilitation of athletic injuries. As we know, the injured athlete will experience a psychophysiological response to trauma, and this dictates that both the physical and psychological needs of the athlete must be considered when designing a rehabilitation protocol (Lynch, 1988; Weiss & Troxel, 1986; Wiese & Weiss, 1987). It is inappropriate to treat tissue damage, but not trauma to the psyche. As Chesterfield remarked, "I find by experience, that the mind and the body are more than married, for they are most intimately united; and when one suffers, the other sympathizes" (cited in Frost, 1971, p. 191).

Recovery from major injury, both physically and psychologically, is a long and arduous process requiring adherence to a comprehensive rehabilitation program. As we know, "compliance may currently be one of the greatest challenges facing the health professions" (Cerkoney & Hart, 1980 cited in Turk, Meichenbaum, & Genest, 1983, p. 177). Any strategies that are effective in encouraging persistence in the face of obstacles to recovery are vital components of any rehabilitation protocol. One of the most effective means of conveying information and psychological strategies for injury rehabilitation that may be helpful to the recovering athlete is modeling, and, after all, "now that I have seen that others can recover from serious injury, then so can I!"

REFERENCES

Anderson, L.A., DeVellis, B.M., & DeVellis, R.F. (1987). Effects of modeling on patient communication, satisfaction, and knowledge. *Medical Care, 25,* 1044-1056.

Anderson, K.O., & Masur, F.T. (1983). Psychological preparation for invasive medical and dental procedures. *Journal of Behavioral Medicine, 6,* 1-40.

Bandura, A. (1969). *Principles of behavior modification.* New York: Holt, Rinehart & Winston.

Bandura, A. (1977). Self-efficacy: Toward a unifying theory of behavioral change. *Psychological Review, 84,* 191-215.

Bandura, A. (1986a). *Self-efficacy mechanism in psychological activation and health-promoting behavior.* Stanford University, Department of Psychology, Stanford, CA.

Bandura, A. (1986b). *Social foundations of thought and action: A social cognitive theory.* Englewood Cliffs, NJ: Prentice-Hall.

Byers, J. (1992, February 16). Canadian ski gold an inspiration to others. *The Toronto Star,* p. E18.

Feltz, D.L. (1984). The psychology of sports injuries. In P.F. Vinger & E.F. Hoerner (Eds.), *Sports injuries: The unthwarted epidemic* (2nd ed., pp. 336-344). Littleton, MA: PSG.

Feltz, D.L. (1988). Self-confidence and sports performance. In K.B. Pandolf (Ed.), *Exercise and sport sciences reviews* (Vol. 16, pp. 423-457). New York: Macmillan.

Fisher, C.A. (1990). Adherence to sports injury rehabilitation programmes. *Sports Medicine, 9,* 151-158.

Flint, F.A. (1991). *The psychological effects of modeling in athletic injury rehabilitation.* (Doctoral dissertation, University of Oregon, 1991). (Microform Publications No. BF 357).

Frost, R.B. (Ed.). (1971). *Psychological concepts applied to physical education and coaching* (pp. 191-210). Reading, MA: Addison-Wesley.

Gordon, S. (1986, March). Sport psychology and the injured athlete: A cognitive-behavioral approach to injury response and injury rehabilitation. *Science Periodical on Research and Technology in Sport, BU-1,* 1-10.

Iveleva, L., & Orlick, T. (1991). Mental links to enhanced healing: An exploratory analysis. *The Sport Psychologist, 4,* 25-40.

Johnson, M. (1984). Dimensions of recovery from surgery. *International Review of Applied Psychology, 33*, 505-520.

Kendall, P.C., & Watson, D. (1981). Psychological preparation for stressful medical procedures. In C. K. Prokop & L.A. Bradley (Eds.), *Medical psychology: Contributions to behavioral medicine* (pp. 198-218). New York: Academic Press.

Kulik, J.A., & Mahler, H.I. (1987). Effects of preoperative roommate assignment on postoperative anxiety and recovery from coronary-bypass surgery. *Health Psychology, 6*, 525-543.

Lazarus, R.S. (1966). *Psychological stress and the coping process.* New York: McGraw-Hill.

Lynch, G.P. (1988). Athletic injuries and the practicing sport psychologist: Practical guidelines for assisting athletes. *The Sport Psychologist, 2*, 161-167.

McCullagh, P., Weiss, M. R., & Ross, D. (1989). Modeling considerations in motor skill acquisition and performance: An integrated approach. In K.B. Pandolf (Ed.), *Exercise and sport sciences reviews* (Vol. 17, pp. 475-513). Baltimore: Williams & Wilkins.

McDonald, S.A., & Hardy, C.J. (1990). Affective response patterns of the injured athlete: An exploratory analysis. *The Sport Psychologist, 4*, 261-274.

Melamed, B.G., & Siegel, L.J. (1975). Reduction of anxiety in children facing hospitalization and surgery by use of filmed modeling. *Journal of Consulting and Clinical Psychology, 43*, 511-521.

Purtilo, D.T. (1978). *Health professional/patient interaction* (2nd ed.). Philadelphia: Saunders.

Rotella, R.J. (1988). Psychological care of the injured athlete. In D.N. Kulund (Ed.), *The injured athlete* (2nd ed., pp. 151-164). Philadelphia: Lippincott.

Rotella, R.J., & Heyman, S.R. (1986). Stress, injury and the psychological rehabilitation of athletes. In J.M. Williams (Ed.), *Applied sport psychology: Personal growth to peak performance* (pp. 343-364). Palo Alto, CA: Mayfield.

Samples, P. (1987). Mind over muscle: Returning the injured athlete to play. *The Physician and Sportsmedicine, 15*(10), 172-180.

Schunk, D.H., Hanson, A.R., & Cox, P.D. (1987). Peer-model attributes and children's achievement behaviors. *Journal of Educational Psychology, 79*, 54-61.

Smith, R. (1980). Development of an integrated coping response through cognitive-affective stress management training. In C.H. Nadeau, W.R. Halliwell, K.M. Newell, & G.C. Roberts (Eds.), *Psychology of motor behavior and sport: 1979* (pp. 54-72). Champaign, IL: Human Kinetics.

Thelen, M.H., Fry, R.A., Fehrenbach, P.A., & Frautschi, N.M. (1979). Therapeutic videotape and film modeling: A review. *Psychological Bulletin, 86,* 701-720.

Turk, D.C., Meichenbaum, D., & Genest, M. (1983). *Pain and behavioral medicine*. New York: Guilford Press.

Van der Ploeg, H.M. (1988). Stressful medical events: A survey of patients' perceptions. In S. Maes, C.D. Spielberger, P.B. Defares, & I.G. Sarason (Eds.), *Topics in health psychology* (pp. 193-203). New York: Wiley.

Weinman, J., & Johnston, M. (1988). Stressful medical procedures: An analysis of the effects of psychological interventions and of the stressfulness of the procedures. In S. Maes, C.D. Spielberger, P.B. Defares, & I.G. Sarason (Eds.), *Topics in health psychology* (pp. 205-217). New York: Wiley.

Weiss, M.R., & Klint, K.A. (1987). "Show and tell" in the gymnasium: An investigation of developmental differences in modeling and verbal rehearsal of motor skills. *Research Quarterly for Exercise and Sport, 58,* 234-241.

Weiss, M.R., & Troxel, R.K. (1986). Psychology of the injured athlete. *Athletic Training, 21,* 104-109, 154.

Wiese, D.M., & Weiss, M.R. (1987). Psychological rehabilitation and physical injury: The role of the sports medicine team. *The Sport Psychologist, 1,* 318-330.

Wilson, J.F. (1981). Behavioural preparation for surgery: Benefit or harm. *Journal of Behavioural Medicine, 4,* 79-102.

Yukelson, D. (1986). Psychology of sport and the injured athlete. In D.B. Bernhardt (Ed.), *Clinics in physical therapy* (pp. 175-195). New York: Churchill Livingstone.

Chapter 11

The Use Of Imagery In the Rehabilitation of Injured Athletes*

Lance B. Green
Tulane University

This chapter provides an educational text that (a) cites existing literature supporting a mind-body paradigm for rehabilitation from psychophysiological and psychomotor perspectives, (b) demonstrates the application of imagery techniques within the chronology of an athletic injury, and (c) describes the performance-related criteria to which an athlete can compare his or her progress during rehabilitation. The chronology includes the period preceding the injury, the attention given to the athlete immediately following the injury, and the subsequent rehabilitation program leading to the return of the athlete to practice and competition. Examples of imagery experientials are used to illustrate its application throughout the chronology.

Note: From "The Use of Imagery in the Rehabilitation of Injured Athletes" by L. B. Green, 1992, *The Sport Psychologist*, (Vol. 6, No. 4), pp. 416-428, Copyright 1992 by Human Kinetics Publishers, Inc. Reprinted by permission.

A recent study conducted by Wiese, Weiss, and Yukelson (1991) reported that athletic trainers support the use of psychological strategies when dealing with injury rehabilitation of athletes. Listening to coaches and trainers, intrinsic motivation on the part of the athlete, and social support were identified as key strategies and skills in the recovery process. It was also reported that the use of imagery was not perceived as important relative to the other techniques.

Weise et al. (1991) indicated that the reluctance on the part of trainers to advocate the use of imagery techniques may have resulted from their not feeling qualified to use such techniques and/or not believing in their efficacy. It may be important to educate health professionals involved with the rehabilitation of injured athletes about the "why and how to" of imagery techniques.

Perspectives on Mind-Body Integration
In most cases, athletes are currently left with a rehabilitation program housed in the traditional confines of a medical model that does not include a mind-body orientation. That the athlete may have the capacity to expedite recovery with the use of cognitive strategies such as imagery does not seem to be recognized to the degree that it should be. The purpose of this treatise is to provide an educational text that (a) cites existing literature that supports a mind-body paradigm for rehabilitation from psychophysiological and psychomotor perspectives, (b) demonstrates the application of imagery techniques within the chronology of an athletic injury, and (c) describes the performance-related criteria to which an athlete can compare his or her progress during rehabilitation.

Psychophysiological Perspectives
Substantial evidence exists that speaks to the credibility of using a mind-body approach in explaining human existence and the intricacies of the healing process. By viewing the human being as a package that contains a constant interchange between mental and physiological functions, one recognizes the interdependence of one's actions. Historically, patients' beliefs about the efficacy of the treatment they received and their own input into the process have been at the forefront of both Chinese and Navajo practices (Porkert, 1979; Sandner, 1979). Indeed, Gardner (1985) speaks of multiple intelligences that an individual possesses to varying degrees. One of these is the "body-kinesthetic intelligence... the ability to use one's body in highly differentiated and skilled ways." These "skilled

ways" include "the body being trained to respond to the expressive powers of the mind" (p. 206). At the cornerstone of this position, however, lies the principle of homeostasis advanced by Cannon (1932, cited in Ievleva & Orlick, 1991), which establishes "a process of interaction between the brain and the body toward maintaining internal stability."

Green, Green, and Walters (1979) adhere to what they call the psycho-physiological principle. It suggests that for every physiological change that occurs in the body, there is an appropriate change in the mental-emotional state. They also suggest that the converse of this phenomenon is equally true. Others have established that imagery triggers similar neurophysiological functions as does actual experience (Leuba, 1940; Perky, 1910; Richardson, 1969).

Surgent (1991) suggests that there is a mind-body connection that facilitates the healing process. He indicates that

> your immune system doesn't work alone... your mind also has a voice in what goes on. There is a communication network between your brain and your immune system, like telephone lines between a general and his field commanders... . Feelings, attitudes, and beliefs are organized in your brain and communicated to your immune system by chemical messengers. These can have an effect on the healing process which can be either positive or negative. (pp. 4-5)

This claim has been substantiated by findings reported by Hall (1983), who revealed an increased immune response when he tested the effects of hypnosis and imagery on lymphocyte function. The most recent support for the interplay between the use of imagery and immune system responses has been reported by Achterberg (1991), AuBuchon (1991), and Post-White (1991). They have provided evidence that describes the positive effects the immune system experiences when triggered by imagery.

Literature pertaining to psychoneuroimmunology further establishes the plausibility of the mind-body paradigm during rehabilitation. Achterberg, Matthews-Simonton, and Simonton (1977), as well as Fiore (1988), have reported that certain psychological characteristics of patients influenced recovery from cancer. Simonton, Matthews-Simonton, and Creighton (1978) provide evidence that supports the use of imagery in the treatment for cancer. Others have reported positive effects of the use of imagery during the rehabilitation of various illnesses and injuries such as psoriasis (Gaston, Crombez, & Dupuis, 1989); stress management (Hanley & Chinn, 1989); ulcers, paraplegia, fractures, hip disarticulations, and intra-abdominal lesions (Korn, 1983).

In addition, a large number of studies have indicated that the use of imagery produces physiological responses such as salivation (Barber, Chauncey, & Winer, 1964), increase in pupillary size (Simpson & Paivio, 1966), increased heart rate (May & Johnson, 1973), changes in electromyograms (Sheikh & Jordan, 1983), increases in blood-glucose, inhibition of gastrointestinal activity, and changes in skin temperature (Barber, 1978).

Taken to its logical end, it may be worth considering that when one takes physiologic measurements, one is in fact taking corresponding psychological indicators simultaneously. The results reported may depend entirely on the category of measurement being taken and the perspective from which the investigator originates, for example, psychology, physiology, psycho-physiology.

The possibility exists that the specialization in professional orientation prevalent in today's scientific community is merely part of the lasting ripple effect created by the Cartesian medical model and does nothing but perpetuate an all too narrow perspective from which to draw conclusions concerning the human condition. As a consequence, the thoughts of Diderot from the middle 18th century may be applicable today. He spoke of the intentional that time of scholars to reinstate holism as an appropriate perspective for medicine so that it "may be advanced to the point of where it was two thousand years ago" (cited in McMahon & Sheikh, 1986, p.12).

Psychomotor Perspectives

From a sport psychology perspective, it appears that there is, at the very least, a logical leap from the relationship between imagery and sport performance to the impact of imagery on the healing process of injuries. The concept that the use of mental rehearsal facilitates the execution of certain motor skills under certain conditions is well documented (for reviews see Corbin, 1972; Feltz & Landers, 1983).

In addition, Hecker and Kaczor (1988) have summarized existing theoretical models that have been advanced to explain the processes involved with mental imagery and its influence on athletic performance, for example, motor skill development. These include (a) the symbolic learning theory that posits that symbolic rehearsal advances the development of skills requiring cognitive processes (Sackett, 1935); (b) the psychoneuromuscular theory associated with Jacobsen's work (1938), which identified muscular innervations during imagery that are similar to those occurring during actual performance; (c) the attention-arousal set that integrates cognitive and physiological aspects of rehearsal in order to distinguish between relevant and irrelevant cues (Feltz & Landers, 1983; Vealey, 1987); and (d) the bioinformational theory of Lang (1979) in which imagery processes the stimulus characteristics of an imagined scenario and the physiological/behavioral responses that accompany them.

Other models such as Greene's (1972) multilevel hierarchical control of motor programs and Pribram's (1971) two-process model of imagery have been applied to the development of motor programs and further describe the interdependence of mind and body. Greene maintains that a motor movement is the result of a mind-body system composed of a number of levels. The higher levels initiate a "ballpark" motor response to environmental input that is then refined by lower levels of neuromuscular processing. The result is the motor movement that meets the requirements of the task.

Pribram's two-process model of imagery includes neuropsychological processes identified as TOTE and TOTEM systems. The TOTE system refers to the exchange of feedback and feed-forward mechanisms between the environment and the organism in order to produce movement. The TOTEM system is an application of these processes in which images conduct TOTE operations on each other exclusively within the mental environment.

It seems reasonable to suggest, therefore, that the same models used to explain psychophysiological and psychomotor processes used in athletic performance can be applied when describing the place of imagery during the rehabilitation associated with the healing of athletic injuries, for example, the reestablishing of fine and gross motor movements, the reestablishing of psychoneurological pathways. However, as Hecker and Kaczor (1988) have indicated, when each of these theories is taken alone, it proves inadequate in explaining the complex, mind-body process of imagery. Therefore, a more encompassing approach must be advanced such as a "systems theory" suggested by Schwartz (1984).

He maintains that systems theory "has the potential to provide a metatheoretical framework for integrating the biological, psychological, and social consequences of imagery on health and illness" (Schwartz, 1984, p. 35). In describing the synthesis attained by implementing systems theory, he elaborates on the metaprinciples of systems theory.

A system is an entity (a whole) which is composed of a set of parts (which are subsystems). These parts interact. Out of the parts interaction emerge unique properties that characterize the new entity

The Chronology of an Injury	The Potential Use of Imagery
Pre-injury	**Preventive Medicine** • enhances relaxation • facilitates • enhances perspective toward stressors
Immediately Subsequent to Injury	**Developing Awareness** • knowledge base of the injury • what is to be expected during rehabilitation (instant pre-play of rehab program) • maintenance of positive attitudes • reinforce efficacy of treatment • knowledge of potential emotions associated with rehabilitation
During Rehabilitation	**Creating the Mind Set for Recovery** • eliminating counterproductive thoughts • develops "possible selves" • facilitates goal setting • affirmation imagery • performance-related mental rehearsals • rehabilitative imagery • copes with pain • brings closure to the injury

Figure 1. The uses of imagery during rehabilitation.

or system as a whole. These emergent properties represent more than the simple, independent sum of the properties of the parts studied in isolation. It is hypothesized that the emergent properties appear only when the parts are allowed to interact. (p. 39)

Thus, independent theories that appear to be in competition can be integrated into a comprehensive perspective that appears to be both logical and substantiated by scientific evidence. It is proposed that this may provide the necessary body of knowledge from which the education of health professionals (i.e., athletic trainers) may be enhanced. The use of psychophysiological techniques such as imagery may increase once the educational barriers are weakened. It is hoped that this will lead to the use of psychological techniques that go beyond the traditional skills of communication and motivation.

What follows is an example of how the mind-body perspective might be applied in the development of a rehabilitation program for injured athletes. It is offered with the understanding that it is not all-encompassing. However, it should provide a starting point from which sport medicine teams can develop programs of rehabilitation from a mind-body perspective.

The Chronology of an Injury

The following is a chronology of athletic injuries adapted from Nideffer's scheme (1987). Although his scheme included factors related to the onset of the injury as well as the athlete's coping and recovery, this chronology addresses three periods of time associated with injuries: pre-injury, attention to the athlete immediately following the injury, and the rehabilitation program leading to the recovery and re-integration of the athlete into the competitive situation. Each will be described with the intended purpose of demonstrating the application of imagery techniques within the context of an integrated mind-body approach to rehabilitation.

Pre-injury

Any athlete is subject to periods in his or her life during which injury is more likely to occur. In keeping with Selye's (1974) classic work on stress, these periods are characterized by stressors that cause "distress" rather than eustress (an exhilarating and positive force) or stress (that energy necessary for daily existence and the body's search for homeostasis). These agents of distress may be categorized as either General Life or Athletic Stressors.

General Life Stressors may include the transition to college life for incoming freshmen, the homesickness experienced by athletes of all levels, or the feelings of sorrow and anguish that accompany the death of someone close. Athletic stressors might include trouble with a coach, teammate, or fans; loss of playing status; or the athletic event itself (Bramwell, Holmes, Masuda, & Wagner, 1975; Kerr & Minden, 1988; Lynch, 1988; Rotella &

Heyman, 1986). The resultant injury may be the function of the fatigue associated with having to deal with these situations or the divisive effect on concentration the athlete may experience (Kerr & Minden, 1988). Inasmuch as an athlete may experience any of these, or other circumstances that have an adverse effect on the "normal" life pattern, injury is often the result.

As a form of preventive medicine that would serve to lessen the impact of stressors and, thus, reduce the potential for injury, imagery techniques that enhance relaxation and perspective toward specific situations of stress may be developed and implemented throughout the season as circumstances mandate. For example, an athlete may experience stress as the result of homesickness. An imagery experiential can be developed that puts the immediate needs of the athlete in a long-term perspective while enhancing a relaxed state of mind. It could be implemented by introducing a relaxed state, possibly with some form of Jacobsen's (1938) progressive relaxation. This may then be followed by guided imagery intended to gain perspective on the situation. This has also been described by Samuels and Samuels (1975) as developing the ability "to see... to look at an object from different mental points of view, as well as from different vantage points" (p. 115). For example, the following imagery exercise could be administered to athlete subjects:

Imagine yourself as a freshman entering college. As soon as the Thanksgiving break arrives, you can't wait to get on the first plane home. Same for the December/January break. Same for the summer break.

Now, you are a sophomore. When Thanksgiving comes, you definitely want to go home, but now you'll miss some of your college friends. Same for the December/January break. Same for the summer break.

Now, you're a junior. You've established your "place" on campus. You have developed close relationships with both male and female friends. As Thanksgiving break approaches, you weigh the pros and cons of going home or staying on campus. You decide to go home as usual. The same thoughts happen, but not as strongly when December rolls around. But with summer, you make plans to travel with your friends and tell your parents you'll see them when you finish your trip.

Now, you're a senior. Your apartment or room seems more like home to you than your parents' home. Because Thanksgiving and the December break are family occasions, it's your parents who want you home more than you wanting to go. But, still, you go. Then its summertime, and your parents are calling you to come home instead of you calling them. What does it feel like to be self-reliant, self-sufficient?

Attention Immediately Subsequent to the Injury

Once the injury occurs, standard first aid procedures should be followed so that further complications are not created unnecessarily. The athlete should be accompanied to the physician by someone associated with the program (e.g., trainer, coach, sport psychologist, parent) and should be given at least "the illusion of hope" at the outset (Nideffer, 1987).

Once the athlete has seen a physician, there should be an exchange of information concerning the injury between the attending medical personnel, the athlete, the team trainer/physician, and coaches. This should include specifics about the anatomy and physiology of the injured area. By using anatomical models and photographs, the abstraction of the injury is translated into more tangible and recognizable terms. In addition, the injury might be explained in lay terms that facilitate an image, for example, "the rubber bands (ligaments) need to grow back onto the bone." This knowledge is critical as it may be applied to the use of rehabilitative imagery that would be employed later (Surgent, 1991).

Rehabilitation of the Injury

The structure of the rehabilitation program (e.g., an instant pre-play of the program) should be discussed by all parties directly involved as the sports medicine team, for example, trainers, coaches, athletes. This may include the expected time associated with recovery, as well as the general parameters of the physical as well as mental program to be used during rehabilitation. Expectations of the athlete such as appointments with trainers, coaches, and sport psychologists; attendance at practice and games; and the criteria to be used to determine when the athlete is ready to return to practice and competition should also be identified. In addition, who will make the final decision (e.g., the athlete, the coach, the physician) as to the athlete's readiness may also be discussed as part of the criteria used for return (Thomas, 1990).

Of considerable importance are the factors relating to the athlete's adherence to the rehabilitation. These should be identified and discussed with the athlete. It should be pointed out that successful rehabilitation is characterized by specific behaviors associated with adherence to the rehabilitation process. Wiese et al. (1991) have identified the following: (a) the willingness on the part of the athlete to listen to the trainer, (b) the athlete's maintaining a positive attitude, and (c) intrinsic motivation on the part of the athlete. In addition, characteristics described by Duda, Smart, and Tappe (1989) include the athlete's belief in the efficacy of the treatment, the presence of a social support system, and the athlete's orientation toward task-related goals in his or her sport. Imagery experientials in which the athlete envisions the overt behaviors associated with these factors may become an integral part of daily treatments in the training room.

As example of such an application of imagery may be created by adapting the work of Lazarus (1984), who has developed procedures that depict an individual taking psychological risks. Once the behaviors associated with carrying out specific instructions from the trainer, personifying positive attitudes, demonstrating intrinsic motivation, and task-related goal setting are imagined, the athlete is then encouraged to go out and perform them. Finally, Rotella and Heyman (1986) and Lynch (1988) have discussed the application of Kübler-Ross's (1969) work concerning the emotional recovery from the death of a loved one to the athletic setting and the recovering athlete. It is suggested that athletes may experience similar patterns of emotional reaction during their rehabilitation. This might include denial, anger, bargaining, depression, and acceptance. Were an athlete given insight into the process of recovery with imagery depicting each stage, he or she may be able to facilitate the transition from one stage to the next.

For example, an experiential entitled "Time Projection or Time Tripping" (Lazarus, 1984, pp. 131-7) may facilitate the development of an athlete's awareness concerning potential emotional reactions throughout rehabilitation. By projecting him or herself back or forward in time and describing the emotions associated with different stages of rehabilitation from retrospective or futuristic perspectives, the athlete is encouraged to recognize various stages of recovery. For example, the athlete may recognize the possibility of becoming depressed during the rehabilitation. But the athlete may also recognize that depression may be part of the process that eventually leads to recovery.

In summary, the following four examples have been described to demonstrate how imagery might be applied to the first two phases of the chronology of an injury: for the pre-injury phase–(a) relaxation and perspective imagery as preventative medicine; and for the time immediately following the injury–(b) an instant pre-play of the rehabilitation program, (c) attitude and belief imagery, and (d) imagery depicting emotional stages of transition during recovery.

The Mind-Body Rehabilitation Process

The rehabilitation program for athletes should be devised by a sports medicine team composed of the attending physician, the athlete, trainers, coach, and sport psychologist. The resulting program should reflect a mind-body approach to the process of recovery (Gordon, Jaffe, & Bresler, 1984; Peper, Ancoli, & Quinn, 1979). It should address the creation of the appropriate mind set for the recovering athlete as well as the physical dimensions of rehabilitation.

Creating the Mind Set for Recovery

A character named Socrates from Dan Millman's (1984) book *The Way of the Peaceful Warrior* describes the part one's mind plays in creating one's being. Socrates suggests that

"Mind" is one of those slippery terms like "love." The proper definition depends on your state of consciousness... We refer to the brain's abstract processes as "the intellect"... The brain and the mind are not the same. The brain is real, the mind isn't. The brain can be a tool. It can recall phone numbers, solve math puzzles, or create poetry. In this way, it works for the rest of the body, like a tractor. But when you can't stop thinking of that math problem or phone number, or when troubling thoughts and memories arise without your intent, it's not your brain working, but your mind wandering. Then the mind controls you; then the tractor has run wild. (p.62)

In essence, an athlete in rehabilitation must accomplish the same task of getting rid of a mind full of negative and counterproductive wanderings. Only then might the brain be able to do its work. These counterproductive wanderings might include certain fears associated with being injured: the fear of re-injury, the fear of the pain associated with the original injury and/or of that experienced during rehabilitation, the fear of not returning to previous levels of ability, the fear of the loss of status. In addition, Ievleva and Orlick (1991) reported that recovery time for injured athletes was faster for those who did not engage in injury-replay imagery. Thus, athletes must use their intellect to guide the neuropsychological processes of the brain in such a manner as to facilitate recovery.

Developing "Possible Selves"

Upon injury, athletes are faced with what Cantor and Kihlstrom (1987) refer to as a life task. They are immediately confronted with a problem that must be resolved before normal existence can continue. In truth, the athletes must make a conscious effort to redirect their attention from playing the game to playing a new game called rehab. The game in which they must now perform becomes that associated with recovery. They must adopt a mind-set that focuses all of their energies toward that end. The immediate life task then becomes one of rehabilitation. It's a brand-new game that requires a conscious shift of attention that has as its ultimate goal their return to competition.

In addressing the task of goal setting associated with the rehabilitation process, sport psychologists might consider applying the theoretical framework of Markus and Ruvolo (1989). This framework depicts the development of "possible selves." Their notion of developing possible selves addresses the potential for "personalized representations of goals" (p. 211). They discuss goal setting in terms of "constructing a possible self in which one is different from the now self and in which one realizes the goal" (p. 211). Thus, a progression of possible selves assists in developing the working self-concept (Markus & Kunda, 1986; Markus & Nurius, 1986).

What is critical is the ability of the athletes to formulate and maintain the possible selves that lead toward the desired goal. They must be able to repress possible selves that are inconsistent with the task of recovery, for example, a possible self depicting injury-replay or negative attitudes. The desired possible selves might depict the athlete as an individual having a positive outlook, descriptive self-talk, or performance-related goals. As a number of authors have suggested, the athlete should engage in affirmation imagery that portrays him or her fulfilling short-term goals (Ievleva and Orlick, 1991; Korn & Johnson, 1983). To the extent that they are able to accomplish these tasks the athlete's behavior will be "focused, energized, and organized by this possible self" (Markus & Ruvolo, 1989, p.214).

For example, imagery scenarios could be patterned after the work of Maxwell Maltz concerning the self-image. Ishii (1986) describes a number of provocative experientials that focus on developing positive, assertive, and successful self-images as well as attitudes pertaining to happiness and willpower. One in particular places the client in an empty theater. From this setting, the client is asked to imagine a movie unfolding in which he or she handles a problem successfully. Another technique requires that the client visualize an unerasable chalkboard on which he or she lists past successes.

The task of the sport psychologist then becomes the creation of a series of "programmed visualizations" (Samuels & Samuels, 1975, p. 229) that reflect the rehabilitative tasks and outcomes established by the sports medicine team. That possible selves may depict performance goals as well as outcome goals presents the sport psychologist with the task of identifying specific scenarios depicting each. In fact, Bandura (1986, 1988) maintains that performance and outcome selves should be separated.

Korn (1983) agrees that there should be a progression from product to process goals. That is, as an initial step, athletes should imagine themselves as completely recovered and able to do all the things they were capable of doing prior to the injury. Once they have become reasonably proficient at this form of product-oriented image, they may then progress to more specific, process-oriented images.

These process-oriented possible selves should reflect instrumental selves. That is, they should represent a sequence of possible selves that depicts the athlete in the process of performing specific motor skills, each leading to a self that is one step closer to total recovery. In essence, the instrumental possible selves are intended to result in a summation effect, with the eventual result matching or surpassing the initial product oriented image.

For example, a female basketball player undergoing rehabilitation for a knee injury consisting of a torn anterior crutiate ligament with cartilage strains used the following series of possible selves over nine months of rehabilitation.

Possible Self #1—"Knee at 90 degrees, I Want to be a Success Story" (e.g., following surgery, getting out of bed and out of the hospital, establishing image of desired outcome).

Possible Self #2—"Strut Your Stuff" (e.g., getting off crutches, watching other people walk, establishing own gait.

Possible Self #3—"Hurt to get Better" (e.g., progression of physical therapy which included, in part, weight training, electric stimulation, stationary bike, stair master).

Possible Self #4—"Spring Forward" (e.g., running @ 75 %, jumping exercises, increasing work load).

Possible Self #5—"Let's Play" (e.g., pick up games).

Possible Self #6—"Dribble, Drive, and Dive!" (e.g., playing with no fear of failure).

Possible Self #7—"No brace" (e.g., the final stage due to school policy of mandatory use of brace following such an injury.

Other Uses of Imagery

The processes of guided and nondirected imagery can also be utilized by the athlete in the form of relaxation techniques, motor skill rehearsals, and rehabilitative experientials (Surgent, 1991). Rehabilitative imagery has been shown to have significant effects on recovery time (Ievleva & Orlick, 1991). As described earlier during the chronology of an injury, information gathered from the physician concerning the anatomy and physiology of the injury facilitates the use of rehabilitative imagery. In addition, Day (1991) has developed an educational discourse on the im-mune system through the use of cartoon imagery that uses immune cell caricatures to explain the function of each cell involved in the rehabilitation process. Korn (1983) described a technique of rehabilitation imagery that

consists of envisioning the wounds as filling from the inside out rather than just being covered over at the surface. The filling material was cement and the repair process was analogous to the method of repair of a hole in a concrete walkway. (p. 28).

Specific mind-sets that might be addressed through the use of imagery may include the following: maintaining a positive outlook, controlling stress, using positive and descriptive self-talk, and sustaining belief in the rehabilitation process. Performance-related imagery may take the form of mental rehearsal while attending practices and competitions in which the athletes imagine themselves as if they were playing. In addition, imagery has been shown to be effective in coping with pain (Achterberg, Kenner, & Lawlis, 1988; Korn, 1983; Samuels & Samuels, 1975; Simonton et al., 1978; Spanos & O'Hara, 1990).

Rotella and Heyman (1986) recommended the use of videotapes of past performances. This technique may serve to reinforce the symbolic learning and psychoneuromuscular processes. Imagery may also be used to facilitate closure of the rehabilitation process once the athlete has returned to competition.

Physical Rehabilitation

The use of targeted performance criterion facilitates the athlete's return to pre-injury performance levels on specific tasks associated with the individual's sport. Such criterion may also serve as the impetus for creating specific instrumental and performance-related possible selves. The groundwork for this, however, must be laid at the onset of training prior to the season and, most certainly, prior to injury.

At the beginning of the season's training, baseline data should be gathered for the athletes on specific tasks associated with their training such as maximum weight, sets, and repetitions for a variety of weightlifting routines; range of motion measurements for flexibility; physiologic parameters such as heart rate, time of recovery, max VO_2 for endurance; and recorded times on specific distances for indication of speed. These data provide the target criteria to which athletes can compare their progress during rehabilitation.

In addition, a functional progression of specific sport skills should be identified that represent being back to the athlete. For example, baseball pitchers who have been out with elbow injuries may wish to use a particular pitch (e.g., breaking off a hard slider) to gauge effectiveness upon return. Tennis players may engage in the side shuffle used on the base line as an indicator that they have recovered from the pain associated with shin splints.

Each of these tasks, in addition to other methods of progressive resistance exercises and cross-training, forms the foundation for physical rehabilitation with tangible indicators of recovery. Of course, these are undertaken in proper sequence relative to the initial training room duties prescribed by the trainers and physician (e.g., whirlpool, electrical stimulation, iced therapy).

SUMMARY

Wiese et al. (1991) have reported that many athletic trainers agree with the need for further education in the area of psychology and, in particular, for methods that can be applied in the athletic setting. The purpose of this treatise has been to provide an educational text that supports a mind-body paradigm for rehabilitation from psychophysiological and psychomotor perspectives, demonstrates the application of imagery within the chronology of an injury, and describes performance-related criteria used in physical rehabilitation. The chronology includes that period preceding the injury, the attention given to the athlete immediately following the injury, and the subsequent rehabilitation program leading to the return of the athlete to practice and competition. It is suggested that imagery techniques may be applied during the pre-injury stage as a tool for preventive maintenance. During the actual rehabilitation program, its purpose is (a) to facilitate the healing process, (b) to promote the development of a positive and relaxed outlook toward recovery, (c) to create the mind set required for optimum performance, and (d) to bring closure to the injury experience.

REFERENCES

Achterberg, J. (1991, May). *Enhancing the immune function through imagery.* Paper presented to the Fourth World Conference on Imagery, Minneapolis, MN.

Achterberg, J., Kenner, C., & Lawlis, G.F. (1988). Severe burn injury: A comparison of relaxation, imagery and biofeedback for pain management. *Journal of Mental Imagery, 12*(1), 71-88.

Achterberg, J., Matthews-Simonton, S., & Simonton, O.C. (1977). Psychology of the exceptional cancer patient: A description of patients who outlive predicted life expectancies. *Psychotherapy: Theory, Research, and Practice, 14*, 416-422.

AuBuchon, B. (1991, May). *The effects of positive mental imagery on hope, coping, anxiety, dypsnea, and pulmonary function in persons with chronic obstructive pulmonary disease: Tests of a nursing intervention and a theoretical model.* Paper presented to the Fourth World Conference on Imagery, Minneapolis, MN.

Bandura, A. (1986). *Social foundations of thought and action: A social cognitive theory.* Englewood Cliffs, NJ: Prentice-Hall.

Bandura, A. (1988). Self-regulation of motivation and action through goal systems. In V. Hamilton, G.H. Bower, & N.H. Frijda (Eds.), *Cognitive Perspectives on Emotion and Motivation* (pp. 37-61). Dordrecht: Kluwer Academic Press.

Barber, T.X. (1978). Hypnosis, suggestions and psychosomatic phenomena, a new look from the standpoint of recent experimental studies. *The American Journal of Clinical Hypnosis, 21*, 13-27.

Barber, T.X., Chauncey, H.M., & Winer, R.A. (1964). The effect of hypnotic and nonhypnotic suggestions on parotid gland response to gustatory stimuli. *Psychosomatic Medicine, 26*, 374-380.

Bramwell, S.T., Holmes, T.H., Masuda, M., & Wagner, N.N. (1975). Psychosocial factors in athletic injuries: Development and application of the social and athletic readjustment rating scale (SARRS). *Journal of Human Stress, 1*(2), 6-20.

Cannon, W. B. (1932). *The wisdom of the body.* New York: Norton.

Cantor, N., & Kihlstrom, J. (1987). *Personality and social intelligence.* Englewood Cliffs, NJ: Prentice-Hall.

Corbin, C. (1972). Mental practice. In W. Morgan (Ed.), *Ergogenic aids and muscular performance* (pp. 93-118). New York: Academic Press.

Day, C.H. (1991). *The immune system handbook.* North York, Ontario: Potentials Within.

Duda, J.L., Smart, A.E., & Tappe, M.K. (1989). Predictors of adherence in the rehabilitation of athletic injuries: An application of personal investment theory. *Journal of Sport & Exercise Psychology, 11,* 367-381.

Feltz, D.L., & Landers, D.M. (1983). The effects of mental practice on motor skill learning and performance: A meta-analysis. *Journal of Sport Psychology, 5,* 25-27.

Fiore, N.A. (1988). The inner healer: Imagery for coping with cancer and its therapy. *Journal of Mental Imagery, 12*(2), 79-82.

Gardner, H. (1985). *Frames of mind: The theory of multiple intelligences.* New York: Basic Books.

Gaston, L., Crombez, J. & Dupuis, G. (1989). An imagery and meditation technique in the treatment of psoriasis: A case study using an A-B-A design. *Journal of Mental Imagery, 13*(1), 31-38.

Gordon, J.S., Jaffe, D.T., & Bresler, D.E. (1984). *Mind, body, and health: Toward an integral medicine.* New York: Human Sciences Press.

Green, E.E., Green, A.M., & Walters, E.D. (1979). Biofeedback for mind/body self-regulation: Healing and Creativity. In E. Peper, S. Ancoli, & M. Quinn (Eds.), *Mind/body integration: Essential readings in biofeedback.* New York: Plenum Press.

Greene, P.H. (1972). Problems of organization of motor systems. In R. Rosen & F.M. Snell (Eds.), *Progress in theoretical biology* (Vol.2, pp. 304-333). New York: Academic Press.

Hall, H.R. (1983). Hypnosis and the immune system: A review with implications for cancer and the psychology of healing. *American Journal of Clinical Hypnosis, 25*(3), 92-103.

Hanley, G.L., & Chinn, D. (1989). Stress management: An integration of multidimensional arousal and imagery theories with case study. *Journal of Mental Imagery, 13*(2), 107-118.

Hecker, J.E., & Kaczor, L.M. (1988). Application of imagery theory to sport psychology: Some preliminary findings. *Journal of Sport & Exercise Psychology, 10,* 363-373.

Ievleva, L., & Orlick, T. (1991). Mental links to enhanced healing: An exploratory study. *The Sport Psychologist, 5,* 25-40.

Ishii, M.M. (1986). Imagery techniques in the works of Maxwell Maltz. In A.A. Sheikh (Ed.), *Anthology of imagery techniques,* (pp. 313-323). Milwaukee, WI: American Imagery Institute.

Jacobsen, E. (1938). *Progressive relaxation.* Chicago: University of Chicago Press.

Kerr G., & Minden, H. (1988). Psychological factors related to the occurrence of athletic injuries. *Journal of Sport & Exercise Psychology, 10,* 167-173.

Korn, E.R. (1983). The use of altered states of consciousness and imagery in physical and pain rehabilitation. *Journal of Mental Imagery, 7*(1), 25-34.

Korn, E.R., & Johnson, K. (1983). *Visualization: The uses of imagery in the health professions.* Homewood, IL: Dow Jones-Irwin.

Kübler-Ross, E. (1969). *On death and dying.* New York: Macmillan.

Lang, P.J. (1979). A bio-informational theory of emotional imagery. *Psychophysiology, 16,* 495-512.

Lazarus, A. (1984). *In the mind's eye: The power of imagery for personal enrichment.* New York: The Guilford Press.

Leuba, C. (1940). Images as conditioned sensation. *Journal of Experimental Psychology, 26,* 345-351.

Lynch, G.P. (1988). Athletic injuries and the practicing sport psychologist: Practical guidelines for assisting athletes. *The Sport Psychologist, 2,* 161-167.

Markus, H., & Kunda, Z. (1986). Stability and malleability of the self-concept. *Journal of Personality and Social Psychology, 51,* 858-866.

Markus, H., & Nurius, P. (1986). Possible selves. *American Psychologist, 41,* 954-969.

Markus, H., & Ruvolo, A. (1989). Possible selves: Personalized representations of goals. In L.A. Pervin (Ed.), *Goal concepts in personality and social psychology* (pp. 211-241). Hillsdale, NJ: Erlbaum.

May, J., & Johnson, H. (1973). Psychological activity to internally elicited arousal and inhibitory thoughts. *Journal of Abnormal Psychology, 82,* 239-245.

McMahon, C.E., & Sheikh, A. (1986). Imagination in disease and healing processes: A historical perspective. In A.A. Sheikh (Ed.), *Anthology of imagery techniques* (pp. 1-36). Milwaukee, WI: American Imagery Institute.

Millman, D. (1984). *The way of the peaceful warrior*. Tiburon, CA: H.J. Kramer.

Nideffer, R. (1987, October). *Psychological aspects of injury*. Paper presented to the National Conference on Sport Psychology, Arlington, VA.

Peper, E., Ancoli, S., & Quinn, M. (1979). *Mind/body integration: Essential readings in biofeedback*. New York: Plenum Press.

Perky, C.W. (1910). An experimental study of imagination. *American Journal of Psychology, 21*, 422-452.

Porkert, M. (1979). Chinese medicine: A tradition healing science. In D.S. Sobel (Ed.), *Ways of Health: Holistic approaches to ancient and contemporary medicine* (pp. 117-146). New York: Harcourt, Brace, & Jovanovich.

Post-White, J. (1991, May). *The effects of mental imagery on emotions, immune function and cancer outcome*. Paper presented to the Fourth World Conference on Imagery, Minneapolis, MN.

Pribram, K. (1971). *Languages of the brain*. Englewood Cliffs, NJ: Prentice-Hall.

Richardson, A. (1969). *Mental imagery*. London: Routledge & Kegan Paul.

Rotella, R.J., & Heyman, S.R. (1986). Stress, injury, and the psychological rehabilitation of athletes. In J.M. Williams (Ed.), *Applied sport psychology: Personal growth to peak performance* (pp. 343-364). Palo Alto, CA: Mayfield.

Sackett, R.S. (1935). The relationship between the amount of symbolic rehearsal and retention of a maze habit. *Journal of General Psychology, 13*, 113-128.

Samuels, S., & Samuels, N. (1975). *Seeing with the mind's eye*. New York: Random House.

Sandner, D.F. (1979). *Navajo symbols of healing*. New York: Harcourt, Brace, & Jovanovich.

Schwartz, G.E. (1984). Psychophysiology of imagery and healing: A systems perspective. In A.A. Sheikh (Ed.), *Imagination and healing* (pp. 35-50). Farmingdale, NY: Baywood Publishing Company.

Selye, H. (1974). *Stress without distress*. Philadelphia: J.B. Lipincott.

Sheikh, A.A., & Jordan, C.S. (1983). Clinical uses of mental imagery. In A.A. Sheikh (Ed.), *Imagery: Current theory, research, and applications* (pp. 391-435). New York: Wiley.

Simonton, O.C., Matthews-Simonton, S., & Creighton, J. (1978). *Getting well again.* New York: St. Martin's Press.

Simpson, H.M., & Pavio, A. (1966). Changes in pupil size during an imagery task without motor involvement. *Psychonomic Science, 5,* 405-406.

Spanos, N.P., & O'Hara, P.A. (1990). Imaginal dispositions and situation-specific expectations in strategy-induced pain reductions. *Imagination, Cognition and Personality, 9*(2), 147-156.

Surgent, F. S. (1991, January). Using your mind to beat injuries. *Running & FitNews, 9*(1), 4-5.

Thomas, C. (1990, October). *Locus of authority, coercion, and critical distance in the decision to play an injured player.* Paper presented to the Philosophic Society for the Study of Sport, Ft. Wayne, IN.

Vealey, R.S. (1987, June). *Imagery training for performance enhancement.* Paper presented at the Sports Psychology Institute, Portland, ME.

Wiese, D.M., Weiss, M.R., & Yukelson, D.P. (1991). Sport psychology in the training room: A survey of athletic trainers. *The Sport Psychologist, 5,* 15-24.

Chapter 12

Mental Paths to Enhanced Recovery from a Sports Injury

Lydia Ievleva
Florida State University
Terry Orlick
University of Ottawa

> The greatest discovery of my generation is that human beings, by changing the inner attitudes of their minds, can change the outer aspects of their lives... .It is too bad that more people will not accept this tremendous discovery and begin living it. (William James, 1950, p. 258)

This chapter discusses mental strategies for enhancing recovery from sports injury, drawing from the authors' extensive field experience, as well as from results of a comprehensive study that examined a number of psychosocial factors related to sports injury rehabilitation using subjects diagnosed with the same degree of ankle or knee injuries (Ievleva & Orlick, 1991). A survey format was used in the study, and the scores between those identified as either fast- or slow-healing subjects based on recovery time were compared. The rate of recovery was found to be significantly related to the extent to which certain mental activities were engaged in, most notably goal setting, healing mental imagery, and positive self-talk.

Given the demands of contemporary sport and the high rate of sports injuries, virtually all high performance athletes experience some sort of injury at some time during their athletic career. Depending on the sport, an athlete can expect to endure at least one significant, and often several, interruptions to training and competition due to injury. Although much of the attention of coaches and sport psychology consultants is focused on preparing athletes for competition, this attention is often cut off completely when an athlete becomes injured. Because of this, an injured athlete may feel excluded, neglected, or of little importance. Many athletes feel abandoned or alone when they are injured. This is partly because they are out of the limelight, inactive and watching from a distance, and partly because the prior support and reinforcement from important people in their sport is often directed elsewhere, to those still actively competing. It is particularly difficult for injured athletes when the coaching staff and the organization fail to demonstrate any concern or genuine interest in those injured individuals. For example, some coaches do not call, visit, write, or maintain contact for extended periods of time. Many athletes are left feeling they are on their own when trying to cope with debilitating and sometimes career-ending injuries, unless they are fortunate enough to have a strong support base. Much of this depends upon the approach, treatment, and attention that an injured athlete receives from the outset from coaches, doctors, physiotherapists, and sport psychologists. It is important that each of these professionals recognizes that there is a person connected to the injured leg, arm, or other body part. The extent to which each of these professionals can make the athlete feel positive, optimistic and in control of his or her own healing, greatly influences the extent to which the athlete will heal fully and quickly.

Fortunately, the mental side of healing is gaining greater recognition among sports medicine practitioners as evidenced by comments in recent sports injury journals. Dunn (1983), former head athletic trainer at Western Kentucky University at Bowling Green, Kentucky, asserts that despite all the highly sophisticated resources in expertise and equipment "designed to cure the injured athlete, most trainers would agree that correcting the physical malfunctioning is only half the battle" (p. 34). Steadman (1982), Chairman, Medical Group of the U.S. Alpine Ski Team, divides rehabilitation into three categories: "psychological rehabilitation, physiologic rehabilitation, and rehabilitation of the injured area" (p. 289). Faris, a certified trainer and staff psychologist at the Fort Collins Sports Medicine Clinic in Colorado, agrees that in order to attain the goals of rehabilitation, one must address the emotional state as well as the physical:

To treat a knee and ignore the brain and emotions that direct the choreography of that knee is not consistent with total care of the patient. Any comprehensive rehabilitation plan will want to interface the proper *external* rehabilitation procedures with proper *internal* state of mind of the patient. When these two factors come together, successful results are tremendously enhanced. A positive state of mind promotes better attendance and attentiveness to, and more intensity toward the external rehabilitation procedures, which yield successful results. (Faris, 1985, p. 546)

This current trend in sports injury rehabilitation in particular, and the health care community in general, towards a greater integration of mind and body in the treatment of illness and injury, has a very long history. Although it may represent a new wave in contemporary medical thinking, the ideas that have spawned the fields of behavioral medicine, health psychology, and psychoneuroimmunology are far from *new*. In fact, the role of visualization and belief in healing–psychological tools that are gaining increasing acceptance for enhancing physical healing–are considered the most ancient healing techniques ever used by humans (Achterberg, 1985; Samuels & Samuels, 1975).

It is clear that psychological factors play a vital role in injury rehabilitation. Which are the most important factors and how they function in the recovery process, however, have yet to be determined. Nevertheless, there is much anecdotal as well as empirical evidence to suggest that certain psychological characteristics either enhance or retard healing. This is based on a classic mind/body principle posited by pioneers in biofeedback research–Green, Green, and Walters (1970):

Every change in a physiological state is accompanied by an appropriate change in the mental-emotional state, conscious or unconscious; and conversely, every change in the mental-emotional state, conscious or unconscious, is accompanied by an appropriate change in the physiological state. (Green, Green, & Walters, 1970, p. 3)

Considerable support for the mind-body relationship is found in contemporary behavioral medicine literature (Achterberg, 1985; Borysenko, 1987; Cousins, 1989a, 1989b; Gordon, Jaffe, & Bresler, 1984; Locke & Colligan, 1986; Peper, Ancoli, & Quinn, 1979; Rossi, 1986; Siegel, 1986, 1989; Simonton, Matthews-Simonton, & Creighton, 1978).

For instance, in those studies investigating biofeedback benefits and placebo effects, it has been found that the triggering mechanism for

personal control and healing lies totally within the subject. With biofeedback training one becomes aware of direct control over one's body. A
placebo produces only an *awareness* that the healing process has begun,
because of the belief that it has begun.

Mental imagery plays a leading role in directing the physical changes
produced by biofeedback training and placebos. It is believed that healing
may be triggered or accelerated through positive, constructive and goal
directed imagery (Barabasz & McGeorge, 1978; Cousins, 1989a, 1989b;
Green & Green, 1977; Korn & Johnson, 1983; Schwartz, 1984; Simonton
et al., 1978). Similarly, it is the symbolic or imagined processes in action
that determine the placebo effect. The placebo, a symbol of healing,
triggers a healing visualization in the patient (Borkovec, 1985; Brody,
1985; Frank, 1961). The placebo has been shown to be effective even
while patients are fully cognizant of the inert property of the placebo (Park
& Covi, 1965; Vogel, Goodwin, & Goodwin, 1980). This indicates that
the mere suggestion that healing should take place may spontaneously
result in a healing image.

Psychological Considerations in Recovery

Certain attitudes and psychological factors may either hinder or enhance the effectiveness of a particular treatment, as well as an injured
athlete's ability to cope. Among these are the athlete's belief in his or her
own self-healing capacity, the nature of emotional support available, the
athlete's faith in the physician's or physiotherapist's skill, and the degree
to which the athlete wants to heal.

The support an athlete receives from family, teammates, friends, etc.,
can have a significant impact on the ability to cope. How this support
system responds to the athlete's injury can affect the athlete's response. It
is, therefore, important to understand the nature of these influences that
occur outside the officially recognized therapeutic environment.

It is important for anyone working with an injured athlete to allow for
full expression of feeling, to listen, and to show empathy. With the
unburdening, the injured athlete may then feel freer to focus on proceeding
forward. As Faris asserts, "It is time well spent, for if the athlete's mental
attitude is sour, the outcome will be retarded" (Faris, 1985, p. 549). It can
also be helpful to remind athletes that it is normal to have ups and downs
during the recovery process. Some days are better than others.
Sometimes there are doubts. Moving forward generally occurs in a series
of waves. Athletes should be encouraged to "hang in there"—all great

athletes experience these ups and downs. Persistence is important here, just like in practice and competition.

The best physical and psychological care is no guarantee of a speedy and successful rehabilitation. In the final analysis, it is the athlete who is responsible for the success of his or her own recovery. As Arnheim (1985) stated, "Trainers must educate all of their injured charges to understand that rehabilitation and full recovery are a cooperative venture, with major responsibility resting on the athletes' shoulders" (p. 207). This is no different from striving to improve and excel in sports. The athlete alone is ultimately responsible for making it happen.

A commonly cited factor mediating injury rehabilitation is "secondary gain." This term refers to an injury providing such benefits as attention from trainers and sympathy from peers, an honorable way of disengaging from the pressures of living up to high expectations or freeing up time and energy to pursue other personal goals. This has been a relatively rare occurance with national team athletes with whom we have worked. Most are highly motivated to get back to active training and competing as quickly as possible. However, some athletes who are unable to acquire time off to rest or to balance their lives in any other way may see some value in an injury in that it lessens the expectations placed upon them and may give them an honorable way out.

An example of this occurred with an accomplished university tennis player.

Patty found herself faced with enormous demands placed on her time and energy. In her senior year, she desperately sought to balance a difficult academic course load while performing as the #1 player on the team. There were numerous time-consuming tennis-related demands that included not only those activities inherent with practice and competing (e.g, traveling to tournaments), but also team social events such as a camping trip; this schedule left her with only one weekend of the entire semester to herself. Despite feeling increasingly distressed and overwhelmed, she did not feel herself to be in a position to make the decision to take time off from either the team social or practice activities to keep up with her studies, because this would have been frowned upon by both her coach and her teammates. The coach felt she should just "tough it out." It was not long before Patty sustained an ankle injury, which finally excused her from enough practices to regain control and stability over her school and personal life.

In fact, in her own words, she described the injury as a "God-send." It was the only way that she was able to seize control over her life. Balancing the demands of training, traveling, classwork, and social life is a common challenge for college athletes. When things become too unbalanced for too long, we can lose people psychologically, or physically.

In some cases, therefore, an injury may provide a valuable *time-out* that the athlete may not have initiated on his or her own. As such, the injury may be perceived as an opportunity to bring back into balance one's life towards an improved quality of life.

Mental Paths To Recovery From Injury

This section discusses specific mental activities that have the capacity to enhance injury recovery, in much the same way that they enhance sport performance. They are as follows:
- Commitment
- Seeing the Opportunities
- Goal Setting
- Attitude and Belief
- Positive Self-Talk
- Relaxation
- Mental Imagery
- Coping with Fear of Reinjury

Commitment

The first element critical to rapid recovery is one's *commitment* to heal. The athlete must want to recover fully and must fully commit to doing so. Persistence and patience are necessary when confronting any challenge, and this applies to full recovery from injury as well (Orlick, 1992).

Seeing the Opportunities

The process of recovering from an injury also involves personal learning and growth. Just as the word for *crisis* in Chinese has two characters–one meaning *danger*, and the other meaning *opportunity*–an injury may be viewed as a chance to learn and to grow and as a challenge to overcome, rather than as a catastrophe.

In the applied behavioral medicine community it is strongly held that if one treats only the physical symptoms and neglects the psychological component of health and healing, an underlying problem will likely resurface in some other form or symptom until the original issue is addressed and resolved satisfactorily. In fact, for most forms of illness, a health crisis is viewed as a "wake-up call." Our bodies are constantly sending us messages; some are benign, happy, and joyful, whereas others are indicative of stress, conflict, and imbalance. Often, personal life-style, health habits, or intra- or extra-personal conflicts may be the problem sources. If we choose to ignore early warning signs, the body may require more drastic measures to get our attention. It is said that first we get a knock on the door, then a tap on the shoulder, and if that doesn't do the trick, then a knock on the head! This is exemplified by injuries and illnesses resulting from overtraining, overworking, and overfatigue, as, for example, in the Epstein-Barr Syndrome.

An illness may indeed serve as a signal of something that has been neglected in the psychological domain which has been neglected. Positive psychological perspectives are needed to promote faster recovery, health and well-being. This is supported by a great deal of evidence shared at a recent conference on the application of behavioral medicine, where there was general consensus that all dramatic improvement and recovery from serious, if not terminal, illness is coincident with a major psychological or spiritual insight and positive transformation (The 2nd National Conference on The Psychology of Health, Immunity and Disease, sponsored by The National Institute for the Clinical Application of Behavioral Medicine, Orlando, 1990). This implies, that in order for a health breakthrough to occur, a psychological one needs to precede it. It is therefore important to *listen* to our bodies and heed those *inner* voices conducive to wellness. This may be accomplished both as a preventive measure, as well as be directed towards enhanced healing and enhanced performance. Commonly suggested methods for enhancing inner awareness are meditation, progressive relaxation, and yoga.

Athletes in our study were asked whether the "time out" from their sport accompanying their injury resulted in any valuable lessons or new perspectives that contributed to their future achievement. Subjects in the fast-healing group derived greater benefits in the form of enhanced insight and enjoyment in their sport, whereas those in the slow-healing group found no benefits at all. In addition, those athletes who learned from the experience and accepted it as a challenge and opportunity fared better in terms of their recovery time. In other words, these athletes made the "most of a bad situation." They turned crises into blessings. This is consistent with the findings from world class athletes where there was always a substantial gain in insight or approach to training that subsequently substantially improved the athlete's training and/or performance (Ievleva, 1988).

Following are examples of valuable lessons learned from the injury experience by some athletes with whom we have worked.

Ann, while a top-ranked squash player in the world, learned about the importance for rest by experiencing recurring injuries. For most developing athletes, the need to train is paramount. Having reached certain heights of competitive success, however, it then becomes more important to discipline oneself to rest. It was Ann's tenacity and drive that enabled her success, but these very same qualities applied to her training made her increasingly at risk to overtraining and injury. She discovered that she was most likely to become injured during a lull in the competitive season, when she would find herself bored and with an excessive drive to train harder and recklessly. Whereas her willingness to train hard had been her strength on her rise in the world rankings, she now had to learn to back off training and remain well in order to maintain or advance her position. Initially, this notion went directly against her grain, but she soon realized the wisdom of rest, to the point where she found delight in her new-found ability to take days off and enjoy and express herself in other, healthier ways. She discovered that, indeed, sometimes less is more. She learned to focus and appreciate herself not only as a human doing but also as a human being.

Alison, a member of the 1991 World Cup champion U.S. rugby team, broke her ankle the week before selections were being made to the national team. Initially, it appeared that she would be denied any chance of participating in the World Cup championships just months away. After much discussion, she resolved to seize the opportunity and rise to the challenge. Alison was not known for her discipline in training: She relied on her exceptional natural ability to carry her through. With the increased caliber of competition, however, she reluctantly under- stood that sooner or later, she was going to have to train if she was going to maintain and advance in her position. She was now faced with the task of commitment to arduous rehabilitation training in order to have any chance of pursuing her dream of a World Cup

Championship. Alison risked the possiblity of great disappointment and chose to view the injury as an opportunity to grow both as a player and as a person. It was an opportunity to slow down the hectic pace of her work life and focus inward, to appreciate and allow herself to be a human being (rather than a human doing), to address certain personal issues; to acquire the training discipline–both mentally and physically. She also found that once she made the commitment to a speedy and full recovery, she was surrounded by many who were quick to assist her. For the first time, she discovered the extent to which others cared about her and her progress. Her rehabilitation became a gratifying experience. Alison also grew to enjoy her mental training, which included relaxation, and performance and healing imagery. She began availing herself of these strengthening mental tools, which she then carried with her after recovering from the injury. In the end, her outcome was very fulfilling in that not only was she ready to play, but she was also able to lead her team to victory.

Another case where injury led to valuable lessons involved an Olympic 10 Kilometer runner. Due to an injury, Lynn was forced to train in a swimming pool, which she soon discovered to be more efficient than road training, because water training enhanced both her technique and her concentration, as well as prevented the wear and tear on her body that roadwork inevitably entailed. She subsequently implemented pool training even while healthy and attributed her successful performance at the Olympics to this new training regime.

To enhance the recovery process, exceptional athletes accept the injury and do everything in their power to initiate a positive and complete recovery. They also take advantage of what can be learned from the experience (e.g., about themselves or their relationship to their sport). This is depicted in a comment made by an exceptionally fast, self-directed healer–a professional dancer who experienced a knee injury due to overuse/overtraining. "I would have a conversation with my other self and ask myself why I had created this situation, where it stemmed from in me, what it made me realize about me and how to go about it to make the most of what could be done" (Ievleva, 1988, p. 85).

Care-givers should help athletes to explore the benefits and insights permitted by a time-out, and personal commitment to recovery, which may ultimately prove fruitful and healthy for the athlete in the long run.

Goal Setting

Setting specific relevant goals for each session, day, week, month, etc., is an important element in any training program, including programs for regaining optimal health. Goals translate commitment into specifically relevant action. Minimal and ideal targets can be set, and the specific steps required to reach them can be listed. The results from our study with injured athletes clearly showed that the fast healers were much more involved in goal setting than were the slow healers, especially where daily goals were concerned (Ievleva & Orlick, 1991).

End result or affirmation imagery, where athletes imagine themselves accomplishing their goals, as well as process imagery, where athletes imagine themselves engaged in their daily goals, is recommended. The procedure for end result imagery, described in *Getting Well Again* by Simonton et al. (1978), is adapted here for recovery from sports injury.

1. Select a goal.
2. Relax.
3. See yourself with a goal already met.
4. Imagine, with as many details as possible, the feelings you would have having reached your goal.
5. See the response of others close to you regarding your achievement.
6. Go over the steps it took to reach your goal and experience satisfaction at each level.
7. Allow yourself to feel happy about reaching your goal.
8. Gradually come back to the present.
9. And then open your eyes and commence action on that first step.

Those who have difficulty seeing or feeling their goals being achieved, or who get negative images should stop and acknowledge their doubts and fears and then make a list of all the positive attributes that will enable them to reach the goal (e.g., talent, treatment, tenacity). This is done to help them believe or to recognize that they have the tools necessary to meet the goals and that they are in control.

A beneficial feature of goal setting is that it usually involves some form of imagery. When one thinks of a goal or thinks through a plan to accomplish a goal, images normally flash through one's mind. Goal setting, therefore, may be an indirect link to the extent of mental imagery taking place. Setting a goal in itself is a statement of expectation, and hence, a conceptualization of success is likely to occur. It is highly probable that once a goal is set, a person will periodically re-contemplate, or re-imagine, achieving that goal. This may serve to conjure up an image of success, control, or those activities in which one can engage that are consistent with achieving that goal. It also follows that daily goals are the most effective means towards this end. The results from our study confirm this, in that Daily Goal Setting was found to be more related to Recovery Time than either the Long Term or Returning to Sport Goals (Ievleva & Orlick, 1991).

Attitude and Belief

Belief in one's ability to influence personal healing and attain full recovery greatly influences the healing process. Once goals are set, it is important to believe that they may be accomplished. This requires persistence and ongoing positive reminders in longer rehabilitations where the end may seem so distant. It is important for the athlete to realize that the quality of continued recovery depends on maintaining a positive attitude to allow the physiological healing processes to take place. Although one cannot control the fact that one is injured and may be facing a lengthy rehabilitation process, one *can* direct and control the way one thinks about it. In other words, rather than thinking about all that has gone wrong and how one's life has been disrupted due to the injury, it is more conducive to focus on the positive and what *can* be done. In tune with this view, Dunn (1983) suggests the following prescription for achieving goals that he adapted from *The Magic of Thinking Big* (Schwartz, 1978):

1. Refuse to talk negatively about health. A person may receive a little sympathy but will never get respect or loyalty by complaining. This is particularly true in athletics.
2. Refuse to worry about poor health. Worry is a negative emotion and fear of ill health or injury in athletics often results in injury or illness due to unconscious adjustment in activity.
3. Be genuinely grateful of good health. This will help keep a person's thoughts focused on the positive aspects of their health.
4. Finally, a person should understand that the body responds to its own needs. Very gradual exercise, not in excess, is an important tool in rehabilitation. (p.34)

Positive Self-Talk

The degree of optimism injured athletes display is indicative of their coping style. A positive outlook indicates adjustment to the new condition

Table 1. Examples of positive self-talk from the fast healing group, and examples of negative self-talk from the slow healing group.

Positive Self-Talk:

- How can I make the most out of what I can do now.
- I can beat this thing.
- I can do anything.
- I told myself, "I can do it'. I can beat the odds and recover sooner than normal."
- I want to go spring skiing. I'll be totally healed by then.
- I have to work to get my leg as strong as the other one.
- It's feeling pretty good.
- It's getting better all the time.

Negative Self-Talk:

- It's probably going to take forever to get better.
- I'll never make up for the lost time.
- What a stupid thing to do. --Dumb mistake.
- What a useless body.
- It will never be as strong again.
- Stupid fool! Stupid injury. Stupid leg.
- I talked to myself about how frustrated I was. There is nothing good about this and there is nothing I can do about it.
- Why me?

and an orientation towards improvement. In contrast, a negative outlook indicates preoccupation with the injury's implications which leads to little effort towards improvement. Outlook may, therefore, have an important impact on recovery time. This is supported by the results about self-talk in our study (self-talk being reflective of one's attitude, belief, and outlook), where those whose self-talk was positive, self-encouraging, and determined healed much more rapidly than did those whose self-talk can best be described as whining and self-pitying; that is, it tended to be totally negative, self-deprecatory, and unforgiving. See Table 1 for representative examples.

Positive thinking can influence one's belief and perspective, and belief is often translated into action through positive self-talk. Monitoring internal dialogue can be effective in taking control, guiding positive thoughts, and reducing negative thoughts. This is done first by planning to think in positive terms and secondly, by responding to negative thoughts that may still occur, as a cue to switch to a positive thought.

Thinking and acting in positive ways contribute to personal well-being and enhanced health. Focussing on the positive, on what is within personal control and what can be done to enhance the situation and recovery is much more effective than dwelling on the negative. Kabat-Zinn (1990) emphasizes in his book *Full Catastrophe Living* that there is usually much more *right* with one's body than there is ever *wrong*. It therefore pays to focus on, and appreciate more, what is going well, than to focus on what is not. It is also very helpful to carry on a positive dialogue with one's body, particularly on those areas that one is focussed on rehabilitating.

Injured athletes invariably have moments when they make disparaging remarks to their injured body part (e.g., "You stupid, useless knee."). They should be asked to reflect on how they would feel and respond if spoken to in such terms, and then invited to consider speaking positively, kindly, and lovingly to the injured part, much as one might speak to one's injured child (e.g., "It's o.k. knee. I'm going to take care of you; you're going to take care of me. You're getting stronger all the time; together we're going to make you as good as new... ").

Relaxation

Relaxation practice in any of its various forms, whether it be physical relaxation, meditation, progressive relaxation, breath control, yoga, etc., plays an integral role in behavioral medicine and stress reduction programs. The health benefits accrued from engaging in relaxation on a regular basis have been well documented (Benson, 1975, 1984; Borysenko, 1987; Bresler, 1984a, 1984b; Kabat-Zinn, 1990; Patterson, 1979; Rossman, 1984). Relaxation helps open avenues in our minds that regulate our bodies (Green et al., 1979). Through relaxation practice we can become more aware of, and connected to, our bodies, and thereby more able to direct their activities. Using relaxation in combination with imagery, we can also initiate physical and behavioral change (Green et al., 1979; Korn & Johnson, 1983; Patterson, 1979; Rossman, 1984).

It is common for one's tension level to increase due to the stress of being injured, especially in the injured area. Regularly practicing a relaxation routine can be effective in relaxing the area and relieving the tension. Staying loose and relaxed facilitates recovery. When the body is more relaxed, blood circulation is enhanced. The greater the blood flow, the faster injured tissues are repaired (Benson, 1975; Bresler, 1984a, 1984b).

Swearingen, an orthopedic surgeon and clinical instructor at the University of Colorado School of Medicine, has seen many skiing injuries that tend to fall into the "severe" category. He employs mental techniques to lower activation and tension levels right in the emergency room in the attempt to couple the injury with a state "conducive to body rest and healing" (Swearingen, 1984, p. 102). Following treatment at the hospital, Swearingen then instructs his patients in relaxation and meditation. Believing that the state of rest generated is beneficial to healing (Swearingen, 1984), he draws upon the work of Benson (1975) for relaxation.

Mental Imagery

Positive images of healing, as well as images of being fully recovered, are useful in enhancing one's belief and mobilizing one's own healing powers both inside and outside sport. The value of imagery in healing has a long history in Eastern philosophies and is currently gaining increasing acceptance in the West.

There are many clinical reports of therapeutic benefits that result from imagery. Although most are anecdotal, there is increasing documentation of cases to support the healing benefits of engaging in healing imagery (Achterberg, 1989; Cousins, 1989a, 1989b; Epstein, 1986, 1989; Krippner, 1985; Siegel, 1986, 1989).

Simonton et al. (1978) have reported positive findings as a result of implementing a relaxation and imagery program with patients diagnosed as having medically incurable cancer. Forty-one percent showed improvement, where 22.2% demonstrated total remission and 19.1%, tumor regression. It was their contention that the practice of relaxation and imagery enhanced the immune system. A subsequent study by Hall (1983) supports the above conclusion. His study tested the effects of hypnosis plus imagery on lymphocyte function. The results showed an increased immune response, but only for those who scored high on hypnotizability.

In our own study on recovery from athletic injuries (Ievleva & Orlick, 1991), it was found that athletes used three types of imagery. These included healing imagery in which athletes tried to see and feel the body parts healing; imagery during physiotherapy in which they imagined the treatment promoting recovery; and total recovery imagery in which they imagined being totally recovered, returning to their sport, and performing well again. Athletes felt that all three types of imagery were helpful; however, healing imagery evidenced the greatest relationship to recovery time. Case studies with athletes have been reported (Foster & Porter, 1987) in which negative images (e.g., of the injury as it occurred, inflamed, torn) have interfered with positive imagery of healing and recovery, and hence impeded recovery. This tendency of negative imagery to have the opposite effect of positive imagery was supported in our study.

It is generally considered more effective to use healing imagery after first eliciting some form of "relaxation response" to *quiet* and enhance the receptivity of the mind. According to Jaffe and Bresler (1984), "Attaining a state of bodily relaxation is a prerequisite for all work with therapeutic guided imagery, for it provides inhibition of somatic muscle activity and verbal thoughts and allows mental images to become dominant" (p. 61). The usual procedure is to engage in some form of progressive muscle relaxation or meditation before beginning the healing imagery. Other methods involve hypnosis, and some have even taken advantage of a patient's being under anesthesia. It was originally thought that while anesthetized, patients were totally oblivious to events around them including casual conversation. It has since been discovered that patients, when later hypnotized, can recall all that was said during and/or following surgery. Apparently, what is said can significantly influence the patient's recovery in either a positive or negative way, depending on what was said (Green & Green, 1977; Korn & Johnson, 1983). Pearson (1961) demonstrated that patients receiving positive suggestions about a quick recovery while "unconscious" (i.e., under anesthesia) had an average hospitalization stay of 2.4 days less than the control group.

Green and Green (1977) have reported the successful results of a doctor who used postsurgical suggestions:

After testing reflexes to make certain that the patient was coming to consciousness, he would begin talking in a very low voice, telling the patient how well the operation had gone, how nicely the body had responded, how well the repairs were made. He planted the idea that there would be little pain, and possibly none at all; the tissues would recover very quickly; there would be no infection; the patient would be walking in a very short time. Nurses in intensive care soon noticed that his patients recovered more rapidly than others and asked him to work with other patients too (Green & Green, 1977, p. 327).

The preceding evidence supports the programmability of the unconscious mind for promoting the healing process. Although anesthesia and hypnosis may be efficient in accessing the unconscious in certain cases, a much more practical method that offers similarly effective results involves

Table 2. Basic components involved in self-directed healing.

1. Relaxing mentally and physically.

2. Maintaining a positive attitude.

3. Mentally connecting with the injured body part and imagining healing taking place within—seeing, feeling, and experiencing healing, using as much detail as possible.

4. Seeing and feeling the body exactly as one would like it to be.

5. Imagining the body fully functioning and performing well at desired activities.

6. Reminding oneself that one is feeling good and improving more and more each day.

self-directed relaxation and imagery. Table 2 outlines the basic components involved in self-directed healing.

Daily practice is recommended for best results. What precisely is to be imagined is determined individually. An image that works for one person may not be as effective for someone else. For example, among the cancer patients studied by Simonton et al. (1978), one patient saw her white cells as "killer sharks" attacking the cancer cells, whereas another saw the white cells as white knights. The important feature is that one see one's own bodily resources as being powerful and effectual. Simonton et al. (1978) also included suggestions of chemotherapy or radiation treatment being effective, although the emphasis is on one's own body leading the battle towards recovery. This can be applied to the physiotherapy setting, for example, seeing/feeling the treatment minimizing scar tissue, increasing blood flow, and strengthening the muscle or tissue. Athletes should be clearly informed about what the treatment is designed to do so they can imagine those effects taking place.

Arnheim (1985) and Swearingen (1984), both medical practitioners who draw upon the mind's capacity to heal, explain healing imagery as follows:

It is important that the athlete be educated about the physiological process of healing. Once the healing process is understood, the athlete is instructed to imagine it taking place during therapy and throughout the day. If an infection is being fought, the body's phagocytes can be imagined as "Pac Men" gobbling up infectious material. When tissue is torn, clot formation and organization can be imagined, followed by tissue regeneration and healing. . . . [This] helps the athlete psychologically to be part of the process and to take major responsibility for rehabilitation (Arnheim, 1985, p. 217).

[Swearingen draws] pictures depicting the four stages of the healing process–clot formation around the fracture, the change of the clot into fibrous tissue lattice, calcium crystallization on the lattice-work, and restructuring of new bone around the fracture site... . My impression is that since I adopted this approach [i.e., meditation and visualization], the necessary time in the cast and the morbidity during the healing process have both been significantly reduced. (Swearingen, 1984, p. 104).

Imagining the healing process can be enhanced by knowing precisely what it looks like physiologically. It is not essential that it be realistic, but it must symbolize positive change (Green & Green, 1977; Jaffe & Bresler, 1984; Simonton et al., 1978).

Because injured athletes are unable to practice physically, mental practice becomes that much more important if they are to maintain a certain skill level. Imagery can also be a powerful tool in this regard. Not only does it provide a medium by which to rehearse sport skills, but it also helps preparation for situations that are infrequently encountered in physical practice or competition. Imagery practice can be effective in preparing injured athletes for any number of competitive or practice situations and can thus help them to retain confidence in their ability and to dissipate any lingering fears they may have of reinjury upon return to competition.

When approaching return to training and competition, it is important to incorporate details in the performance imagery of the use of such protective devices as taping or braces, etc., as would be required for actual activity. An omission of such detail in the imagery may result in the kind of pain, soreness, or discomfort that would typically occur if one were physically performing the activity without the protective device. This occurred with a university basketball player with whom we worked, who habitually taped his previously injured ankles before every practice and game to avoid soreness. He had, however, inadvertently neglected to do so in his imagery. Once the taping was included in subsequent imagery, the soreness did not recur.

Timing is an important consideration concerning the athlete's readiness to practice certain forms of imagery. For example, it may be advisable

Table 3. Summary of imagery application during rehabilitation.

1. Visualizing the healing taking place to the injured area internally.

2. Visualizing effectively moving through specific motions and situations that put the most demand on the injured area.

3. Reexperiencing or imagining individual skills required for best performance— to stay sharp mentally.

4. Calling up the feelings that characterize best performances.

5. Visualizing returning to competition and performing at one's best.

6. Engaging in imagery that involves feeling positive, enthusiastic, and confident about returning to training and competition.

to focus solely on relaxation and pain management immediately following knee reconstruction surgery, before commencing with healing imagery. It may not be feasible to practice performance imagery until enough healing has taken place for the athlete to feel ready to contemplate being active and performing again. In some cases, the injury may have been so dramatic or traumatic that it would be unreasonable to expect the athlete to have sufficiently recovered psychologically, let alone physically, to apply the mental energy required to implement self-directed healing, if there has not been enough opportunity for rest. Table 3 summarizes how imagery may be used in rehabilitation.

Coping With Fear of Reinjury
Once full recovery has been attained, fear of reinjury may hold back some athletes. Such fear can result in additional muscular tension that can contribute to the increased possibility of reinjury. The fast healers in our study reported being generally less fearful or worrisome about reinjury as compared to the slower healers. When fears of reinjury did surface in the faster healers, they were modified by a desire to look for positive lessons, exercise greater caution, and exert greater personal control in the future. Respondents in the slow-healing group tended to dwell just on the negative possibilities.

A combination of relaxation and imagery (systematic desensitization) has been reported useful in counteracting fear of reinjury (Nideffer, 1976; Rotella & Campbell, 1983). This technique is based on the principle that it is impossible to be both relaxed and anxious at the same time. First the athlete is asked to identify the fear. Then a relaxed state is elicited using a relaxation technique, following which the athlete is asked to visualize the situation he or she is fearful of. In this way the anxiety-provoking scenario becomes associated with the relaxed state.

Physical Activity

When possible, the athlete should be encouraged to remain physically active in an alternative activity (providing it does not impede the recovery process). Aside from the fitness aspect, staying active has several benefits: dissipating the excess energy resulting from the sudden inability to train, maintaining a sense of control, reducing stress, and keeping up self-image (Crossman, 1986; Salisbury, 1984; Steadman, 1982; Willis, 1983). For those whose injury precludes any form of physical activity, meditation or relaxation training may assist coping with anxiety or depression that accompanies exercise deprivation (Massimo, 1985).

RECOMMENDATIONS

Athletes who are very determined and positive about rehabilitation, as well as those who imagine or *see* and *feel* their recovery and successful resumption of their sport activity, fare much better than do those with negative outlooks. The following is a summary of practical suggestions for use with recovering athletes:

For the injured athlete:
• Stay involved with the sport as much as possible.
• Set daily goals for healing and improvement as well as long-term goals for recovery.
• Develop a physiotherapy plan and plan to mentally prepare for optimal healing each day.
• Do mental imagery of healing and of achieving goals.
• Emphasize positive aspects of the recovery.
• If the injury must be described, always attempt to follow it with a positive statement or image about recovery (if not out loud, at least to yourself).
• Say positive things to yourself about your rehabilitation and your future performance possibilities, every day.
• Be alert to any negative thoughts, imagery or "replays" of the injury.

Change the image to a positive, healing one.
• Take advantage of the "time out" as an opportunity to rest and reflect.
• Practice relaxation techniques particularly if under stress.
• Use audio-tapes such as the one by Orlick (1988), and the sample script at the end of this chapter to promote healing imagery and relaxation.

For those helping an injured person to enhance recovery:
• Maintain contact and involvement with the injured person (e.g., coaches can make a point in their agenda to call once a week).
• Show compassion while encouraging and supporting progress.
• Point out the opportunities the "time out" may provide.
• Speak of possibilities as opposed to limitations.
• Point out and name other athletes who have had similar injuries who are now at the top of their game again.
• Reinforce the fact that the athlete has the capacity to directly influence his or her own healing.
• Encourage the athlete to set specific daily recovery goals for rehabilitation (in conjunction with his or her physiotherapist or trainer), to *think* into his or her body in helpful ways, to use relaxation and mind/body imagery strategies to enhance recovery.
• Mention the fact that the same mental skills that enabled the athlete to excel in sport can be applied to excel at healing (e.g., commitment, belief, positive imagery, full focus, mental readiness, refocusing and constructive evaluation).
• Listen closely to the athlete's concerns.
• Adapt your program to individual input and needs.
• Be flexible in your attitude and approach and encourage athletes to be flexible while on the path to recovery.
• When you provide committed athletes the psychological principles and concepts related to healing they can play with, they are likely to develop creative and imaginative ways of implementing them to enhance their own healing.

To guard against injury and illness:
• Avoid overtraining athletes (consider individual recovery times required).
• Avoid overloading athletes (consider overall schedule and demands the athlete is facing).
• Provide athletes with adequate time to rest and recover between practice,

workouts, and games.
- Encourage good nutritional habits.
- Teach athletes good stress reduction and stress control strategies and perspectives.

It is our hope that healers and *healees* alike will begin to make greater use of mental skills for enhanced injury rehabilitation and personal well-being.

REFERENCES

Achterberg, J. (1985). *Imagery and healing: Shamanism and modern medicine.* Boston: New Science Library.

Achterberg, J. (1989). Mind and medicine: The role of imagery in healing. *Journal of the American Society of Psychical Research, 83(2)*, 93-100.

Arnheim, D.D. (1985). *Modern principles of athletic training.* St. Louis: Times Mirror/Mosby College Publishing.

Barabasz, A.F., & McGeorge, C.M. (1978). Biofeedback, mediated biofeedback and hypnosis in peripheral vasodilation training. *American Journal of Clinical Hypnosis. 21*, 28-37.

Benson, H. (1975). *The relaxation response.* New York: William Morrow.

Benson, H. (1984). *Beyond the relaxation response.* New York: Berkeley Books.

Borkovec, T.D. (1985). Placebo: Defining the unknown. In L. White, B. Tursky, & G.E. Schwartz (Eds.), *Placebo: Theory, research, and mechanisms* (pp. 59-64). New York: The Guilford Press.

Borysenko, J. (1987). *Minding the body, mending the mind.* Reading, MA: Addison-Wesley Publishing Company.

Bresler, D.E. (1984a). Conditioned relaxation: The pause that refreshes. In J.S. Gordon, D.T. Jaffe, & D.E. Bresler (Eds.), *Mind, body, and health: Toward an integral medicine* (pp. 19-36). New York: Human Sciences Press.

Bresler, D.E. (1984b). Mind-controlled analgesia: The inner way to pain control. In A.A. Sheikh (Ed.), *Imagination and healing* (pp. 211-230). Farmingdale, NY: Berkley Books.

Brody, H. (1985). Placebo effect: An examination of Grunbaum's definition. In L. White, B. Tursky, & G.E. Schwartz (Eds.), *Placebo: Theory, research and mechanisms* (pp. 37-58). New York: The Guilford Press.

Cousins, N. (1989a). *Head first: The biology of hope and the healing power of the human spirit.* New York: Penguin Books.

Cousins, N. (1989b). Belief becomes biology. *Advances, 6*(3), 20-29.

Crossman, J.E. (1986, May/June). Psychological and sociological factors supporting athletic injury. *Coaching Review,* 54-58.

Dunn, R. (1983). Psychological factors in sports medicine. *Athletic Training, 18*(1), 34-35.

Epstein, G. (1986). The image in medicine: Notes of a clinician. *Advances, 3*(1), 22-31.

Epstein, G. (1989). *Healing Visualizations: Creating health through imagery.* New York: Bantam Books.

Faris, G.J. (1985). Psychologic aspects of athletic rehabilitation. *Clinics in Sports Medicine, 4*(3), 545-551.

Foster, J., & Porter, K. (1987). *Mental training for healing athletic injury.* Unpublished manuscript.

Frank, J. (1961). *Persuasion and healing.* Baltimore, MD: Johns Hopkins University Press.

Gordon, J.S., Jaffe, D.T., & Bresler, D.E. (1984). *Mind, body, and health: Toward an integral medicine* (pp. 56-69). New York: Human Sciences Press.

Green, E.E., & Green, A.M. (1977). *Beyond biofeedback.* New York: Delacorte Press/Seymour Lawrence.

Green, E.E., Green, A.M., & Walters, E.D. (1970). Voluntary control of internal states: psychological and physiological. *Journal of Transpersonal Psychology, 2,* 1-26.

Green, E.E., Green, A.M., & Walters, E.D. (1979). Biofeedback for mind/body self-regulation: Healing and creativity. In E. Peper, S. Ancoli, & M. Quinn (Eds.), *Mind/body integration: Essential readings in biofeedback* (pp. 125-140). New York: Plenum Press.

Hall, H.R. (1983). Hypnosis and the immune system: A review with implications for cancer and the psychology of healing. *American Journal of Clinical Hypnosis, 25,* 92-103.

Ievleva, L. (1988). *Psychological factors in knee and ankle injury recovery: An exploratory study.* Unpublished master's thesis, University of Ottawa.

Ievleva, L., & Orlick, T. (1991). Mental links to enhanced healing: An exploratory study. *The Sport Psychologist, 5*(1), 25-40.

Jaffe, D.T., & Bresler, D.E. (1984). Guided imagery. In J.S. Gordon, D.T. Jaffe, & D.E. Bresler (Eds.), *Mind, body, and health: Toward an integral medicine* (pp. 56-69). New York: Human Sciences Press.

James, W. (1950). *The principles of psychology.* Vol. I. New York: Dover Publications.

Kabat-Zinn, J. (1990). *Full catastrophe living: Using the wisdom of your body and mind to face stress, pain, and illness.* New York: Delacorte Press.

Korn, E.R., & Johnson, K. (1983). *Visualization: The uses of imagery in the health professions.* Homewood, IL: Dow Jones-Irwin.

Krippner, S. (1985). The role of imagery in health and healing: A review. *Saybrook Review, 5*(1), 32-41.

Locke, S., & Colligan, D. (1986). *The healer within: The new medicine of mind and body.* New York: New American Library.

Massimo, J. (1985, April). Psychological recovery from injury. *International Gymnast,* pp. 42-43; 58.

Nideffer, R. (1976). *The inner athlete.* San Diego: Enhanced Performance Associates.

Orlick, T. (1988). *In Pursuit of Personal Excellence* (Audio-tape on relaxation, imagery and healing). Ottawa: Coaching Association of Canada.

Orlick, T. (1992). The psychology of human excellence. *Contemporary Thought in Sport Psychology and Human Performance, 1*(1), 112-127.

Park, L.C., & Covi, L. (1965). Nonblind placebo trial: An exploration of neurotic outpatients response to placebo when its inert content is disclosed. *Archives of General Psychiatry, 12,* 336-345.

Patterson, D.M. (1979). Progressive relaxation training: Overview, procedure and implication for self-regulation. In E. Peper, S. Ancoli, & M. Quinn (Eds.), *Mind/body integration: Essential readings in biofeedback* (pp. 187-200). New York: Plenum Press.

Pearson, R.E. (1961). Response to suggestions given under general anesthesia. *American Journal of Clinical Hypnosis, 4,* 106-114.

Peper, E., Ancoli, S., & Quinn, M. (1979). *Mind/body integration: Essential readings in biofeedback.* New York: Plenum Press.

Rossi, E.L. (1986). *The psychobiology of mind-body healing.* New York: W.W. Norton & Company.

Rossman, M.L. (1984). Imagine health! Imagery in medical self-care. In A. Sheikh (Ed.), *Imagination and healing* (pp. 231-258). Farmingdale, NY: Berkley Books.

Rotella, R.J., & Campbell, M.S. (1983). Systematic desensitaization: Psychological rehabilitation of injured athletes. *Athletic Training,*

18(2), 140-142; 151.

Salisbury, N. (1984). The comeback trail. *New Body, 3*(6), 56-58.

Samuels, M., & Samuels, N. (1975). *Seeing with the mind's eye.* New York: Random House / Berkeley: The Bookworks.

Schwartz, D. (1978). *The magic of thinking big.* New York: Prentice-Hall.

Schwartz, G.E. (1984). Psychophysiology of imagery and healing: A systems perspective. In A.A. Sheikh (Ed.), *Imagination and healing* (pp. 35-50). Farmingdale, NY: Berkley Books.

Siegel, B.S. (1986). *Love medicine & miracles.* New York: Harper & Row.

Siegel, B.S. (1989). *Peace, love, and healing.* New York: Harper & Row.

Simonton, O.C., Matthews-Simonton, S., & Creighton, J.L. (1978). *Getting well again.* New York: Bantam Books.

Steadman, J.R. (1982). Rehabilitation of skiing injuries. *Clinics in Sports Medicine, 1*(2), 289-294.

Swearingen, R.L. (1984). The physician as the basic instrument. In J.S. Gordon, D.T. Jaffe, & D.E. Bresler (Eds.), *Mind, body, and health: Toward an integral medicine* (pp. 101-106). New York: Human Sciences Press.

Vogel, A.V., Goodwin, J.S., & Goodwin, J.M. (1980). The therapeutics of placebo. *American Family Physician, 22*, 105-109.

Willis, H. (1983). Some psychological effects of athletic injuries. *Physiotherapy in Sport, 5*(3), 16-17.

HEALING IMAGERY SCRIPT AND GUIDELINES
Preface

The following is a sample script and guideline that a Canadian Olympic fencer used for an ankle injury. It should be noted that although this example incorporates many of the important elements for most effective imagery, it is always best to collaborate with the athlete when developing an individualized script for healing. In addition, it can be very useful to provide the athlete related reading material.

Guidelines

Imagery. Set aside several times per day to do your healing imagery (even if for brief periods of time). For at least one of those sessions, use the healing tape. In the other two sessions, try to generate your own imagery of healing or active involvement in your sport. In your imagery, try to experience and feel the event vividly and exactly as you would like it to happen, and then choose a trigger word or phrase that represents this image and repeat it as you do your mental imagery and throughout the day.

Relaxation. Practice relaxation twice a day, preferably just before doing your imagery or going to physiotherapy.

Physiotherapy. Find out what each aspect of your physio is designed to do to help your recovery. Then *during* your treatment, imagine your body getting the maximum gain from that treatment.

NOTE: Athletes may need reminders to continue to take care of the remainder of their body during recovery. Some find that their healing imagery is enhanced by imagining colors (e.g., a cool blue, aqua or white for reducing inflammation; emerald green or violet for healing tissue).

Personalized Healing Script–Sample

Before beginning, take a moment to get comfortable and relax ... Now, close your eyes, and take a few slow, deep abdominal breaths ... Make the exhale long and steady ... completely emptying out your lungs before each fresh new breath you take . . . .

Focus your attention on your breathing throughout this entire exercise .... Slowly and deeply.... As you focus on your breathing, feel your whole body relaxing.... With each breath, allow yourself to become more and more relaxed... inhaling slowly and deeply...exhaling fully and steadily... . As you exhale, imagine any tension, tightness, pain, or discomfort flowing out of your body... inhaling slowly and deeply, exhaling fully and steadily... and with each breath, becoming more and more relaxed.... Just continue with your breathing for a moment... relaxing your body and mind ... inhaling slowly and deeply, exhaling fully and steadily... becoming more and more relaxed... .(Pause for about one minute).

When you find yourself quiet and fully relaxed, take a moment to enjoy it... . Sense the gentle warmth and feeling of well-being all through your body... . If any extraneous thoughts try to interfere, simply allow them to pass through and out of you.... . Disregard them and go back to your breathing, inhaling slowly and deeply, exhaling fully and steadily.... . Enjoy this nice state of gentle relaxation.

By directing your body to relax, you increase your blood flow and improve circulation, and thereby improve tissue regeneration and promote faster healing.

Your body already has healing power that is now in progress. You can enhance that power by using your mind to mobilize your body's healing resources to the fullest. Your determination, will, and imagination have a tremendous influence on your capacity to direct and control your own healing process.

By imagining the healing process occurring within your body you are using your mind to program your body to heal more effectively. Through your images, you are sending messages to your body of how you want it to be, and your body responds accordingly. Your body follows the directives of your mind.

Now, as you continue to relax, inhaling slowly and deeply, and exhaling fully and steadily, imagine this feeling of relaxation flowing through your body and down your legs... washing away any remaining tension and injury... and providing nourishing, healing oxygen to every fiber and cell in your left ankle... . Feel the blood flow increase deep within your left ankle, providing healing energy... and flushing away any broken down tissues. (Pause about 30 seconds)

Feel your entire ankle encircled with warm, soothing flow of healing nourishment... . See it being enveloped by white light... . Now, with your mind, go inside your left ankle and feel and visualize the ligament knitting together smoothly, and efficiently... . See it healing and getting stronger...

See your ankle exactly as you want it to be... . Feel your ankle healing, mending, and strengthening . . . mending and strengthening ... . You may want to check with your healthy right ankle as an example of how your left ankle should be ... send a message to your healing ankle to be like your other healthy ankle... . Freely use your imagination... . Imagine your entire leg and ankle feeling and functioning harmoniously and efficiently again ... . Really try to feel and experience these images. (Pause)

Good.

Now, imagine your whole body healthy and strong again... able to take on any demands that you place upon it... . It is strong and flexible... . Your ankle has healed, and is strong and flexible...ready for any activity you want... . You are relaxed and ready to fence... . Imagine being able to fence again... . Your ankle is cooperative and ready to support your every move ... . You are ready to be the best you can be...knowing that you can rely on your body to perform as your direct it... . See and feel yourself fencing your best again, moving freely, without hesitation...doing what you love most to do...feel all the sensations of your movement... . Freely use your imagination... . Allow yourself to be confident and in control... . Enjoy yourself and smile. (Pause about 30 seconds.)

Great!

You are getting better and better...stronger and stronger...more and more flexible.... . You are healing quickly and efficiently.... . You are restoring all of your strength, power, and motion.

Just continue with your imagery for as long as you like.... . And when you are finished, remember to take a few seconds to slowly come back to the "here and now"...and give yourself a mental "pat on the back" for participating with your body towards a speedy recovery.

SECTION 4

Counseling Athletes
With Permanent Disabilities

SECTION 4

Counseling Athletes With Permanent Disabilities

In the lead chapter in this section, **Keith P. Henschen** and **Gregory A. Shelley** employ vignettes of real-life athletic injuries that resulted in permanent physical disability. They describe counseling efforts employed in successful rehabilitative programs used with these athletes.

The second chapter, written by **Edward F. Etzel** and **A. P. Ferrante**, emphasizes the need to go beyond the exclusive employment of the "medical model" in assisting disabled injured college athletes. Detailed descriptions of the roles of athletic trainers and psychological counselors are provided by way of two case studies. A number of difficulties encountered in working with this population are discussed.

In the book's very last chapter, **Bruce W. Tuckman** provides an account of his own battle with a debilitating athletic injury. He shares personal insights and describes a step-by-step account of his self-counseling strategies.

Chapter 13

Counseling Athletes with Permanent Disabilities

Keith P. Henschen
Gregory A. Shelley
University of Utah

Two actual vignettes of athletes experiencing permanent disabilities are presented, and information concerning the transitional period as well as the general reaction pattern to injuries is discussed. Next, a number of general guidelines to which the sport psychologist should adhere during the various stages of the psychological rehabilitation are presented. Finally, psychological interventions that would be beneficial in each scenario are discussed. A team approach to handling athletes with permanent disabilities is advocated.

VIGNETTE I

On a snow covered football field in mid-December an all-pro wide receiver streaks down the sideline, intently concentrating on the long, arching pass headed in his direction. As the ball gently nestles into the receiver's soft hands, simultaneously a defensive player's helmet is planted in the middle of the receiver's back with unbelievable force. The force of the two players colliding is analogous to that of two cars crashing head-on at about 30 miles per hour with neither applying the brakes. At the instant of impact, the receiver suffers a severing of the spinal cord and is immediately transformed into a paraplegic.

VIGNETTE II

On a stormy summer night an Olympic, world-class pistol shooter is involved in a terrible automobile accident. She is severely injured, with numerous broken bones and a deep concussion that leaves her in a coma for about two weeks. After awakening from the coma, she continues to experience migraine headaches and blurred vision. It is determined that the neurological damage is permanent and that her vision impairment is uncorrectable. She will remain, throughout her lifetime, legally blind in one eye.

These vignettes describe true-life experiences that create a variety of special circumstances that must be handled by the medical science specialists. Of particular interest are the problems or challenges that these situations create for the sport psychologist. What are the similarities the sport psychology consultant must be cognizant of in both scenarios? What are the obvious and subtle differences? How, when, and where should counseling and intervention techniques be applied in each situation? Also, what are the major concerns that need to be addressed before total reintegration back into society can be achieved? The remainder of this chapter will attempt to provide salient information on how to proceed in each of these cases, as well as to discuss the setbacks or problems that could possibly arise for the sport psychologist.

To begin our discussion, it should be understood, unequivocally, that sport termination trauma is real, and often initiates a life crisis for which very few athletes are prepared. An elite athlete initially receives a great deal of publicity and support when injured. Soon the injury becomes "yesterday's news." The athlete eventually is left to deal with the trauma with the help of his or her family or intimate support group. The long-term consequences of such injuries can be devastating.

Not only is high-level athletic participation no longer probable, but the athlete's entire quality of life is also in jeopardy. Permanent physical damage may significantly hamper the person's ability to lead a productive, fulfilling life and may severely limit possible career options (Ogilvie & Howe, 1986). When adjustment to new circumstances must be made, it is likely that counseling interventions will be required to assure functional transitions and achieving "a new normalcy in life."

The Transition Period

Irrespective of the specific cause of the athletic termination, as illustrated by the two previous vignettes, each injured athlete must address a crucial period of adjustment with only the tools or techniques acquired in past experiences or personal growth. The demands of this transition are specific to the individual and handled differently by all those forced to experience it. Any injury is mentally, emotionally, and behaviorally challenging. The athlete's state of mental health prior to the injury will have a great influence on how the athlete reacts to it (Samples, 1987). It is a time when vital issues, such as permanent retirement, identity crises, and the transition from athlete to ex-athlete status emerge. It is difficult to actually terminate any important relationship on an objective basis because the motives to do so are absent or very weak. This is exactly the difficulty in a career-ending sports injury. In general, how athletes handle this period of adjustment is most dependent upon the strength of their identification with sport, their perceptions about self-worth, and the importance they place on the expectations held for them by others. For many, the identity of being an athlete is an important part of their feelings of self-worth and interpersonal needs.

A heavy investment in the "sport identity" may be troublesome for the person making the transition from athlete to nonathlete. Such an individual has thrived on the recognition and accolades derived from competitive endeavors. When deprived of these reinforcements, the injured athlete suffers a serious loss because he or she may no longer have opportunities to develop in other areas and cultivate other talents (Ogilvie & Howe, 1986). Sports management tends to emphasize single-mindedness relative to the athletic commitment. Athletes, particularly those who compete on elite levels, are encouraged to invest heavily in training and maintain an almost exclusive focus on sports.

In making a smooth and healthy transition from athlete to nonathlete status, the injured athlete's perceptions of self are crucial. Many athletes, even world-class competitors, do not have high levels of self-worth and therefore require much positive reinforcement from significant others (Henschen, 1992; Poole, Henschen, Shultz, Gordin, & Hill, 1986). Cessation of such reinforcement, heretofore provided by successful competitive experiences, may result in further decreases in self-worth and difficulty in coping with the demands of transition. Injured athletes who believe they are worthwhile and important persons exclusive of their involvement in sport are likely to adjust more easily to their status change than are those with low self-worth. It should be noted that perceptions of helplessness regarding the physical self may undermine the entire concept of self.

Loss of recognition and status, as well as the unavailability of an exciting life-style, may complicate the injured athlete's transition to nonathlete status. Injured athletes are no longer acknowledged in the same manner by other athletes, peers, significant others, and by a previously adoring mass media. Often, so-called "close friendships" fade, and the injured athlete must rely on primary bases of support–frequently, family members. Unfortunately, members of the immediate family also are obliged to confront serious interpersonal, financial, and time management challenges related to injury of one of its members. Consequently, the preparedness to help the athlete may be compromised. The period of adjustment to the injury (the transitional period) may be difficult for athletes due to the need to relinquish center stage, the "roar of the crowd and the smell of the greasepaint," and the loss of opportunity to showcase their talent. They still must deal with unfair expectations that they have been exposed to for years: the expectation that they must "be tough," "play with pain," "never quit," etc. In addition, debilitating injury to a professional athlete may result in serious loss of family income in the face of increased medical expenses.

General Reaction Pattern To Sport Injury

The period of adjustment to injury involves a number of predictable directions taken by the athlete. Although each athlete is unique in many physical and psychological ways and so personal reactions to disabling injury will be different, even so, certain common experiences that may be referred to as stages seem to be shared by many. In the athlete's quest to accept the inevitable consequences of termination from sports, variations in defense mechanisms and coping strategies are employed. No serious physical injury occurs without psychological consequences, and these are contingent upon the personal attributes of the athletes themselves (Wiese & Weiss, 1987). According to Kübler-Ross (1969), Ogilvie and Howe (1986), and Rotella and Heyman (1986), these stages in sequence, are: (1) denial, (2) anger, (3) grief, (4) depression, and (5) reintegration.

The *denial* and/or disbelief phase is normally experienced first. Initially, the athlete is shocked, numb, and has difficulty in accepting his or her physical trauma. Often injured athletes will seek second, third, or as many medical opinions as they can afford, in order to disprove the inevitable diagnosis. This approach is compatible with their well-developed "athletic attitude" that emphasizes "never giving up" and "striving to beat insurmountable odds." Sport heroes and heroines are recognized for their staunch implementation of these philosophies. However, other, less helpful attitudes also prevail that may be inhibitory, such as "something like this cannot happen to me–only to other people." The ability to relinquish this denial and to accept the reality of the injury depends upon how well the athlete is prepared for the eventual outcome. If the athlete subscribes to the myth of athletic invulnerability or invincibility, then the denial phase can be long and traumatic (Ogilvie, 1987).

When denial is no longer an effective coping strategy, the athlete enters the *anger* phase. Here, emotions such as anger, rage, envy, resentment, hostility, and aggression are frequently displayed. Friends, loved ones, and family members are commonly targeted as subjects. The "why me?" and "why not you (or someone else)?" thinking is prevalent here. Often the athletes will also direct anger against themselves. Self-abuse, as well as unpredictable mood swings and resentment towards others, are evident during this phase.

Although the first two stages, denial and anger, are usually temporary, they may be experienced by the athlete with intensity and cause pain to others in the environment. Well-adjusted individuals pass through these phases relatively quickly, but individuals with more problematic adjustments may remain in the denial phase for an extended period of time or harbor extreme rage (Ogilvie & Howe, 1986).

The next phase is usually that of *grief* and bargaining. Grieving and depression are frequently extensions of each other. A grief response involves a series of feelings related to the sense of separation or loss. It is not static, but rather a dynamic state of fairly unpredictable behaviors. Again, the "why me?" attitude is prevalent with a slightly different twist. Here, acceptance of permanent change due to injury is present; however, also involved is the attempt to determine "why?" The injured party longs for "what he/she used to be" and spends a great deal of time in past memories and fantasies about the future. Factors influencing the grief reaction include the unique nature of the loss; the social system of the person who is grieving; the injured party's coping behaviors, personality, and mental health; the athlete's level of maturity and intelligence; and the athlete's social, cultural, ethnic, and religious/philosophical background (Rando, 1984). Actually, the grief phase is the initial step to recovery. Almost as a last gasp effort, the individual, in the waning stages of the grief phase, resorts to bargaining. Here is where the athlete talks to a personal supreme deity and attempts to "make a deal." In exchange for complete healing, the athlete will promise always to be good, faithfully attend church, never run again, be a pillar of the community, etc. This desperate effort is probably the final attempt or coping strategy used to avoid the reality that must be faced. When the injured party finally realizes that no miracles are forthcoming, then and only then is he or she ready for the final phase–*acceptance* and reintegration.

The fourth phase of the general reaction pattern is *depression*. Depression in this context is usually defined as a sense of great loss. During this phase, it is common for the athlete to withdraw from teammates, friends, and family members. In other words, the depressed individuals distance themselves from the very people who could provide the most meaningful support. Other characteristics of this phase are verbalized helplessness and perceived loneliness. Enthusiasm and vibrancy are replaced by loneliness. Confusion prevails, and a sense of purpose seems to be lost. This phase can be of short duration or can last for a long time. Its length depends on many factors, such as the injured athlete's personality and the persistence of significant others in providing support.

Factors that significantly determine how quickly the injured athlete reaches the final phase (reintegration) relate to each athlete's overall physical, emotional, and psychological foundation. Once an athlete is able to accept the consequences of disability, then he or she can effectively face the challenge of reintegration into society. It would be nice to be able to describe, or present, an outline of the behaviors that would indicate that the reintegration phase is underway; however, a general description is virtually impossible because of the multitude of individual factors involved. It can be safely stated, though, that acceptance should not be mistaken for a happy stage; rather, it is almost void of feelings. Suffice it to say that an athlete's progression through the general reaction response is dependent upon (a) prior psychological level of functioning; (b) the meaning of the disability to the athlete; (c) the nature, location, severity, and duration of the injury; and (d) the resulting changes in the individual's life-style (May & Sieb, 1987). The one thing that the sport psychologist should provide throughout all these stages is *hope*.

Now that we have discussed the general reaction pattern and the transitional period associated with catastrophic injury, let us examine each of the vignettes that were used to introduce this chapter, according to counseling techniques that can be used in each circumstance. It should be remembered that the following are recommended counseling methods based upon the authors' experiences and are not presented as exclusive or definitive approaches.

VIGNETTE I

Putting aside the questionable sociable acceptance of such sport violence, the issue becomes how to work most effectively with the injured athlete in order to facilitate his transitional period. This football player must overcome two major issues: (a) retirement from athletics, and (b) adjustment to permanent disability. The first issue is relatively meaningless in this scenario. It is inevitable, and the athlete will come to this realization almost immediately upon awakening from surgery. The crucial issue for this person is not one of realizing how to become a productive ex-athlete, but rather how to deal with being a permanently disabled individual for the remainder of his life. It is not even a question of the severity of injury, because this injury is so severe that the athlete thinks it threatens any semblance of a normal quality of life.

In this case rehabilitation should involve a medical team approach with special emphasis placed on three stages–preoperative, postoperative, and long-term recovery. Prior to discussing the three stages of rehabilitation for this scenario, it should be made abundantly clear that the most effective procedures will be accomplished by a team approach. No individual can provide all of the services necessary for this athlete as he struggles through the stages of rehabilitation. The team should consist of family, friends, teammates, athletic trainers, medical personnel, and the sport psychologist. Each of these individuals has significant contributions to make to the injured athlete and his reintegration to society. Let us examine these contributions in reverse order from how they were presented previously.

In reality, the most crucial portion of the medical rehabilitation team is the sport psychologist. This person will be the *only* individual remaining in close, personal contact throughout all the stages of rehabilitation. The sport psychologist, because of the professional relationship, will also be the sole member of the sportsmedicine team who can provide compassionate but objective evaluations and reinforcement to the injured party in an unbiased fashion. Specific procedures and techniques used by the sport psychologist will be presented as the stages of rehabilitation are discussed.

The second category of the team includes all the medical personnel. The operating surgeons, the personal medical doctor, and the physical therapists are part of this category. These people are all professionals and are experts at what they do–providing medical services. Sadly, these individuals are typically not trained in counseling techniques, which are essential in this scenario. That is why the sport psychologist must have the confidence and cooperation of the medical staff in order to be effective.

The athletic training staff is normally a crucial element in most injury rehabilitation situations, but this vignette is slightly different. After the initial on-the-field treatment for the injury, the athletic trainers will really have little contact with the athlete; but they can be invaluable to the sport psychologist. They can be a source of much needed information concerning the personal aspects of the athlete that will be needed in the counseling. Nideffer (1983) identified several personality characteristics in athletes that interact with the personalities of the sportsmedicine team: information-seeking, self-confidence, self-esteem, and extroversion or introversion tendencies. Athletic trainers can provide the sport psychologists with this personal information about the athlete, thus saving the time and energy of the sport psychologist.

Friends and teammates can also provide the injured athlete with an enormous amount of support and love, or they can be a source of potential problems. Many times friends and teammates demonstrate enormous interest in the injured athlete, but often only initially. As the severity of the disability becomes apparent, these same individuals may become conspicuously absent. Their visits will be frequent in the beginning, but diminish and ultimately become nonexistent over time. Many persons feel uncomfortable in the presence of disabled individuals, and the easiest solution is "out of sight, out of mind." Although sometimes difficult for the injured athlete to accept, friends and teammates have full agendas and committed lives of their own. It is often difficult for active people to spend time with inactive individuals, especially disabled ones. In addition, friends, relatives, and former teammates may be burdened with psychological fears and limitations that inhibit their interaction with permanently disabled persons. The sport psychologist should therefore prepare the injured athlete for this "abandonment" as the rehabilitation process proceeds.

Perhaps the most important members of the team approach are the family. This group can be as directly affected by the disability, as is the injured person. The family goes through the initial trauma of the accident, the slow transition period, and the long-term rehabilitation. Family members' lives may be as influenced as the athlete's own life by the disabling injury. The sport psychologist must be prepared to counsel family members through their transitional periods. This may prove to be very difficult. Emotions such as anger, depression, and resentment will be prevalent. In fact, the sport psychologist should recommend general family counseling in all cases involving permanent disability. A number of general guidelines should be adhered to during psychological rehabilitation:

1. athlete entry into counseling as soon as possible;
2. establishment of a positive relationship by the counselor with all family members;
3. as much positive support as possible;
4. continuity of care by the same counselors.

Constantly changing counselors, for whatever reasons, often sends an inappropriate message, so this should be avoided.

Preoperative Stage

It is very important that counseling begin immediately after the injury and prior to surgery. A great deal of psychological preparation for surgery and other invasive procedures is almost always necessary. Fear of surgery is very common, and dealing with pain is difficult. The sport psychologist can prepare an injured athlete for surgery by providing accurate information about what is to happen and what to expect. Fear is often associated with the unknown, and by virtue of providing explanations of the forthcoming surgical experience, the counselor may alleviate this emotion. Training in anxiety reduction and relaxation skills is also frequently appropriate at this time. It would seem appropriate for medical personnel to provide such services to patients, but for various reasons this normally fails to occur. It is wise for the sport psychologist to anticipate providing counseling services that the medical staff is not providing to athletes with disabilities.

Postoperative Stage

In this vignette, surgery resulted in return of all bodily functions with the exception of motor activity. In other words, the football player was ultimately able to do almost everything except walk. The mandate facing the sport psychologist is to deal with the general reaction of this athlete to his tragic locomotive inability and to guide him through the period in which he accepts his serious liability. This is a difficult and time-consuming challenge. One positive psychological aspect is that in the postoperative context, problems are more accessible, closer to the surface, and more likely to be revealed. Again, postoperatively, the sport psychologist needs first to handle the transition of the athlete and then to lay the foundation for reintegration into society.

Long-Term Stage

The long-term stage of counseling has two purposes: learning to deal with the disability and reintegrating into society. These two aspects are interrelated, but learning to deal with the disability is the most crucial. If coping with the disability is accomplished, then reintegration is likely. The sport psychologist must assist in the cognitive restructuring of many aspects of the injured athlete's perceptions. The athlete must be convinced that he is still a viable, productive, and important individual, even if he is no longer a sports hero. Ogilvie & Howe (1986) stated that once athletes are resigned to the facts of retirement, they will experience an interesting shift in values. Instead of valuing such things as being first, travel, money, and popularity, they will redirect their emphases to reflect higher value being placed on family and friends. The counseling should focus on what the reality of the disability actually is and what the athlete will be able to do. The counselor should always present this information in a positive fashion.

It is our contention that the athlete described in Vignette I will respond positively to the challenge of rehabilitation. He has, since childhood, flourished on competition and has been exposed to conflict and conflict resolution challenges in the sports arena. Challenges and competition are an integral part of his life and can be used in his rehabilitation. This athlete must be convinced that even though physical participation in sport, as once experienced, is no longer possible, nevertheless, there is still the challenge to channel many of his abilities and skills towards successful rehabilitation. The object of competition now becomes himself, his own muscles and nervous system, instead of other football players. Counseling this individual should include some, if not all, of the following interventions: cognitive restructuring, visual imagery, thought stopping, panic mitigation, relaxation, goal setting, and positive self-talk. Exactly how to employ these with this particular disabled athlete is dependent upon a variety of factors, such as personality, previous psychological training, and progress through the transition phases. Rather than describe these skills here we indicate that previous authors have advocated and offered detailed descriptions of programs using these techniques (Lynch, 1988; Rotella, 1982; Samples, 1987; Wiese & Weiss, 1987). The counseling in this scenario may continue for years.

VIGNETTE II

This case is totally different from the last one. Here the high-level competitor is not faced with an obvious lifetime disability and in fact can function very effectively in society with her impairment. Counseling in this case must focus primarily on retirement from competition rather than on dealing with a restrictive permanent disability. Again, two stages of counseling are recommended: (a) the postoperative stage; and (b) the long-term stage.

Postoperative Stage

The athlete in Vignette II, as is the case with almost all injured individuals, will experience the same general reaction pattern during the transition. The emphasis during the postoperative stage will be to regain a normal level of health and to involve her husband, family, and friends in the transition period. Due to the visual demands of pistol shooting, this athlete will need to accept the termination of her competitive shooting career. She will be able to continue as a recreational shooter, but intense high-level competition is improbable. The athlete's motivation and readiness for rehabilitation and counseling in this stage will be determined by what she thinks happened, how she feels about what happened, and what she plans to do about the accident (Wiese & Weiss, 1987). Once she is physically healthy, it is quite likely she will attempt to shoot again, but understandably with poor results. The counselor must be ready for the anger and frustration that will follow. After she has proven to herself that she is no longer physically capable of competitive pistol shooting, the long-term stage of counseling will commence.

Long-Term Stage

Counseling in this scenario should focus on retirement from competitive athletics. In this case the key people in the athlete's total reintegration efforts will be the counselor and the athlete's husband. If there are "significant others" in this athlete's life, they will also be important factors. Through interaction with the athlete, the counselor must locate the influential variables that are causing her to experience frustration in the retirement process.

Previous research has identified the following factors that frequently influence the "stress" of retirement: degree of marital satisfaction, the personality of the athlete, level of self-esteem and self-concept, self-motivation and self-direction, social and emotional support, value orientation, life satisfaction, educational level, present and future financial situation, and perceived career opportunities. This list is not exhaustive but provides many of the most common factors necessary to consider when dealing with forced athletic retirement. Again, the counselor must address some of the aforementioned variables but also can aid the athlete's readjustment by teaching her a number of psychological skills. These skills are taught with the intent of providing a greater quality of life. The following psychological skills could be beneficial to this athlete: relaxation, imagery, cognitive restructuring, hypnosis, positive self-talk, and concentration training. The long-term objectives for counseling this athlete involve having her accept the termination of her competitive athletic career and helping her to proceed with her life in a positive manner. This injured athlete should be encouraged to remain socially integrated with her former teammates in terms of personal needs. Also, her coach should maintain a relationship with the athlete even though she may never compete again. The athlete should be allowed to move away from her sport (pistol shooting) at a pace commensurate with her emotional reintegration.

SUMMARY

Counseling athletes with permanent disabilities is indeed a formidable challenge because each athlete's response to injury is unique. Sport trauma is real, and often initiates a life crisis for which very few athletes are prepared. Counselors should recognize the importance of the transitional period and the many psychological factors that affect readjustment. Also, the general reaction pattern phases (denial, anger, depression, grief, and reintegration) must be worked through appropriately prior to successful readjustment. Counselors also need to recognize that the way in which athletes respond to permanent disability is dependent upon their physical, emotional, and psychological foundation. An athlete's adjustment to injury is dependent upon (a) prior psychological functioning; (b) the meaning of the disability to the athlete; (c) the nature, location, severity and duration of the injury; and (d) the resulting changes in the individual's lifestyle.

We advocate a team approach to handling athletes with permanent disabilities. Sport psychologists, medical personnel, athletic trainers, family, friends, and teammates are all important contributors to the team approach. Each of these groups have significant influences during the preoperative, postoperative and long-term stages of rehabilitation.

REFERENCES
Henschen, K. (1992). Developing the self-concept in track and field

athletes. *Track and Field Quarterly, 92* (1), 35-37.

Kübler-Ross, E. (1969). *On death and dying.* New York: Macmillan.

Lynch, G.P. (1988). Athletic injuries and the practicing sport psychologist: Practical guidelines for assisting athletes. *The Sport Psychologist, 2,* 161-167.

May, J.R., & Sieb, G.E. (1987). Athletic injuries: Psychosocial factors in the onset, sequelae, rehabilitation and prevention. In J.R. May & M.J. Asken (Eds.), *Sport psychology: The psychological health of the athlete* (pp.157-185). Great Neck, NY: P.M.A. Publishing Corporation.

Nideffer, R.M. (1983). The injured athlete: Psychological factors in treatment. *Orthopedic Clinics of North America, 14,* 373-385.

Ogilvie, B. (1987). Counseling patients with career-ending injuries. Unpublished Manuscript.

Ogilvie, B., & Howe, M. (1986). The trauma of termination from athletics. In J.M. Williams (Ed.), *Applied sport psychology* (pp. 365-382). Palo Alto, CA: Mayfield.

Poole, C., Henschen, K., Shultz, B., Gordin, R., & Hill, J.(1986). Psychological profiles of elite collegiate athletes according to performance level. In L.E. Unesthal (Ed.), *Contemporary sport psychology* (pp. 65-72). Orebro, Sweden: Veje Publishing.

Rando, T.A. (1984). *Grief, dying, and death.* Champaign, IL: Research Press Company.

Rotella, R.J. (1982). Psychological care of the injured athlete. In D.N. Kolund (Ed.), *The injured athlete* (pp. 138-149). Philadelphia: J.B. Lippincott.

Rotella, R., & Heyman, S. (1986). Stress, injury and the psychological rehabilitation of athletes. In J.M. Williams (Ed.), *Applied sport psychology* (pp. 343-364). Palo Alto, CA: Mayfield.

Samples, P. (1987). Mind over muscle: Returning the injured athlete to play. *The Physician and Sportsmedicine, 15*(10), 172-180.

Suinn, R.M. (1967). Psychological reactions to physical disability. *Journal of the Association for Physical and Mental Rehabilitation, 21* (1), 13-15.

Wiese, D.M., & Weiss, M.R. (1987). Psychological rehabilitation and physical injury: Implications for the sports medicine team. *The Sport Psychologist, 1,* 318-330.

Chapter 14

Providing Psychological Assistance to Injured and Disabled College Student-Athletes

Edward F. Etzel
West Virginia University
A.P. Ferrante
The Ohio State University

Numerous college student-athletes regularly incur athletic injuries and disabilities. The authors discuss difficulties working with this special population, the unique consequences associated with their losses in functioning, and ways of providing psychological assistance. Two cases are offered illustrating the nature and course of work with injured and disabled student-athletes.

In the summer of 1987, The National Collegiate Athletic Association's (NCAA) Presidents' Commission hired The American Institutes for Research (AIR) to conduct a comprehensive survey of college student-athletes. The endproduct, The National Study of Intercollegiate Athletes (NSIA) (1988), provided an unprecedented view of the reported experiences of both female and male NCAA Division I sport participants from 42 institutions throughout the country. Among many other things, slightly more than half of the respondents said that they had incurred an injury during their college days. As the NSIA summary results indicate, this figure would not be too shocking, given the frequency and intensity of physical activity associated with sport, if it were not also learned that 70% of football and basketball players and 50% of those who participated in other sports also said that they had experienced "intense" or "extremely intense" pressure to disregard their injuries (American Institutes for Research, 1988, p.52). Other authors have also noted high rates of injury across intercollegiate sports (Lanese, Strauss, Leizman, & Rotondi, 1990; Zemper, 1989). Taken together, these data reveal the pervasiveness of injury experienced by college student-athletes as well as the need to help members of this special on-campus population cope with losses in functioning that they are either discouraged from addressing or denied.

Difficulties Providing Psychological Services To Student-Athletes

Assistance to injured student-athletes is typically provided by well-trained and caring athletic trainers and physical therapists, as well as by various sport medicine physicians. Their rehabilitative efforts traditionally focus on the physical insult with treatments directed toward returning the student-athlete back to the field, court, track, or pool as soon as possible, unless the injury is disabling (i.e., it is a condition that is characterized by long-term or permanent losses in functioning). However, as Rotella and Heyman (1986) pointed out, injured athletes often are not prepared to return to participation because they have had little time to adjust to loss, given the efficiency of modern rehabilitative interventions, and therefore commonly experience a wide range of concomitant psychological responses (e.g., anxiety, fear, depression). Unfortunately, these psychological responses appear to be infrequently addressed by collegiate sports medicine professionals, even in the case of distressing, disabling conditions.

Several reasons seem to underlie this rather narrow approach to rehabilitating physically impaired student-athletes. First, sports medicine professionals are usually not formally trained to consider psychological aspects of assisting the injured and disabled. They may not understand the potential usefulness of psychological consultation or intervention for the impaired student-athlete who is attempting to cope with loss of functioning. Although there occasionally are on-campus helping professionals (e.g., psychologists, counselors, or psychiatrists) who are formally or informally affiliated with the college or university sports medicine team and who could be helpful to the psychological rehabilitation of injured or disabled student-athletes, this does not seem to be the norm. What seems to be a common situation is one in which athletic department staff are not aware of the availability of helping professionals or the ways in which this expertise can be relevant to the rehabilitative process. If they are aware, they may not know how or when to refer an injured student-athlete.

Another obstacle is the prevalence and influence of the so-called "medical model" adhered to by the majority of sports medicine professionals, which does not place much emphasis on psychological approaches to the treatment of injury. Accordingly, helping professionals see fewer numbers of referrals of injured student-athletes from sports medicine professionals to on-campus psychological services than might be warranted. Limited consultations are likely to occur between sports medicine staff and mental health professionals, despite the frequency of injuries and the severity of many of them. Seeing what they believe, many sports medicine staff often may not sense the need to consult a professional or refer an injured person.

In the end, such concern with physiology and not adjustment is seen as not helpful to injured and disabled student-athletes. Although it may be argued that sports medicine staff know the student-athletes they serve very well, adhering closely to the medical model may not provide injured people with the amount and range of care that can help in the holistic rehabilitation of those who are injured or have a disability. It has been shown that psychological support can be a very useful adjunct to medical interventions because the effects of injury are not limited to the afflicted body part(s) (Eldridge, 1983; Lynch, 1988).

Reluctance to involve helping professionals is somewhat understandable. Even in the 1990s, psychological treatment remains a mystery for many people. Stereotypic images of the couch and the bearded analyst persist; misconceptions about who seeks help from such people (i.e., only those who are mentally ill or crazy) contribute to the avoidance of on-campus helping professionals (even if they are affiliated with the athletic department staff) and their services. In fact, college students in general, and student-athletes in particular, tend to underuse psychological services for many reasons (Pinkerton, Hinz, & Barrow, 1987).

Even if student-athletes know about psychological services and are referred for help, several obstacles exist that make such assistance typically difficult to tap or completely inaccessible to them. Some of those barriers are (a) the "high visibility" of student-athletes on campus, (b) the limited amount of time available to seek outside help, (c) misconceptions about the personalities of student-athletes, (d) the restrictive nature of the athletic environment, and (e) certain attributes of student-athletes (Ferrante & Etzel, 1991).

Visibility. Student-athletes are often high-profile members of their school's community. Their names and faces regularly appear in the media. They may stand out in a crowd because of their size: A well-known personality on crutches is quite recognizable. Accordingly, student-athletes often avoid places like counseling and psychological service centers because they cannot easily seek assistance as privately as others can. There is often reluctance manifested in the forms of anxiety and shame that make it difficult for students in general to seek help. Student-athletes' notoriety can further compound the problem.

Time demands. Whether in or out of season, student-athletes lead hectic, stressful lives (American Institutes for Research, 1988; Etzel, 1989). Time is a precious commodity. Although recent NCAA legislation has put a cap on the number of hours that those who participate in intercollegiate athletics may be involved in sport-related activities (i.e., 20 hours per week), historically they have spent much more than 20 hours conditioning, practicing, and competing. The National Study of Inter-collegiate Athletes revealed that in 1987-88 student-athletes reported participating in excess of 30 hours per week in their chosen sport(s). Participants in that same study reported that they spent more time participating in athletics-related activities than they did preparing for and attending classes. Clearly, there are individual differences in the amount of time devoted to participation across schools and programs of differing competitive levels. Nevertheless, when combined with the amount of time that must be devoted to academic responsibilities, daily individual respon-sibilities and a personal life, little time is left during a highly structured day to get professional help from service centers that are typically open from 8AM to 5PM. Student-athlete frustration with this situation is common. We cannot recall the number of times a student-athlete has said to us, "Doc, I just can't seem to make it in."

Misconceptions about student-athletes. Student-athletes, in particu-lar football and men's basketball players, and members of other athletic teams on certain campuses, are often seen by the community as a spoiled, "overprivileged" group (Remer, Tongate, & Watson, 1978). Some may assume that the athletic department is taking care of all of their needs. Therefore, on-campus helping service providers who could be of assistance to those who become injured or disabled may not see a need to reach out to a group perceived as "pampered" or they may be reluctant to do so because they are anti-athletics. Although some student-athletes may be "spoiled," if they are young people who truly have a need for personal assistance in the wake of an injury, it should be as available to them as it is for any other student.

Restrictive environments. Over the years, many athletic departments have come to be seen by others, and often by themselves, as autonomous organizations on campus. Sperber (1990) goes so far as to say that many athletic departments are merely entertainment businesses that have essentially no real connection to the mission of their respective academic institutions. Independent-minded athletic department staff may not trust mental health professionals or other "outsiders" with the care of their student-athletes. Somehow, it is erroneously assumed that all student-athlete needs can be met by athletic department staff alone (except in times of true crisis). Indeed, the "we can take care of our own in house" attitude appears to be held by many athletic department staff (e.g., coaches).

Student-athlete attributes and developmental tasks. Other barriers to injured college student-athletes seeking psychological assistance are various personal characteristics (e.g., behaviors and attitudes), as well as certain so-called "developmental tasks" that all college students face.

As a group, student-athletes tend to be a rather independent lot. This is understandable in view of some of the messages they may learn from influential others in the athletic world. Also, individualism is characteristic of college students in general. Indeed, one of the major developmental tasks of college students involves struggling to become an independent adult (Chickering, 1969). Over time, many student-athletes seem to acquire a sense that they can solve most (if not all) of their difficulties. They also seem to learn through sport to be strong and to minimize or deny physical and emotional pain. If one is not tough or "macho," one is somehow an inferior peer. Therefore, injured or disabled student-athletes may not ask for or seek help even though they may be experiencing considerable distress. "When rugged individualism ... leads to, or heightens, an unwillingness to seek or accept assistance, athletes will find themselves separated from existing and potential sources of social support"(Pearson & Petitpas, 1990, p.9). Consequently, persistent encouragement to seek outside psychological assistance on the part of referral sources (e.g., athletic trainers) is often necessary to get an independent-minded, injured or disabled student-athlete assistance from helping professionals.

Another developmental task that this group must work through involves learning to deal effectively with authority (Farnsworth, 1966). Those who have problems relating to powerful others often will not respond to their guidance or direction. Consequently, referral for psychological assistance may be met with resistance, even though it is in the best interest of the injured person. Therefore, if people with such difficulties who do come to obtain help or are forced to do so by others (e.g., coaches or trainers), they must be handled with sensitivity so as not to alienate them.

It is not uncommon for those who do ultimately make contact with a helping professional to expect that they can obtain relief in a very brief amount of time and/or without much personal effort. Upon becoming aware of this agenda (the "quick fix"), the astute clinician must carefully educate the injured person about the nature of psychological treatment (e.g., roles of client and therapist, goal setting, who is responsible for change and how it may occur) so as to create realistic expectations for their work together.

Finally, for those who can have an impact on assisting injured or disabled student-athletes, it will be helpful to assume a broader view of the individuals who are both college students and participants in athletics. Student-athletes are not students or athletes first and foremost. Rather, they are developing young *people* in transition who are in the process of becoming adults. They are continuously working through the many developmental tasks that people at their stage in life are confronted with such as (a) becoming independent; (b) dealing with authority; (c) learning to deal with uncertainty and ambiguity; (d) developing personal standards; values, and a sense of purpose; (e) developing a mature sexuality; (f) developing feelings of security and competence; (g) establishing personal identity and attaining prestige and esteem; and (h) managing emotions (Chickering, 1969; Farnsworth, 1966). Further, their roles of students and entertainers frequently make the transition from childhood to adulthood more complicated (Ferrante & Etzel, 1991). Therefore, it is most useful to view their experiencing of athletic injury and disability within the context of their uniquely demanding lifestyles.

Clearly, our position underlines the importance of taking a "holistic" approach to the treatment, rehabilitation, and aftercare of injured and disabled student-athletes. We believe that the student-athlete is a *person* first, and it is from this "person-ness" that their athletic, academic, developmental, and career needs evolve. Accordingly, athletic injury can be regarded as both an obstacle and a threat to the realization of long- and short-term needs and goals. Injury and disability can leave student-athletes vulnerable to distress that can complicate and inhibit the process of physical and psychological rehabilitation. We believe that injured or disabled student-athletes can best be served by understanding their unique needs within the context of their individual histories, personalities, current experiences, and aspirations.

The Unique Consequences Of Incurring
An Injury For College Student-Athletes

The ways that people characteristically respond to sport-related injury and the theoretical concepts that help us to understand why they respond in these ways have been discussed in previous chapters of this book and in other resources (Astle, 1986; May & Seib, 1987; Rotella & Heyman, 1986; Silva & Hardy, in press; Tunick, Etzel, & Leard, 1991). Therefore, we will not review them here. There are, however, several points that we believe can help the reader understand how college student-athletes respond to injury and/or disability and how to better assist them as they struggle to cope with their losses.

The Novelty of loss. First, when young student-athletes' physical capacities are suddenly or progressively not what they have been throughout life, it may simply be the first time this has ever been encountered. They typically have been successful, highly functioning people. The world of injury and loss is foreign territory for many student-athletes. Indeed, many young people aged 18-21 often have a limited, if any, history of significant losses. They may have little appreciation of the finite nature of human capacities. When student-athletes are not capable of doing what they have taken for granted all their lives, it can be a very frustrating, unwanted revelation. For adults in a position to assist injured or disabled young athletes (who usually own a more extensive loss history), it may be difficult to appreciate the magnitude and complexity of the problem. Therefore, it is important that coaches, sport medicine, and helping professionals not underestimate or discount the impact of injury on student-athletes.

The Effects of changed status. As is the case with noncollegiate athletes, when student-athletes become injured or disabled, their lives may change in various ways psychosocially. Over time, student-athletes often become isolated and alienated from their peers, experience changes in their social status, and may encounter new academic/developmental concerns (Ermler & Thomas, 1990; Pearson & Petitpas, 1990; Tunick et al., 1991).

Student-athletes who cannot participate in day-to-day athletic activities (e.g., conditioning, practicing, traveling, and competing) become separated from their teammates, coaches, and others with whom they normally interact. Because they can no longer function in their customary roles, injured people become gradually or suddenly estranged from their previously predictable and supportive social network. Sadly, they sometimes are intentionally ignored, set aside, or criticized by insensitive coaches or peers for being injured (which somehow implies that one is weak, less valuable or not committed enough to "tough it out"). More commonly, the impaired student-athlete becomes gradually separated from others. The time once spent on the field or in the weight room is now spent in the care of athletic trainers in the athletic training room–if fortunate–with some time sitting on the bench watching others do the now impossible. One disabled client succinctly described the confusion and frustration of being in this unfortunate situation in the following way: "It's like I'm on the team, but I'm really not. I don't know what else to do."

Other relationships change for injured or disabled student-athletes. Although their conditions often make them the focus of public attention for a while, as time passes they fade from the spotlight, their stories become old news, and healthy others take their places. Students and media do not pay as much attention to the student-athlete as they did in the past. Social opportunities often become fewer for the former "BMOC" or "BWOC." There are no tales to relate about the upcoming game or meet: Only recollections of bygone accomplishments and the unglamorous rehabilitation process are left to tell. Special status is lost or at least diminished.

Confronted with the reality of assuming a radically different, usually unanticipated, life-style, injured and disabled student-athletes face different academic situations and challenges. More free time is often available to injured student-athletes whose rehabilitation activities do not consume a large part of the day (although they may–witness the case of an injured yet active player who receives four hours of rehabilitation daily to stay in playing condition). In such situations, academic priorities can come more to the forefront, and the injury may serve as a "blessing in disguise" for those who have neglected their studies. Previously flexible professors who do not appreciate the need for continued accommodation, however, may become less sympathetic to the impaired student-athlete who may still need occasional special arrangements in view of the demands and inconveniences of the rehabilitation process (Tunick et al., 1991).

For disabled student-athletes, especially those whose injury is career ending, academic priorities and career paths will probably need to be reexamined over time. When faced with this major life transition, school frequently assumes a higher priority in life. A reassessment of interests, skills, and abilities is often warranted. On-campus helping professionals who are trained in career-vocational counseling can be great assets in such cases. (See Riffee & Alexander, 1991, for a discussion of career counseling strategies for student-athletes.) In the case of disabled student-athletes, educational-vocational counseling and supportive psychotherapy can be undertaken concurrently and interactively as there is considerable overlap in the concerns seen in such cases (Pinkerton, Etzel, Rockwell, Talley, & Moorman, 1990).

Injured and disabled student-athletes may benefit from such combined psychological interventions to address questions about changing personal identity (i.e., confidence in maintaining a sense of continuity and sameness of the self) (Chickering, 1969). (The reader will recall that developing a sense of identity is one of the major developmental life tasks of college students.) When impaired student-athletes are forced to examine who they are when they cannot be who they once were for themselves and for others, they are often left with an overwhelming sense of confusion and numbness. Kir-Stimon's (1977) discussion of the mind-set of severely disabled persons at the onset of emotional rehabilitation is very similar to what we often hear injured and disabled student-athletes say to themselves:

> Who am I?
> I am different than I was.
> I don't like me.
> Nobody likes me.
> I am not worthwhile.
> Perhaps I never was worthwhile.
> Who was I?
> I have no real identity anymore.
> I have changed. Nothing is the same as before.
> My friends, my family, the world about me has changed.
> I am lost. (Kir-Stimon, 1977, p.365)

Answering the question of "Who am I if I'm not an athlete?" becomes very difficult because many student-athletes have "foreclosed" on their identities early in life. That is, many have learned to identify themselves as athletes at a young age and so act in ways that are consistent with their self-perceptions (Chartrand & Lent, 1987). Therefore, it can be very disturbing to student-athletes (especially for the alarming number of male baseball, basketball, and football players who expect to become professionals) when the identity of being an athlete must be abandoned. Indeed, research indicates that many student-athletes are less mature than their nonathlete peers in terms of being able to make mature educational and career plans (Blann, 1985; Sowa & Gressard, 1983). Consequently, referring injured and disabled student-athletes to obtain professional assistance for personal-social and educational-vocational concerns is often very timely from a developmental standpoint.

Methods Of Providing Psychological Assistance
To Injured Or Disabled Student-Athletes

Although the number seems to be growing, only a few universities today appear to have professionally trained psychologists, counselors, and/or psychiatrists whose duties specifically involve providing direct psychological service to student-athletes. Most of these institutions utilize professionals who are members of counseling services. Some have a staff member who serves as a liaison with the athletic department. A small number of schools have a professional who is affiliated with both the athletic department and a helping service. Whatever the administrative arrangement, on-campus helping professionals who are interested in or who have been hired to provide assistance to student-athletes in general, and in particular those who are injured and disabled, face many challenges.

As mentioned above, several barriers serve to separate helping professionals from injured or disabled student-athletes who could benefit from their expertise. To begin to bridge the gaps that exist, the helping professional must have the outside support of the athletic director and the chief student affairs officer. These two influential people can assist the helping professional in the initial efforts to establish credibility within the often closed athletic community. These people have the power to create an inroad to staff and student-athletes that the helping professional may otherwise never develop alone.

Given a crack in the door, the helping professional must begin the process of educating the athletic community about the potential usefulness of psychological assistance to injured and disabled student-athletes. In general, coaches, student-athletes, sports medicine staff, and administrators do not appear to readily understand how such services can be helpful (or they may be resistant for reasons mentioned earlier). Establishing credibility is a long-term project that can be quite frustrating. Indeed, one of the authors of this chapter was reminded by an athletic department administrator: "Remember, 95% of the people here don't care about what you do."

Meeting with coaches, sports medicine staff, and each team is an effective way of introducing the professional to potential referral sources and consumers of services. Given the permission of coaches and sports medicine staff, regularly attending practices and visiting athletic training rooms are also effective ways of familiarizing people with the helping professional and the services available to injured and disabled student-athletes. Such visits may also serve to undo some of the stigma associated with psychologists (i.e., "Dr. X is an OK person who is interested in helping us and who can be trusted").

Perhaps the most important relationship to establish and nurture is the one between athletic trainers and the helping professional. Athletic trainers historically have a very special relationship with coaches and student-athletes (Compton & Ferrante, 1991). They are perhaps the most trusted people within the athletic community. Indeed, their services are clearly understood, needed, and used on a daily basis. This is typically not the case with mental health professionals and their services, unless such services have been used for some time. Developing close ties with the athletic training staff can be very helpful to the accessing of injured and disabled student-athletes and their coaches. Such a relationship can enhance the extent to which helping professionals are accepted and trusted by the athletic community. Also, athletic trainers can be good referral sources of student-athletes who have been injured or who have other difficulties of which the athletic trainer becomes aware (e.g., personal problems, substance use, performance decrements). Given the opportunity, presenting to student trainers on mental health issues, psychological aspects of injury and disability, communication skills, and referral methods can help develop good working relationships between helping professionals and the athletic training staff. With such training student athletic trainers can become effective referrers of injured and disabled student-athletes.

Finally, another method of facilitating the provision of psychological assistance to injured or disabled student-athletes is to conduct needs assessments and other surveys. For example, collecting data on the psychological responses to loss of functioning can help establish the need to provide counseling or therapy. Undertaking research in collaboration with interested sports medicine staff members can provide a wealth of useful information and can further promote the cooperative efforts of athletic trainers and helping professionals.

The Effects of Injury And Disability On College Student-Athletes: Two Case Examples

The following case examples are offered to provide further insight into the psychological impact of sport injuries and the role of psychological services in the treatment and follow-up of injured and disabled student-athletes. Each case describes the general course of counseling with an NCAA Division I-A student-athlete. Due to ethical considerations relating to issues of confidentiality, these cases are presented in composite form. Although these situations may have involved both female and male clients, the following examples are referenced only in the male gender.

Case 1

A student-athlete was referred for consultation and recommended by the Director of Sports Medicine following extensive neurological and other medical examinations. Several months prior to the referral, the student-athlete had experienced a number of symptoms including paresthesias (i.e., numbing and tingling sensations in the hands and feet and part of the face)with accompanying motoric changes, blurred vision, and generally decreased coordination. Results of subsequent examinations revealed that the student-athlete had experienced a demyelinating episode, a phenomenon that is seen in several disorders of unknown etiology. Of these, multiple sclerosis (MS) is the most prominent. The diagnosis of MS becomes quite difficult in that it requires the occurrence of a second demyelinating episode: Remission can be quite long-term (e.g., up to 25 years). Consequently, a firm diagnosis could not be made. However, the student-athlete was provided with information to help better understand his general medical situation as it existed. Then, the student-athlete was referred for psychological services, to assess his current psychological functioning and to obtain emotional support and decision-making assistance.

In the initial session, the student-athlete complained of feeling frustrated, discouraged, and intermittently angry and sad. He also reported feeling anxious in view of the "incomplete diagnosis," its potential limitations regarding the questions of his continued sport participation, and uncertainties regarding his personal functioning in the future. Further exploration of the situation revealed that his parents appeared to be denying the implications of the medical examinations. They were pressing him to continue to participate in his sport, stating that they "didn't raise a quitter." He was also afraid of disappointing his teammates and coach and felt threatened by the possibility of not meeting their expectations. Unfortunately, the student-athlete was physically incapable of performing at the high skill level that he had previously achieved, and as a result was experiencing considerable dissonance.

In consultation with the referring physician, it was agreed that a treatment team would be formed consisting of the physician, an athletic trainer, and a clinical/counseling sport psychologist. The treatment team plan involved (a) monitoring the student-athlete's medical progress and providing information about the condition; (b) developing and implementing a "controlled" workout/training regimen; and (c) providing supportive counseling/psychotherapy to help him cope with various stressors and assist with decision making relative to the situation.

The student-athlete's participation in regular counseling provided a confidential, professional setting in which he was continually encouraged to explore his concerns and feelings. Over the course of several months, he received help dealing with the personal-social stress surrounding the need to make important decisions (e.g., whether he should prematurely end his sports career, how to interact with his coaches and parents) without the aid of a firm diagnosis. With the assistance of the psychologist, he also was able to resolve issues surrounding his parents and their expectations, as well as the pressures of his coach and teammates.

The role of the athletic trainer and the controlled workout/training regimen held special, strategic significance to the process and outcome of the case. More specifically, the student-athlete faced a number of difficult decisions–each without the benefit of a concrete diagnosis, information that would have made decisions more clear cut. The controlled workout setting allowed for the development of progressive training goals and the monitoring of any physiological distress, if it occurred. In that setting the student-athlete was encouraged to test progressive limits comfortably, away from the coach's watchful eye and any teammate's pressures. With the support of the athletic trainer, the student-athlete was able to gain confidence and experience-based insight into his current level of functioning by seeing gradual increases in performance with or without symptoms.

Having made significant progress in the controlled training program, the student-athlete ultimately rejoined his team with the permission of the physician. Although it was gratifying for him to be a part of his team again, he had experienced ongoing discouragement for some time in view of the fact that his athletic abilities were still well below their previous level. As a consequence of this dissatisfaction, following the conclusion of his season, he announced to his psychologist that he had decided to pursue a medical release and resign from the team–something he had considered and processed in counseling. His plan was to focus on academics and to continue with other campus and community involvements. The student-athlete continued his counseling relationship for some time, obtaining assistance with concerns surrounding his premature retirement from sport, as well as issues concerning his personal adjustment to a different life-style.

Case 2

K. was an eighteen-year-old freshman student-athlete who was referred by an athletic trainer to the psychologist for athletics soon after the beginning of the first semester of the academic year. K. had been a very successful high school student and athlete who had no previous history of injury. He was excited about beginning college and had worked hard on a daily basis over the summer to get into shape for his first season of athletic participation. K. had only been on campus for a month when during an informal conditioning activity, he unfortunately incurred a serious orthopedic injury. The injury required immediate surgery. Although the procedure was successful, the injury left K. disabled, facing a painful rehabilitation process that would last several months.

When he came to the first session soon after the surgery, K. reported feeling depressed, angry, and very frustrated in the wake of the totally unexpected turn of events in his life. It seemed unfair to him that despite all his hard work he had fallen victim to this injury. K. had just begun to feel as if he was becoming a part of his team when he was suddenly torn away from them. Although he had begun to receive treatment from a very competent and caring athletic trainer, he suddenly felt alone and alienated from his new-found peers. K. recognized he was still officially part of his team, but in reality he knew that he would have to wait until next season to join them as a healthy teammate. An unprecedented personal struggle against physical and psychological pain lay ahead.

Other difficulties made the effects of the injury even worse. K. had indicated that he was considering psychological assistance before his injury in view of a long-standing conflict with one of his parents with whom he had not lived with for several years. He had struggled with his parents' separation on and off over the years. This parent had been trying to reconnect with him and K. was troubled about whether to do so and if so, how to proceed. The issue appeared to be particularly important at the time given K.'s need for emotional support from primary caregivers. As an aside, he was receiving support from a distance from the parent with whom he lived and from a step-parent, support that was very helpful to his recovery.

From a developmental standpoint, K. was also confronted with the considerable task of becoming an independent person. Adjusting to school in a healthy fashion, he had begun to make the transition from home and family. Before his injury, K. indicated that he was a happy person. After having felt homesick for a short time, the number of phone calls had dropped off, and things were going well. However, his injury forced K. to have to depend on his family once again, slowing down the process of being an independent young adult. He knew that he could not solve his problems alone.

Within a few sessions we established a good working relationship. K. was encouraged to explore his thoughts and feelings about the issues mentioned earlier, and he was comfortable doing so. His mood improved progressively over time as he became engaged in school and in his rehabilitation. However, K. continually struggled with his feelings of isolation from his team. We worked on ways that he could spend time with them, if only briefly. This was quite difficult for K. to do because his rehabilitation was regularly scheduled during the team's practice sessions and because he experienced mobility difficulties. He often saw some of his teammates in the athletic training room and appreciated their contact and concern. Occasionally, K. made it out to their practice site toward the end of practices, something that was enjoyable yet frustrating and depressing, because he could do little else but watch. When the team's season started, K. could not travel with them early on; this was also a source of distress. Eventually, K. was able to travel with them as his condition improved. This was a great relief for him that he saw as a sign of reconnecting with the peers he longed to be with.

Our work also focused on the rehabilitation process itself. K. and his athletic trainer had set challenging yet realistic goals for his recovery. Although he worked hard and made exceptional progress, he had to work through considerable daily pain. K. shared the pain he experienced with his psychologist, something he did not want to share or could not share with others. K. also worked together on fears he had about moving on to increasingly more challenging levels of activity. He received support and encouragement from his athletic trainer and psychologist to continue to take small steps, which he did. With each step he gained confidence and learned to deal with uncertainty.

All the while, K.'s concern about his estranged parent became progressively less important. So much time and energy was taken up with school and rehabilitation that K. chose not to address the issue at the time. It was just too much for him. He decided to work hard in both areas until he was back to normal.

Over the course of counseling, which lasted a few months, K.'s psychologist occasionally visited him in the athletic training room as he went through his rehabilitation activities, something K. appreciated. Ultimately, K. indicated that it was very helpful for him to have had someone who was available to listen to him and support him as he worked to overcome his injury and disability. He performed very well academically during his ordeal and remained a well-adjusted person upon follow-up. Interestingly, K. said he was thinking about becoming an athletic trainer.

SUMMARY

The foregoing has been an attempt to present information about ways to provide psychological support to a special group of young people–college student-athletes. To assist more fully their coping with, and recovery from, injury and disability, it is important to understand their unique lifestyles and the developmental tasks that they must confront, as well as the barriers that exist to their seeking and/or obtaining helping services. The authors hope that our observations and suggestions will prove useful to readers who want to better understand and more effectively assist the considerable numbers of student-athletes who experience sport-related losses in functioning each year.

REFERENCES

American Institutes for Research (1988). *Summary results from the 1987-88 national study of intercollegiate athletes.* (Report No.1). Palo Alto, CA: Center for the Study of Athletics.

Astle, S. (1986). The experience of loss in athletes. *Journal of Sports Medicine, 26,* 279-284.

Blann, F. (1985). Intercollegiate athletic competition and student's educational and career plans. *Journal of College Student Personnel, 26,* 115-118.

Chartrand, J., & Lent, R. (1987). Sports counseling: Enhancing the development of the student athlete. *Journal of College Student Personnel, 66,* 164-167.

Chickering, A. (1969). *Education and identity.* Washington, DC: Jossey-Bass.

Compton, R., & Ferrante, A. (1991). The athletic trainer-helping professional relationship: An essential element for the enhanced support programming for student-athletes. In E. Etzel, A. Ferrante, & J. Pinkney, (Eds.), *Counseling college student-athletes: Issues and interventions* (pp.221-230). Morgantown, WV: Fitness Information Technology.

Eldridge, W. (1983). The importance of psychotherapy for athletic related orthopedic injuries among adults. *Comprehensive Psychiatry, 24,* 271-277.

Ermler, K., & Thomas, C. (1990). Interventions for the alienating effect of injury. *Athletic Training, 25,* 269-271.

Etzel, E. (1989). *Life stress, locus of control, and sport competition anxiety patterns of college student-athletes.* Unpublished doctoral dissertation, West Virginia University, Morgantown.

Farnsworth, D. (1966). *Psychiatry, education, and the young adult.* Springfield, IL: Thomas.

Ferrante, A., & Etzel, E. (1991). Counseling college student-athletes: The problem, the need. In E. Etzel, A. Ferrante, & J. Pinkney (Eds.), *Counseling college student-athletes: Issues and interventions* (pp.1-19). Morgantown, WV: Fitness Information Technology.

Kir-Stimon, W. (1977). Counseling with the severely handicapped: Encounter and commitment. In R. Marinelli & A. Del Orto (Eds.), *Psychological and social impact of physical disability* (pp. 363-369). New York: Springer.

Lanese, R., Strauss, R., Leizman, D., & Rotondi, A. (1990). Injury and disability in matched men's and women's intercollegiate sports. *American Journal of Public Health, 80,* 1459-1462.

Lynch, G. (1988). Athletic injuries and the practicing sport psychologist: Practical guidelines for assisting athletes. *The Sport Psychologist, 2,* 161-167.

May, J.R., & Sieb, G.E. (1987). Athletic injuries: Psychological factors in the onset, sequelae, rehabilitation and prevention. In J.R. May & M.J. Asken (Eds.), *Sport psychology: The psychological health of the athlete* (pp. 157-185). Great Neck, NY: P.M.A. Publishing Corporation.

Pearson, R., & Petitpas, A. (1990). Transitions of athletes: Developmental and preventive perspectives. *Journal of Counseling and Development, 69,* 7-10.

Pinkerton, R., Etzel, E., Rockwell, K., Talley, J., & Moorman, J. (1990). Psychotherapy and career counseling: Toward an integration for use with college students. *Journal of American College Health, 39,* 129-136.

Pinkerton, R., Hinz, L., & Barrow, J. (1987). The college student-athlete: Psychological considerations and interventions. *Journal of American College Health, 37,* 218-226.

Remer, R., Tongate, R., & Watson, J. (1978). Counseling the underprivileged minority. *The Personnel and Guidance Journal, 56,* 626-619.

Riffee, K., & Alexander, D. (1991). Career strategies for student-athletes: A developmental model. In E. Etzel, A. Ferrante, & J. Pinkney (Eds.), *Counseling college student-athletes: Issues and interventions* (pp. 101-120). Morgantown, WV: Fitness Information Technology.

Rotella, R., & Heyman, S. (1986). Stress, injury, and the psychological rehabilitation of athletes. In J. Williams (Ed.), *Applied sport psychology: Personal growth to peak performance* (pp.343-364). Palo Alto, CA: Mayfield.

Silva, J., & Hardy, C. (in press). The sport psychologist: Psychological aspects of injury in sport. In F. Meuller & A. Ryan (Eds.), *The sports medicine team and athlete injury prevention.* Philadelphia: F. A. Davis.

Sowa, C., & Gressard, C. (1983). Athletic participation: Its relationship to student development. *Journal of College Student Personnel, 26,* 236-239.

Sperber, M. (1990). *College sports, inc.: The athletic department vs. the university.* New York: Henry Holt.

Tunick, R., Etzel, E., & Leard, J. (1991). Counseling injured and disabled student-athletes: A guide for understanding and intervention. In E. Etzel, A. Ferrante, & J. Pinkney, (Eds.), *Counseling college student-athletes: Issues and interventions* (pp. 199-220). Morgantown, WV: Fitness Information Technology.

Zemper, E. (1989). Injury rates in a national sample of college football teams: A 2-year prospective study. *The Physician and Sportsmedicine, 17*, 100-102,105-108,113.

Chapter 15

I Cried Because I Had No Shoes...A Case Study of Motivation Applied to Rehabilitation

Bruce W. Tuckman
Florida State University

This is a case study of a 53-year-old recreational marathon runner, intensely ego-involved in his athletic activity, who developed a potentially debilitating chronic condition of the lower back that made further running impossible. The paper describes the initial manifestation of the condition and the ensuing physical rehabilitation process undertaken. It then illustrates how motivation was used to facilitate the rehabilitation process by focusing on attitude (the belief that recovery was possible) and drive (increasing the incentive value of the outcome). The ultimate strategy was to establish a substitute goal activity: racewalking.

INTRODUCTION

"...and then I met a man who had no feet." What does this little adage tell us? That no matter how badly off we are, there will always be someone else who is worse off. Remembering this may help us put our personal calamities in perspective.

This is a paper about sports injury rehabilitation. However, there is a facet of the paper that must be noted. It is about injuries that are so severe that even after rehabilitation, the athlete cannot continue performing the sport at the same competitive level. The purpose of the rehabilitation, therefore, is to enable the athlete to function as a normal human being, not a supernormal one. However, the repair of the physical disability in such a case may be easy compared to the repair of the psychological disability associated with separation from the sport. Thus, considerable attention must be addressed to dealing with, and overcoming the psychological impact of this separation. When we talk about meeting both the physical and psychological demands of recovery, we are talking about motivation.

The "data" for this paper come from an intensive (and exhaustive) case study of a single athlete, one with whom the author is intimately familiar and extraordinarily empathetic, himself. I myself am the single subject of this in-depth examination of the psychological impact of physically necessitated separation from successful competition in one's sport. I will begin my journey through the topic at hand by describing my case in some detail, after which I will apply motivational principles in an effort to draw conclusions, generalizations, and recommendations that can be applied by counselors to others in similar circumstances. If successful, you will clearly recognize that "having no shoes," although a painful and unfortunate predicament to be in, is far better than "having no feet."

The Case: Injury

I am a 53-year-old man who makes his living by being a college professor. How then can I have the temerity to suggest that this is the case of an "athlete?" In the sense that one can only be an athlete if one derives one's livelihood from athletic performance, then this is not the case of an athlete, and the case of a "real" athlete would pose considerably more severe repercussions than this one. However, I would like to contend that an athlete is someone who bases his or her sense of self on the competitive performance of an athletic endeavor, and in that sense I am (or was) an athlete. I was a competitive long-distance runner who had been running for 21 continuous years, had competed in 32 marathons, three ultramarathons, and over 200 shorter races (ranging from 5K's to 20-milers). On average, my training consisted of running 9 or 10 miles a day, every day, with frequent long runs and periodic sessions of interval training on the track.

Yes, I was (and still am) a college professor. But I was also as much a runner as I was a professor although nobody ever paid me so much as a dime for running. In identity terms, however, "runner" and "Bruce Tuckman" were fused and inseparable; remove the one and you might lose the other. This inseparability of self and sport was based not only on the daily training regimen but also on the sense of success derived from competition. I never viewed myself as a "jogger," clearly a recreational term, but as a "runner," and a competitive one at that.

In early December of 1989, I ran a marathon to qualify for the 1990 Boston Marathon. Over the previous seven years, I had been experiencing a steady decrement of my racing performance, especially at the longer distances, which I attributed primarily to a combination of the aging process and of the move to a much warmer climate than that in which I had grown up. During my peak marathon years of 1981-82, at the ages of 42-43, my best marathon times were in the highly competitive 3:08 to 3:10 range. Since then, I had "deteriorated" to the point where running a 3:30—the qualifying time for Boston for someone in my age range–was a real challenge. Hence, I trained very hard for this qualifying race, and despite the cold, windy, and rainy conditions, succeeded in running a 3:29:51, thereby qualifying for Boston with nine seconds to spare!

Soon thereafter, I began to experience severe back pain, so bad that walking and bending were difficult, to say nothing of running. But I had worked so hard to qualify for Boston that I was determined to run it, and to run it I had to train for it. So I began chiropractic treatments and sports massage; after a brief respite, I continued to train despite the pain.

In April of 1990, I ran Boston–terribly–and soon thereafter, my back pain became debilitating again. And so again I followed my prescription of a brief respite from running combined with chiropractic treatments and sports massage. Also, I stretched religiously, both before and after every run, and took a cool dunk in my swimming pool after each run. Incredibly, I continued to run about 60 miles per week simply by "gritting my teeth" for the first two miles of each workout until the back pain subsided, and living with the relatively constant moderate pain and limited mobility experienced during the remainder of each day. In the middle of February 1991, I went to San Francisco for a week and ran there every day, up and down the hills. I also walked a lot. When I arrived home, I could no longer stand erect, and the pain was constant and intense. I knew then the "jig was up," so I went out, bought an exercise bike, and stopped running. I also went back to the chiropractor for treatments three times a week. After about six weeks, with no visible change in my condition, I finally broke down and went to see an orthopedic surgeon who sent me for an MRI (Magnetic Resonance Image), which takes a picture of your soft tissue, in this case my spinal discs.

The result was shattering. All of my discs were in bad shape, particularly in my lower back, added to which I had a condition called spinal stenosis or a narrowing of my spinal column at about the level of my third and fourth lumbar vertebrae. My discs were not cushioning my back very well, and my narrowed spine was putting pressure on the nerves, thereby causing the pain. Twenty-one years of running with very little rest had combined with a genetic disposition to arthritis to create an intolerable situation. I was in constant pain, had trouble walking, could not bend, and could not stand in one place for more than a few moments. I had gone from being a well-conditioned athlete to being a "cripple." Had it not been for my daily exercise bike rides, an activity that was essentially pain free, I would have been ready for a padded cell.

It all seems quite ironic. Over the years that I had run, I had managed to run many running partners "into the ground." While I would show up for every workout, they would often be "down" with some injury or another. They called me the "horse that pulls the milk wagon" because of my reliability and strength. Of course, one day the horse that pulls the milk wagon drops dead as the result of accumulated overuse and is simply replaced by another nag. Was that to be my fate? I was clearly depressed, faced with the pain and immobility of my present condition and the uncertainty of my future as an athlete. Although riding a stationary bike was clearly exercise, it was not sport. I was in need of help, both physically and psychologically.

Rehabilitation
The orthopedic surgeon told me that my condition was inoperable at that time, mainly because of the limitations the surgery would impose on my mobility. He referred me for physical therapy and told me to come back in 5 or 10 years "when you can't stand the pain any longer," and then he would operate. Things looked mighty glum.

And so, for the first time in my life, I undertook physical therapy. I did not, at the same time, undertake psychological therapy—at least in a formal sense. Because I am myself a psychologist, I decided to manage that part of the process itself. I say this up front in order to emphasize that the psychological part of the process is no less important than the physical.

Because of the pain I was experiencing, and the association between that pain and running, I was in no way tempted to run. So, instead, I decided to walk. In physical therapy I learned how to stretch and strengthen my back myself, and was given further opportunities to strengthen it on my tri-weekly workouts on a machine they had (called "MEDEX") that functioned specifically for that purpose. When I began physical therapy, I could barely move 45 pounds of weight with my back. Each time I went on the machine I was determined to move up to a higher level, and by the time I had completed 20 visits, I could move 100 pounds 30 times without pain.

Every morning immediately after arising, I did my back stretching and strengthening exercises. This took an hour. Then, either immediately thereafter or later in the day, I spent about an hour and a quarter walking. Since, as a runner, I had always had the typical runner's obsession of going fast, it transferred to my walking, and I began to try to walk faster and faster. I became a racewalker. I even joined the few other racewalkers who were to be found in my community.

When my medical insurance ran out, I left physical therapy and joined a health club, one that featured Nautilus equipment and had a machine especially designed to strengthen the lower back. It was similar to the MEDEX I had used in physical therapy. I got the physical therapist to design a workout program for me at the health club and began going regularly twice a week. I also began using the Stairmaster as an occasional aerobic alternative to racewalking. I began to use swimming that way as well.

I have gotten immeasurably better. I experience relatively little back pain during normal daily activities while maintaining my weight and aerobic fitness level. Compared to those for whom improvement may not be possible (those who have serious automobile accidents, for example), I realize how well off I am. I have even racewalked a few 5K races and have performed better each time. Racewalking is much less "bouncy" than running, and far easier on my back. However, even on this I will exhibit extreme caution!

Applying Principles Of Motivation

Other than perhaps an interesting or even an inspirational story, what is my case doing in a book like this? The answer is that I would like to use it to illustrate how motivation can be used to facilitate the rehabilition process, particularly in cases where the athlete will never be able to return to his or her sport at the same competitive level as before the injury.

Let me propose that motivation has the following three facets or components: (a) attitude, (b) metacognition, (c) drive.

Attitude. This is the motivational enabler, particularly the attitude of self-confidence or what Bandura (1977, 1986) calls self-efficacy. Believing that you can do something is what enables you to do it (combined, of course, with a suitable amount of skill). People who have this attitude can be called self-believers, and those who do not, self-doubters (Tuckman & Sexton, 1992a). Self-believers have been shown not only to outperform all others, but also to outperform even their own self-expectations (Tuckman & Sexton, 1990). Furthermore, they are largely unaffected by external circumstances, although in a competitive situation, they perform better when they do not know where they stand relative to others (Tuckman & Sexton, 1992b). In other words, if they do not know for sure how far ahead they are, they just keep "pouring it on."

Therefore, in a rehabilitative situation, an athlete will be much more motivated to try to recover if he or she believes that recovery is possible. In my case, I believed that I could fix my back. That belief enabled me to get better. But where did that belief come from? According to Bandura (1977), the most effective way to improve self-efficacy is to try to do something and then succeed at it (what he calls enactive attainment). That, however, is like a catch-22. How can self-efficacy be both a prerequisite and a result? If a person lacks self-efficacy, that person is not likely to try something and so will never experience success. To get that person to try something and have the attempt result in success, you need to create a highly structured situation in which the necessary behaviors can be carried out with assistance and without threat of failure. Bandura (1977) calls this participant modeling. The person models the desired behavior for him or herself. Of course someone else is standing by to see that it is done right.

In my case, the physical therapist was the person standing by to see that I did things right. He was instrumental in helping me to carry out participant modeling leading to success experiences, each one adding to my sense of self-efficacy or belief in my ability to recover. The physical therapist never seemed to doubt that I would be able to move more weight each time I worked out on the machine. Without telling me, he would set the weight a little higher each time, and, after I had succeeded in moving it through the desired number of repetitions, inform me of what I had just accomplished. This process helped me develop the self-confidence I needed to complete my recovery.

Mere pep talks do not have the same effect. Telling someone over and over that he can do something does not necessarily make it happen. Nor does simply showing him how or pointing out to him someone else who is already doing it. There is no substitute for success. But success requires support and assistance. Scale down the rehabilitation task to the level that the recovering athlete can do it and success becomes more likely. Then follow success with positive feedback. Don't tell rehabilitating athletes what they have done wrong (a typical tendency of coaches, for example). Tell them what they have done right. Positive or encouraging feedback following performance has been shown to increase both self-efficacy and subsequent performance (Tuckman & Sexton, 1991). After each workout, my therapist would always say to me something like "You sure know how to focus your energy on that weight." Hearing that always made me feel more competent.

Metacognition. This is the guide, particularly insofar as it includes the strategies of goal setting and planning. Metacognition as applied to motivation means having mental or thought models for accomplishing your purpose. My purpose was to recover physically and psychologically from my disability, at least to the level of normal functioning—that being less than athletic functioning. To accomplish that, I needed to set intermediate or proximal goals and to develop plans for achieving them (Tuckman, 1992; Tuckman & Sexton, 1990). This is particularly necessary when the injured person does not have a lot of confidence in the likelihood of recovery, a particularly prevalent attitude at the beginning of the rehabilitation process. Having the goals and plans also helps to enhance the attitude of self-confidence, so necessary for recovery. My short-term goals were clear: to gradually reduce the pain and discomfort while gradually increasing the strength in my back. Each time I went for physical therapy, I set as a goal the amount of weight I wanted to be able to move on the MEDEX machine. I always tried to select a goal that seemed challenging yet attainable. This way I had a target to aim at, and each time it was a little higher than the time before. Of course there is likely to be an ultimate limit, at which time maintenance goals need to be set.

It also helps to have a plan, a mapping out in your mind of how to meet each goal. The more detailed the plan in terms of specific days, times, and activities the better because that makes it easier to follow. Also, a good plan includes acknowledgment of likely obstacles (what I call UFO's or Unavoidable Formidable Obstacles) and strategies for overcoming them. Otherwise, a miss can cause a major setback, even perhaps be an end to the whole process. Finding an alternate exercise program, namely racewalking, turned out to be an excellent strategy for me. I could set performance goals and could plan out my weekly schedule to include physical therapy workouts and racewalking workouts. I planned for shorter walks and longer walks, slower walks and faster walks. I also planned for days when I did non-weight-bearing exercise such as swimming. Moreover, I had a contingency plan for a diminution of activity should the pain return, that being the major obstacle I could imagine.

Metacognitively, I served as my own coach so to speak, since goal setting and planning are major coaching functions. The existence of an alternative activity, though, was essential to this metacognitive aspect of motivation because it gave me something for which to plan. With competition-ending conditions such as mine, just planning to be pain free is probably not enough. It is much more motivating to plan for some other kind of performance and to believe that you can achieve it.

Drive. This is the energizer, the source of the effort that is required to deal with the physical and psychological demands of rehabilitation. To be motivated to do something means to expend energy or effort on it. Beyond believing that you can prevail and having cognitive strategies to give you direction, you must also have drive. Without it you are not likely to succeed.

Where does drive come from? It comes from valuing or wanting something. You may not know how to get it or even believe that you can get it but if you want it badly enough you will be driven. We could say that the goal or outcome has incentive value for you. For example, some of us have children who do not work hard enough at school. We know they are smart, and they probably do too, but they just do not seem to care as much as we think they should. School seems to lack incentive value for them, and so they are not driven to do well in it.

Sometimes we try, externally, to enhance the incentive value of something, and hence the drive to achieve it, by making a reward available. Some schools reward students materially for attendance, good behavior, and improved grades. The result seems to be positive. However, in the long term, people seem to persist when at least some of the incentive value comes from within.

With athletes, especially older ones, drive is often not a problem. In fact, if anything it can be a problem in the opposite way in that the older athlete has a tendency to put in more effort than is physically productive. Because of the enormous incentive value of competitive success, the older athlete is often driven to train to excess–the result being injury. It is a clear case of the drive factor being so strong as to overshadow the cognitive factor. Then, when the athlete gets injured, the drive to recover is as strong as it ever was in order to be able to return quickly to competition. In that case, the athlete throws him or herself wholeheartedly into the rehabilitation process. But what happens, as in my case, when the likelihood of real recovery, at least to the preinjury level, is not possible?

One possibility is that there will be little incentive value for rehabilitating oneself. Why bother to put in the effort to "get better" if "better" cannot be gotten? What needs to be done is to harness or bring out the old competitive drive, but at the same time to redirect that drive into some other endeavor that the injured person can become capable of doing. Direction is a cognitive function, not a function of drive, but since attitude, cognition, and drive all interact, a change in one cannot help but produce a change in the others. Thus, the solution may be to introduce substitute goals (cognitively) and work to attach the preinjury drive to these new goals.

In my case, the substitute goal was to become a successful racewalker. Because I could not be a competitive runner, I would invest my effort in rehabilitating myself in order to become a competitive racewalker. If my sport was also my livelihood (which, of course, it was not), I would have tried to find a substitute career the attainment of which would have become my new goal toward which I could direct my effort.

In fact, I was faced with exactly that situation not too long ago when I involuntarily gave up administration to return to the faculty. Since the new job lacked incentive value to me, particularly in comparison to the old one, I had nothing to which to attach my drive. In such cases, the result is typically first anger and then depression, given all that drive without an attainable goal toward which it can be directed. I used all my drive to try to find another administrative job, and it was not until I accepted the reality of my situation and was able to see its incentive value that I could get past the anger and depression.

When my back injury came along, I was able to quickly settle on a new goal, racewalking, toward which I could direct my drive. Very possibly, the job experience had taught me the value of goal substitution in avoiding the anger and depression that typically follows a loss.

CONCLUSIONS

From my case, the critical importance of a goal can be clearly seen. A goal serves three purposes, namely: (a) as a direction in which to go (cognitively); (b) as an incentive, thereby providing something to which drive can be attached; (c) as something to believe yourself capable of attaining (attitudinally). Since rehabilitation is a demanding process, both physically and psychologically, it requires a considerable amount of motivation. That motivation, in turn, requires the necessary attitudes, thoughts, and drives. By serving as a key to each, the goal of recovery becomes very possibly the most critical element in the process.

In the case of injuries from which complete recovery is not possible (or certainly not likely), the matter of the goal becomes even more critical. In cases where an obvious goal such as complete recovery does not exist, a substitute goal must be found. The substitute goal should help the injured athlete to detach from the former competitive activity and attach to some other desired outcome. Given the new goal, the athlete can organize his or her beliefs, thoughts, and energies around it. In my case, this approach worked well because of my substitute goal involving racewalking. In cases where an athlete cannot or will not accept a substitute goal, the motivation required for physical recovery is likely to be lacking.

The goal also serves a very important evaluative function in the rehabilitation process. In order to determine whether or not you are getting better, there must be some mental representation of what "better" is. In my case, "better" meant being able to racewalk fast enough and properly enough to be able to enter a race without either embarrassing myself or reinjuring myself. For an injured professional athlete, the goal might be getting a job as a broadcaster or coach. Landing such a job would provide a measure of having gotten "better."

In my case I was fortunate to have arrived at a substitute goal that could meet so many of the needs that had previously been met by running competitively. Whether or not I ultimately carry through on my substitute goal, it has served its purpose in facilitating my physical recovery from serious athletic injury.

REFERENCES

Bandura, A. (1977). Self-efficacy: Toward a unifying theory of behavior change. *Psychological Review, 84*, 191-215.

Bandura, A. (1986). *Social foundations of thought and action: A social cognitive theory.* Englewood Cliffs, NJ: Prentice-Hall.

Tuckman, B.W. (1992). The effect of student planning and self-competence on self-motivated performance. *Journal of Experimental Education, 60*, 119-127.

Tuckman, B.W., & Sexton, T.L. (1990). The relation between self-beliefs and self-regulated performance. *Journal of Social Behavior and Personality, 5*, 465-472.

Tuckman, B.W., & Sexton, T.L. (1991). The effect of teacher encouragement on student self-efficacy and motivation for self-regulated performance. *Journal of Social Behavior and Personality, 6*, 137-146.

Tuckman, B.W., & Sexton, T.L. (1992a). Self-believers are self-motivated; self-doubters are not. *Personality and Individual Differences, 13*, 425-428.

Tuckman, B.W., & Sexton, T.L. (1992b). The effects of informational feedback and self-beliefs on the motivation to perform a self-regulated task. *Journal of Research in Personality, 26*, 121-127.

About the Editor

David Pargman is in his twentieth year at Florida State University where he is Professor of Educational Psychology and Coordinator of Sport Psychology Studies in the Department of Educational Research. Previously, he taught in the Departments of Health and Physical Education at Boston University and the City College of New York. Dr. Pargman received the Master's degree from Teachers College, Columbia University and the Ph.D. from New York University.

Dr. Pargman is author and co-author of two other books that deal respectively with stress and performance, and fitness and wellness. He is currently completing a textbook entitled *Sport Psychology.* He has been major professor to 25 Ph.D. graduates, is a member of the American Psychological Association, International Association of Applied Psychology, the North American Society for the Psychology of Sport and Physical Activity, and a Fellow of the Association for the Advancement of Applied Sport Psychology and the American College of Sports Medicine. He is also a Certified Sport Psychology Consultant, the Association for the Advancement of Applied Sport Psychology.

Dr. Pargman has competed in hundreds of road races, was a member of his college track and cross-country team and continues to train, run and compete as a distance runner. Consequently, he is often injured and in the throes of mental and physical rehabilitative experiences.

Subject Index